RHYMING HISTORY

The Story of England in Verse

RHYMING HISTORY
The Story of England in Verse

by Colin Wakefield

Illustrations by John Partridge

VOLUME FIFTEEN: 1939 – 1945

The Second World War

DHP

Double Honours Publications

RHYMING HISTORY
The Story of England in Verse

VOLUME FIFTEEN: 1939 – 1945
The Second World War

First published in 2023 by Double Honours Publications.

ISBN 978-1-7396882-4-0

Double Honours Publications

Email: info@rhyminghistory.co.uk
Website: www.rhyminghistory.co.uk
Twitter: @Rhyming_History

AUTHOR'S NOTE

This is Volume Fifteen of our *Rhyming History* (still in the writing), which will eventually stretch from Julius Caesar's first arrival in Britain in 55BC to the funeral of Queen Elizabeth the Second in 2022.

Volume Sixteen (Attlee to Wilson) will be published in 2023, with subsequent volumes appearing annually. The published volumes are available for sale through our website, Amazon and selected retailers. Volume One (The Romans to the Wars of the Roses) is also available as an ebook through Amazon Kindle. There is a CD of excerpts from Volume One.

These books of verse are intended for those who want to learn more about our history, but in not too solemn a way. I hope they will also appeal to a wider audience, schools, students and historians, and to those who simply enjoy reading verse.

John Partridge has again provided witty and entertaining illustrations to accompany the text, for which I am as ever most grateful.

My special thanks are due to Jonathan Dowie for his detailed overview of the text and to Janet Marsten for the creation of our new website. I am also most grateful to Alan Coveney for his expert advice.

Please visit our website for updates on future volumes of the *History* and for news of live performances of the verse.

www.rhyminghistory.co.uk

Colin Wakefield – May 2023

The Second World War

GEORGE THE SIXTH (1936 – 1952)

September the 1st, 1939: **1939**
Adolf Hitler's massed forces crossed the line.
Nazi Germany invaded Poland.

For reasons rather hard to understand,
Chamberlain still dithered. Would there be war?
The Germans had already bombed Warsaw.
What more did he want? Would Hitler withdraw?

Some hope! But later the very same day,
That's what Chamberlain asked. Idle, I say,
And craven. "Every minute's delay
"Now means loss of life," claimed Arthur Greenwood,
For Labour. The House of Commons came good:
"Speak for England, Arthur!" cried Amery,
A Tory. No more of this knavery:
Our "national honour" was at stake.

Chamberlain's ultimatum

The Commons were angry, make no mistake,
The Cabinet too. It was make or break.
The PM now knew it had to be war.
He issued an ultimatum, therefore,
To Germany. He received no reply.
He still, poor man, could not understand why.
On the 3rd of September, he broadcast
To the nation. It was war at last.

The British ultimatum had expired
At 11 a.m. Chamberlain, tired,
Grave and restrained, was nonetheless sure
"That right will prevail". He offered no more.

France and Australia entered the war,
Also New Zealand, although Canada
And (less of a surprise) South Africa
Took a tad longer. Nearer home, Eire
Declared herself a neutral area,
Inspired by Éamon de Valera,
No friend to the British. All far too late.
Abandoned, the Poles were left to their fate.

The German advance

For when they crossed the Polish frontier,
The Germans were vastly superior
In manpower, armaments and transport.
One and a half million (with air support)
Made up the massive invasion force,
With well over 400,000 horse
And 200,000 vehicles: tanks,
Mechanised transport… Morale in the ranks
(Many the rawest of recruits) was high.

The Second World War

This was a just war. Few questioned why.
The Führer was beyond criticism.
The defeat of 'Polish barbarism'
Was a moral crusade. Folk believed him.
The Germans, *en masse*, proved signally dim.

Towns and villages, as if on a whim,
Were torched and destroyed, inhabitants shot.
Hitler spouted a lot of racist rot
And the people fell for it. This was war.
When the US embassy in Warsaw
Was bombed, this was despite Roosevelt's plea
To spare civilian targets. To me,
This speaks volumes: no mercy, no pity,
No compassion did the Germans show.

The terror still had a long way to go.
The 'ethnic cleansing', so-called, was ruthless.
65,000 were massacred (yes,
You read that right): mass murder; genocide.
Resistance would amount to suicide.

The German advance was expert and brisk.
The *Luftwaffe* (mark this with an asterisk:
It would be the same story in Norway,
Where Göring enjoyed a free holiday)
Provided key air cover. Moreover,
They guaranteed a German walkover
By bombing Polish airfields in advance.
Where were 'Great' Britain, all the while, and France?
Nowhere! This pathetic, macabre dance
Was staged without our intervention.
We had expressed every intention
Of helping, but omitted to mention
That Britain was rather too far away
To be of much use, far less save the day.

Shameful, but sadly Lloyd George had been right.
We were powerless to relieve the plight
Of the Poles. Solidarity, good night.

Poland suffered another nasty fright
When Russia invaded from the east.
The Nazi-Soviet Pact, that strange beast,
Spawned a further wave of chaos, terror,
Mayhem and murder. This was no error.
The attack had been scrupulously planned.
The Poles, surprised, were totally unmanned.

Russia moves in

Bravely defending Warsaw to the last,
Fighting for survival, they were aghast
When the Soviets moved in from the east.
They had expected, at the very least,
Russian neutrality. When, alack,
'Uncle' Joe Stalin stabbed them in the back,
They'd no means of resisting the attack.

The Red Army crossed the Polish border
On the 17th – well out of order.
What of their non-aggression treaty?
Well, the Kremlin argued (yes, really)
That they were not bound by this anymore,
Because Poland's government in Warsaw
Had ceased to exist! Be that as it may,
The 17th was a very dark day.
The Poles suffered massive casualties –
Over 50,000 fatalities.
This figure does not include, if you please,
Those murdered in 'secret' atrocities.

Stalin loathed the Poles. In 1920
(The Battle of Warsaw) the Red Army

Had been smashed to pieces, shamed and disgraced.
The measure of revenge the people faced
Can be readily explained. Within days,
Poland fell. The dictator lavished praise
On his officers: keep on "cleaning out
"The Polish filth." No shadow of a doubt,
This gave Stalin the opportunity
To kill and torture with impunity.

The fall of Warsaw

The valiant Poles fought to the last man
To save Warsaw. German bombing began
On the 20th day of September.

October the 1st saw the surrender
And the terrible annihilation
Of the capital. A broken nation,
Poland was carved up between Germany
And Russia. The Poles, more's the pity,
Were executed by the Red Army
In dreadful numbers. Mass deportations
Began to Siberia. The nations
Of the west held their noses, looked away,
And reserved judgement for another day.

Stalin as an ally, I have to say,
Sticks in the throat... Winston Churchill was right,
However: if he helped to win the fight
Against Hitler and the Nazis, so be it –
A necessary evil, as I see it.

One advantage, from Stalin's point of view,
Of the pact with Hitler (one of the few)
Was the agreed Russian takeover
Of the three Baltic states, Estonia,

Latvia and Lithuania. Grand –
Unless you were Jewish, you understand,
Or a dissident. Snide and underhand,
Of course, but that's what dictators are for.
As for Hitler, to prosecute the war,
He would soon be running low on supplies.
Now, to the Führer's delight and surprise,
The Soviets could supply manganese
And rubber. Essentials such as these,
Like oil, and copious quantities
Of wheat, could well keep Germany going
For years. For there was no way of knowing
The effect of Britain's naval blockade
On the German economy, and trade.

The Poles felt ignored and badly betrayed.
Several Polish warships, however,
Escaped to the west. Never say never.
In London, a government in exile
Was set up. The Poles, by a country mile,
Displayed more courage, and less resentment,
Than might have been expected. Discontent –
Nay, anger – at the allies' lack of grit
Was more than justified. The Poles saw fit,
Nonetheless, to work for the benefit
Of peace across Europe. They showed respect
To all, more than was deserved, I suspect.

They were generous (and yet circumspect)
In their sharing of secrets. The breaking,
In due course (this is truly breathtaking),
Of the German enigma code machines
Was down to the Poles. For they'd found a means
Of cracking the code (or had made a start).
The Poles were bright and played a vital part
In winning the war. We owe them a debt
That's never been properly paid as yet.

Chamberlain's complacency

Chamberlain never thought the war would last.
Over by the spring? Churchill was aghast.
The Germans continued to rearm fast.
We sat on our hands. It's a sad fact
That by April '40 (to be exact)
Manpower in armaments factories
Had only grown in strength, if you please,
By a pathetic eleven *per cent.*
Now this was little short of indecent,
One sixth of the increase that was needed.
Yet Churchill's warnings still went unheeded.
A key member now of the government,
He took great care, when he made a statement,
Not to rock the boat. Ever in the news,
Old Winston had to mind his p's and q's.
But the great British public quickly saw
That Churchill alone could win them the war.

Chamberlain was convinced that Germany
Was on the brink, economically,
Of a great national catastrophe.
How wrong he was. The British were the ones
Who should have worried. 800,000 tons
(Yes, eight hundred thousand) of merchant shipping
Would be sunk before the end of the spring
By U-boats, potentially crippling;
While Germany (as should have been foreseen)
Was stronger now than she had ever been.
How could Chamberlain have been so green?

The 'phoney war'

The 'phoney war', so-called, was unforeseen.
While the British people's nerve held steady,
Everyone was nonetheless ready

For air attacks the moment war broke out.
They feared aerial bombardment, a rout,
A million dead, no shadow of doubt.
The air raid sirens sounded the warning,
Before midday, on the very morning
Of Chamberlain's broadcast. Yes, bombs away!
It was a false alarm, I'm glad to say,
But they duly trooped down, in single file,
To the shelters. Today it makes us smile,
The thought of this nervous wee crocodile,
But that's all very well in retrospect.
City dwellers had been led to expect
Death and disaster on a massive scale.
Would anybody live to tell the tale?

Chamberlain's name for it was 'twilight war',
Or 'this strangest of wars'. It was called 'bore'
By some ('Bore War', get it?). But 'phoney war',
Coined later by the Americans, stuck.

The Führer, we're told, had been thunderstruck
When Britain and France declared war. Poland
Was his focus. Chamberlain take a stand?
It certainly wasn't what Hitler planned.
The *Luftwaffe* was at full stretch. He knew,
As did his commanders (a motley crew),
That an immediate bombing campaign,
Against British cities, would bring more pain
Than benefit. Hitler hoped against hope
That bombing was also beyond the scope
Of the RAF. Chamberlain, the dope,
Refused to engage, so it's hard to know.
He was never the sort to 'have a go'.

The Tory MP, Leo Amery,
Asked the Air Secretary directly,
Sir Kingsley Wood, why not bomb Germany?

The answer he received (seriously)
Was this: an armaments factory
(Wait for it) was "private property".
It was far too risky, at any rate,
For Hitler was sure to retaliate!

Gas masks and the blackout

Although everyone was braced for war,
Nothing very much happened for two, four,
Six... no, eight months. However, 'be prepared'
Was the message. At first, people were scared.
They all carried their gas masks in the street,
In cardboard containers, all very neat.
Some kids had Mickey Mouse ones, rather sweet.
The hospitals were cleared, every bed
Kept free for victims of air raids instead.
Theatres and cinemas closed their doors,
By order. There was rapturous applause
When they welcomed audiences again,
Just a few weeks later. A constant pain
Was the blackout. Show a mere chink of light,
The ARP were after you all right!
The shops quickly ran out of black fabric:
Old clothes and curtains had to do the trick.

Walking home at night was fraught with danger.
Pitch dark! Bumping into the odd stranger
Was a hazard, but there was worse than that:
Falling down steps, tripping over the cat,
Walking into canals, or through glass doors,
And tumbling over onto all fours.
One person in five sustained injury
In the blackout – crashing into a tree,
Or missing the kerb unexpectedly
And twisting an ankle. Seriously,

The risk was real. In September, we're told,
Accidents on the roads increased twofold,
With twice as many people killed by cars
As in August. Even the twinkling stars
Were of little comfort. A tiny bit
Of light was permitted, a narrow slit
In a car's front headlamps, but that was it.

The streets were still very dark and ill-lit.
Small hand torches were finally allowed
For pedestrians (bloody, but unbowed),
Dimmed by two layers of tissue paper
To minimise the beam. What a caper!

Sandbags protected public monuments,
Offices and government departments
From bomb damage. This made absolute sense –
Or would have done, except for the silence.
Balmy weather added to the pretence.

The people's 'carry on' mentality
Was a sign either of their sanity
Or of wilful blindness. Banality?
Perhaps. Some lovers, on the other hand,
For reasons not that hard to understand,
'Took the plunge'. Well, you have to live your life.

More engaged couples became man and wife
In those first few weeks than ever before,
As soon as they heard there would be a war.
The jewellers even ran out of rings,
Which now came off curtain rods, of all things.
Who knew what might happen? No time for tears.
They could be apart for months, if not years.
They would meet again, though who could say when?
Tens of thousands got married there and then.*

---

*On Thursday the 7th of September,
My parents wed, a day to remember.
My mum wore a red and white spotted dress.
No time to buy white. She couldn't care less,
Though the photos show she dressed to impress!
They had a problem, I have to confess,
Driving to Cornwall for their honeymoon.
The signposts had been removed, all too soon,
For fear of a German invasion.
No one respected the occasion
Of my parents' wedding. Did they get lost?
I've no idea. How on earth they crossed,
Without a compass, the whole of Cornwall…
It doesn't seem to have mattered at all.
I gather, too, they'd forgotten the map.
No signposts to boot. A good-natured chap,
My dad (I'm sure) took it all in his stride,
While my mum just laughed, his beautiful bride.

Evacuees

Others there were heading for the country.
Spare a thought for the poor evacuee.
Over three short days a mighty campaign
For mass evacuation, by train,
From Britain's great cities was underway –
An incredible feat, I have to say.
Had the feared aerial bombing occurred,
The tragic loss of life, you have my word,
Would have been huge. Men, women and children,
Every law-abiding citizen,
Was at the gravest risk of being maimed,
Or worse. Millions of kids, it was claimed,
Were in danger. The expectation
Was that the planned evacuation –
Completely voluntary, by the way –
Would involve four million. Come the day,
About one and a half million went.

This comprised some forty-seven *per cent*
Of schoolchildren from the cities. Others
Included pregnant women and mothers
With children under five. Older children
Travelled unaccompanied, Bill and Ben
(Siblings, perhaps?) or, on her tod, wee Bren.
When I say 'travelled unaccompanied',
A few adults went with them, in a bid
To check things didn't go wholly awry –
Not always with success, but worth a try.

As the trains pulled out of the termini,
Mothers wept. The thought of waving goodbye
(For how long?) was more than many could bear.
The children were travelling… who knew where?
Clutching their gas masks, sandwiches perhaps
(The lucky ones), but certainly no maps,

They had luggage labels with their names on.
Many of the poor souls were woebegone,
With tears streaming down their little faces.
Only a few had bags or suitcases,
Warm clothes for the winter, shoes with laces,
Or the faintest idea what lay in store.

After four long months of the phoney war,
By January, with no bombs falling,
The strain on families was appalling.
Over one million evacuees
Returned home. The majority of these
Remained in the cities throughout the Blitz.
Evacuation had been the pits.

Yet many evacuees, those who stayed,
Had a great time. They were far from dismayed.
Cows, they found, were bigger than dogs! They played
In green fields. What was this? A real bed?
Upon arrival, some had crept, instead,
Into a bottom drawer to go to sleep,
As they used to at home. You want to weep.
Some had never cleaned their teeth in their lives,
Or run hot water. The record survives:
Flannels, clean sheets, pillows… all alien
To these poor, underprivileged children.

There were endless cases of bed-wetting –
Needless to say, extremely upsetting.
For many evacuees were nervous
And unhappy (as well as verminous).
To their hosts, the level of poverty
They witnessed for the first time, properly,
Came as a profound and unwelcome shock.
Their social consciences took a knock –
Those who were sensitive enough, that is.
The whole affair was a dreadful business,
An eye-opener, they came to see that.

This did long-term good or I'll eat my hat.
Even the Prime Minister, Chamberlain,
Expressed his horror. With a war to win,
There was little that could be done right now,
But folk sat up and took notice, and how.

Child poverty

For many children lacked basic hygiene.
A number were riddled with nits, unclean,
And had never seen a lavatory.
They used the carpet (yes, seriously)
Whenever, it seems, they needed a wee.

Whatever the stress, whatever the strain,
This must never, ever happen again.
Ignorance, the old saying goes, is bliss,
But this was now society's business.
Rich and poor alike, no one could opt out.
Britain changed for ever, without a doubt.
In 1945, the Labour rout
(Of the Tories) was hardly a surprise.
The scales had been lifted from people's eyes.

I digress. It is easy to be wise
After the event. Evacuation
Heralded a sea-change in the nation.
The British, though, still had a lot to learn.
Sad to say, it was a very slow burn.

Chamberlain's Cabinet

Pursuit of the war was the top concern,
Though little happened. Chamberlain recalled
Churchill (his Tory critics were appalled:
Winston they dismissed as a maverick,
A loose cannon) and his ardent sidekick
(As some saw him) and co-belligerent,
Young Anthony Eden. Ever the gent,
Eden, though ex-Foreign Secretary,
Accepted the Dominions. Wary,
As he was, of his old adversary
(Churchill), the Prime Minister nonetheless –
A bold manoeuvre, I have to confess –
Appointed him to the Admiralty,
The post he had quitted, reluctantly,
In 1915, and under a cloud.

The signal went out. The Navy was proud –
'Winston is back!' It's worth saying out loud:

The Dardanelles, an utter fiasco,
Was of Churchill's making. Those in the know,
However, were aware of his talent
And drive. Winston, simply, was brilliant.

Eden and Churchill apart, the old guard
Still ruled the roost. Simon, in this regard,
Hoare and Halifax, were appeasers all.
Was this a case of pride before a fall?
Could Chamberlain soldier on? Who knew?

The BEF

The PM's bellicose instincts were few.
The British Expeditionary Force
(Four divisions) set off in due course
For France. An offensive measure? No fear.
They dug in on the Belgian frontier…
And waited… Only when fighting began
Would they advance (at least, that was the plan)
Into Belgium. Maurice Gamelin,
An elderly, arrogant, lazy man,
Was in command of the BEF – yes,
A Frenchman! Crazy, naive and witless.

A cause of not a little bitterness,
Among the French, was the number of Brits
Sent in support of France. This was the pits.
For the French had contrived to mobilise
Six million men. They expressed surprise
At Britain's meagre four divisions –
One of Chamberlain's smarter decisions,
As it turned out. After France's collapse,
The British could feel some relief, perhaps,
That they had not been driven to send more –
Even though, by March, they'd increased the score
By six. Any more, we'd have lost the war.

Chamberlain's optimism

Chamberlain still did not believe, indeed,
In an offensive war. There was no need,
He argued, with Hitler still keen to sue
For peace. What complacency! I ask you!
Austria, Czechoslovakia too,
And Poland... How could the PM believe
That to offer yet another reprieve
Would somehow get the country off the hook?
Peace talks were still, in Halifax's book,
The preferred option. An awful choice.
Well, thank the Lord. Winston now had a voice.

The RAF was busy all the while –
I know I shouldn't, but this makes me smile –
Dropping leaflets on Nazi Germany.
The foe would come to their senses, you see,
Once they discovered the war was in vain.
They had little to lose and all to gain
From peace. *Mein Pamph* cynics called this campaign!

Early losses at sea

Anyway, the blockade would do the trick.
Was the Prime Minister really that thick?
Meanwhile, a U-boat entered Scapa Flow –
Up in the Orkneys, a long way to go –
And sank the great battleship *Royal Oak.*
A month earlier, no word of a joke
(In September), we lost *Courageous*,
An aircraft carrier. Outrageous.
With the war already going badly,
Churchill would have taken over, gladly,
But he chose to bide his time. This was wise.
For the PM (this comes as a surprise)
Was a popular chap in people's eyes.

Some three quarters of a random sample
Felt he was setting a fine example,
And facing a tough and arduous task
With nerve. I beg to differ, since you ask.
The country was in one heck of a mess.
How we'd win the war was anyone's guess.

The *Graf Spee*

The First Lord had the bit between his teeth.
Churchill, it was hoped, would supply the beef.
There was no doubting his strong self-belief.
The Navy got off to a flying start,
Warming "the cockles of the British heart"
(His phrase, in a speech marking the event),
With a famous victory, Heaven-sent,
In the South Atlantic, off Uruguay.
In a fierce sea battle (do or die!),
The German pocket battleship,* *Graf Spee*,**
Was severely damaged. She slunk away,
Hoping, at best, to fight another day.

She sought refuge in Montevideo
To repair the damage and to lie low,
But was refused licence to anchor there.
So the Germans scuttled her, in despair,
And the Captain shot himself. All good news
For the First Lord and the triumphant crews,
Who took part in a victory parade
Through the City of London: unafraid,
Bold and defiant – the stuff of legend.

There might have been a far less happy end.
A whole host of prisoners were taken
By the *Graf Spee* (if I'm not mistaken)
On the River Plate, before she was destroyed.
Hitler was particularly annoyed,

When, in February the following year, **1940**
Three hundred prisoners (or very near),
Held on the German *Altmark*, were rescued
In Norwegian waters. This was construed,
Of course, as another great victory
And, as such, it went down in history.

The ill-fated Norwegian campaign

But Churchill lost some of his mystery,
His golden touch, when it came to Norway.
This is complex. I could go on all day,
But I'll give you the bare bones anyway.

It was linked to exports of iron-ore,
Crucial to Germany for the war,
Which came from Sweden. Owing to the ice,
In winter (the Baltic, to be precise,

---

*Nicknamed 'pocket' by the British. Here's why.
The Germans were limited, by Versailles,
To six small battleships. These 'pocket' ones,
With half a dozen large-calibre guns,
And restricted to just 10,000 tons,
Nonetheless had the advantage of speed –
28 knots. French and British take heed!
They also enjoyed a long cruising range,
Up to 18,000 miles, which was strange,
Given that the Treaty had limited
German capacity. Odd, isn't it?

**For any of you reading aloud, *Spee*,
In German, is pronounced to rhyme with 'pay'.
That's what I was always taught, anyway.

Was frozen over), supplies of the ore
Passed through Norway, to be loaded on shore
At Narvik, in the north of the country.
The cargo then continued its journey
(Benefiting from the neutrality
Of Norway) south to Germany, by sea.

The First Lord, a combative fellow he,
Was keen to mine the waters off Narvik,
To stop the traffic. Unrealistic,
Cried the Cabinet (Halifax and co.).
His plan was met with a resounding 'no'!
Besides, what of Sweden's neutrality,
Norway's too? Unbridled brutality,
They argued, it would be to ride roughshod
Over their 'rights'. It's decidedly odd,
But this ploy was later given the nod
(Amidst a mass of blunders) in the spring.

If this has a faintly shambolic ring,
Read on. The picture was complicated
By the Finns. The Russians they hated,
And the Red Army was poised to invade.
Finland, to her credit, was undismayed.
Sniffing an easy victory, we hear,
The Reds crossed over the Finnish frontier
In large numbers. But the Finns were ready:
Camouflaged skiers, their nerve held steady.

Well used to the worst winter conditions,
They took up key strategic positions
And halted the Russian advance with ease.
The Red Army's best officers, by degrees,
Had been purged by Stalin, leaving the Ruskies
To perish of exposure in the snow.
The poor souls froze at their posts. Death was slow.

This was in December (still '39).
Stalin was livid, a worrying sign,
And sure in time to renew his attack.
Could the Finns continue to hold him back?
Probably not. A new rallying cry
Went up: Aid for the Finns! Well worth a try…

Or was it? Highly risky, I should say,
But the French and Brits agreed – to this day,
The decision fills me with dismay –
To send an expeditionary force
To Finland. It was poorly planned, of course,
Heralding the mother of all mishaps:
Faulty intelligence, out-of-date maps,
Woeful lack of strategy. If, perhaps,
They'd known what they were really about,
Just maybe… But they were riddled with doubt,
Chamberlain and, for France, Deladier,
Whose overriding motive, sad to say,
Was to be seen to be doing *something.*

Winston Churchill (now this was a rum thing)
Saw support for Finland as a back door
For stopping consignments of iron-ore
To Germany, his main obsession.
Once Narvik was in our possession,
The blockade of Swedish ore could go ahead –
And seizing Narvik, you can take it as read,
Was central to the plan to support the Finns.
You will have heard the old adage, Who Dares Wins.
Not in this case, sadly. Finland, for her sins,
Was forced to reach an accommodation
With Stalin, a bruised and broken nation.

The British were set to sail for Norway,
By co-incidence, on the very day

That Finland collapsed. Progress had been slow.
By March the 12th, we were ready to go.
This was fortunate. Had we reached Narvik
One week earlier, there'd have been panic.
For had we arrived even days before,
Bound for Finland, we would have been at war
With the Soviets! A lucky escape.

Yet we were still in one heck of a scrape.
The embarkation was halted, true,
But Chamberlain, bless him, hadn't a clue
(He dithered and swithered) what he should do.

Deladier of France had staked his all
On backing the Finns. He was sure to fall,
And so he did. His successor, Reynaud,
By contrast (only), was a dynamo.
He persuaded Neville to have a go
At mining Norwegian waters! Well,
Some of his Cabinet raised merry hell,
But, strange to say, the PM insisted.
The scheme he had so strongly resisted
Was back on the table. Churchill's baby,
The Narvik adventure, sounded crazy,
But stopping Hitler's iron-ore supplies
Would give the Führer a nasty surprise.

Churchill (and Reynaud) were quick to surmise
That Hitler was sure to retaliate.
Should Germany happen to take the bait,
So be it. The time must come, Churchill knew –
To tell the truth, he was one of the few –
When the conflict would begin in earnest.
Only then could Britain rise to the test.
Chamberlain failed to understand the fuss.
Hitler, he assured us, had "missed the bus".

The Norway campaign was a fiasco.
The planting of mines was given a go
On the 8th of April, the day before
Hitler, without even declaring war,
Invaded Denmark (with ease) and Norway.
The Führer took full charge, as was his way,
Of strategy. The thrust of his attack –
Once it was launched, there was no going back –
Was by sea. He overpowered Oslo,
Then Bergen and Trondheim, then (woe on woe)
Narvik. The Nazis struck a fearsome blow
Against these ports. The allies were too slow,
Too weak, to fight back, but they had a go.

We did have some success reaching Narvik.
The Navy had been remarkably quick,
A relief to all. The snow was heavy.
This hid our ships from the enemy.

Several German destroyers were lost,
But not without considerable cost.
Grievous losses were sustained on both sides.
HMS *Warspite* (nine destroyers besides)
Was despatched, on the 13th of April,
To rescue other vessels in peril.

As for the land forces, without a doubt
Their fate (there's no better word) was a rout.
Where, for a start, were they to be landed?
The strategy, at best, was cack-handed.
Trondheim? Namsos? Effectively stranded,
The Army, unprepared and ill-equipped,
Was offered no air cover. They were whipped
(Again, no better word) by German planes,
The *Luftwaffe*, who had taken great pains
To seize all the airfields. This was the key
To the Germans' success. They came by sea,
But advanced within days, amazingly,
Through all of Norway. It had been snowing.
Did we really have no way of knowing
That our forces would be in need of skis?
The French were abundantly supplied with these,
But sadly neglected to bring any straps –
Just one of a host of terrible mishaps.

Hundreds of our courageous chaps
Became prisoners. Taken to Berlin –
To the utter disgust of Chamberlain –
They were paraded, ingloriously,
Before Adolf Hitler for all to see.

Narvik was taken, temporarily,
After heavy bombardment from the sea,
But was finally evacuated
On June the 8th. The Navy was fated

To lose two destroyers and *Glorious*,
An aircraft carrier. I'm curious
How Churchill survived this dreadful event,
The Norway *débâcle*. But rest content,
It was Chamberlain who suffered the most.
By the end of April, Neville was toast.

There were a couple of compensations.
Of all the Scandinavian nations,
Norway made the greatest contribution
To the war effort. A revolution?
No, but folk showed a dogged resistance
To occupation. Their persistence
In refusing to jump through Nazi hoops
Meant a quarter of a million troops
Were tied up there for the duration.
With ideas well above their station,
Hitler distrusted the Norwegians. Their King,
Haakon, kept his country's flag proudly flying,
In London, with his government in exile.

But a more significant blow, by a mile,
Was to Hitler's navy. They were the losers.
Ten destroyers were sunk, three battle cruisers
And dozens of lesser vessels. Germany
Effectively lost the cream of her navy.
An invasion of Britain, by sea,
Was a present impossibility.
Norway had proved a liability.

The Norway debate

The debate, on the 7th and 8th of May,
In the Commons, was an inquest on Norway –
The most damning indictment, to this day,
Of any government. Backbenchers held sway

(A welcome change), with up to forty Tories
Voting against their party. These brave MPs
Changed the course of history. The government
Was assaulted from all sides. Parliament
Had never witnessed such a fierce debate.

A string of strong speeches sealed Chamberlain's fate.
His record, as Attlee (for Labour) made clear,
Was an "almost uninterrupted career
"Of failure". This was key, I have to say,
For this debate was not just about Norway,
But the conduct of the war as a whole:
"Everywhere" (Attlee was on a roll)
"The story is 'too late'." He took some care
Not to implicate Churchill, well aware
That he might occupy the vacant chair
Should the Prime Minister fall. In despair,
Admiral Sir Roger Keyes (retired)
Spoke for the Navy. As if inspired –
The Admiral, truly, was on top form,
With medals and in full dress uniform,
In the House of Commons hardly the norm –
Sir Roger lambasted the government.
This was his far from happy testament:
The Navy had been ordered to hold back
From launching their planned offensive attack
On Trondheim, which might well have succeeded.
The assault, they'd been told, was not needed,
Owing, apparently, "to the success
"Of the military". Talk about a mess.

This drew a great gasp of astonishment
From the House. For such an admonishment,
From a naval hero of World War One,
Was a near-mortal blow, all said and done,
To the government. To add to the fun,

The highly regarded Tory MP
(And Chamberlain fan), Leo Amery,
Rose to speak. His voice was strong, his eyes shone,
His gander was up. "We cannot go on,"
He said, "as we are. There must be a change."

It may sound disloyal, as well as strange,
To turn on his friend, but that's what he did.
Leo quoted Cromwell's words, unprompted
(Delivered to the Long Parliament,
Three hundred years before), with dark intent:
"You have sat too long here for any good
"You have been doing" (who could have withstood
So awesome a challenge?). "Depart, I say,
"And let us have done with you." Come what may,
This speech, of such majesty and power,
Was Leo Amery's finest hour.

His conscience stirred him. He could not say no.
So he concluded: "In the name of God, go!"

Lloyd George, the cunning little so-and-so,
Twisted the knife. He hated Chamberlain
(It was mutual), whose besetting sin,
In his book, was his lack of enterprise
And daring. So it came as no surprise
When the old Welsh Wizard put the boot in.
By a cruel irony, Chamberlain
Had earlier appealed for sacrifice.
Nothing better, Lloyd George claimed, could suffice,
That would "contribute more to victory
"In this war" (he still had the knack, you see),
Than him laying down his seals of office.

Disaster for Chamberlain

Could the beleaguered PM survive this –
His private and political crisis?
The vote was taken. It was hit and miss.
His majority fell to eighty-one.
Over two hundred in the normal run,
The result was devastating for him.
Chamberlain left the Chamber pale and grim.
Even his worst critics after Munich,
On his own side (this is some statistic),
Never ventured beyond abstention.
Now it was clearly their intention
To bring about a change of government.
Chamberlain, to a limited extent,
Was prepared to listen. Bring in Labour!

Serve under Neville? Do us a favour!
Such was the reaction of Attlee
And his colleagues. They would serve, willingly,

In a national coalition,
But only on the strict condition
That Chamberlain resign. The PM's fall
Was certain. The writing was on the wall.

What no one anticipated at all
(Few, anyway) was that Lord Halifax
Would lose out to Churchill. Here are the facts.
Halifax had long enjoyed the backing
Of the Establishment. He was lacking,
However, in popular support. Why,
People wondered aloud, should the choice lie
With a man who had stood by Chamberlain,
Not least over Munich, through thick and thin?
Appeasement? Sorry, with a war to win
They wanted somebody more bellicose,
Someone to get up Adolf Hitler's nose.

Churchill or Halifax?

Churchill had been warning people for years
Of the scourge of Nazism and his fears
Over Hitler, the *Reich* and the *Wehrmacht.*
Churchill at times could be lacking in tact,
But he spoke his mind and people liked that.

He was a better bet, from where they sat,
Than Halifax. His Lordship was urbane,
Cool, aloof – in short, a bit of a pain.
A fellow of All Souls, he was clever –
Indeed, formidably bright. However,
He was, by definition, a peer.
This disqualified him, it would appear,
From the Premiership. It's said the King
Preferred Halifax, and if anything
Could have been done to help him ('suspending'

His peerage?), he'd have co-operated.
Halifax, sadly, was overrated,
That's the truth of it. Where Churchill was keen,
His Lordship had the air of a has-been.
He appeared reluctant to press his case
And visited his dentist* (a disgrace)
Around the time the choice had to be made.
His supporters were suitably dismayed –
And some among them felt badly betrayed –
But Halifax, when it came to the crunch,
Opted out. So, the best of a bad bunch
(The view of many), Churchill took over –
In the end, something of a walkover.

Churchill's political background

Churchill nonetheless came as a surprise.
Even his close friends wondered: was this wise?
Among the Tories he had few allies,
Having crossed the floor of the Commons – twice!
In terms of supporters, he paid the price.
Elected first as a Conservative
In 1900, he was abrasive
And independent. Quick to criticise
His own leaders, he came to realise
That he preferred the Liberal Party.
Dismissed by some as a little smarty,

---

*John Major visited his dentist too,
In 1990, prior to the *coup*
That toppled Margaret Thatcher. He knew
How smart it was to be out of the way
While the knives were out. And he won the day!
So John owed the job to his wisdom teeth
(Unlike Lord Halifax). Beyond belief,
As both Hurd and Heseltine came to grief.

He was President of the Board of Trade
Under Asquith, when massive strides were made
In pensions, employment and welfare.
Your average Tory did not much care
For such reforms. Churchill was well aware
That conditions for the working man
Were deplorable. Lloyd George was a fan.
As Chancellor, he supported Churchill.
The two men formed a sort of 'double bill'.

Churchill, though, was ever the maverick.
He made the working classes pretty sick
When, as Asquith's new Home Secretary,
He dared to bring in the military
To break strikes in the docks and the railways.
He failed (to put it mildly) to win praise
When, as First Lord of the Admiralty,
He had to take responsibility
For the fiasco in the Dardanelles
In 1915 – the worst of bombshells
In a budding political career.

Churchill bounced back. He had nothing to fear.
Next, as Secretary of State for War,
He advocated (now this I deplore)
British use of force as a solution
To crush the Russian Revolution!
This wild proposal, in 1919,
Was dismissed as little short of obscene.
What was he thinking? How foolish; how green.

Re-elected in 1924,
For the Conservatives (Churchill foresaw
The imminent collapse, you can be sure,
Of the Liberals), he was appointed
New Tory Chancellor. Disappointed?

Hardly, once the PM had made it clear
That this was the Exchequer, not (oh, dear!)
The post of Chancellor of the Duchy
Of Lancaster… I can tell you for free,
Churchill would have been mightily hacked off
With that office, a mere spit and a cough.

Many Conservatives were mystified
By this bizarre choice, if not horrified.
Churchill was a traitor, a renegade.

Yet the novice Chancellor, unafraid
(Nay, reckless), depressed the economy
By returning Britain (utter folly)
To the Gold Standard. Churchill, by golly,
Contrived to do some damage in his time!
His provocative tactics were a crime,
Some reckoned, during the General Strike
Of 1926. What was he like!

When the Tories, in 1929,
Lost office, Churchill's terminal decline
Looked inevitable. His middle years
Should have been his most fruitful. Few shed tears
In '35, when he was overlooked
By Baldwin. The best jobs were fully booked.

He opposed Baldwin over India,
Calling Gandhi a "half-naked fakir".
Offensive and crude, this cost Churchill dear.
All talk of Indian self-government
Was anathema, an experiment
Designed to undermine the Empire.
Churchill, the orator, was on fire,
But in private he was beset by fears
And regrets. These were the wilderness years.

Churchill's character

He suffered from the 'black dog'.* When he warned
Against the rise of Hitler, he was scorned –
Nay, mocked. Poor fellow, he was under strain,
A bit of a lush. A worthy campaign?
Forget it. Winston was at it again.

"Worry," Churchill once wrote, "is a spasm
"Of the emotion." That dark chasm,
Depression, was fed by worry. So,
He needed a hobby. Keep on the go!
He took up oil painting. "Splash it on!"
Advised a friend. No longer woebegone,
Churchill discovered he was good at art.
No cure-all, painting was at least a start.

---

*This was Churchill's favoured expression
When he fell into a depression.

Painting as a Pastime is a fine book.
Unearth a copy, by hook or by crook.

His high-profile stand against appeasement
Was vindicated. In strong agreement
Were the people. Churchill was their hero.
But support in Parliament? Zero –
Among the majority of Tories.
In one of politics' odder stories,
When Churchill's premiership began,
The Labour benches rose to a man.
Among his colleagues? Hardly a fan!
This all changed, of course. But rumour ran
That Halifax was waiting in the wings,
Still – with proposals for peace, of all things.

Churchill was an eccentric, a one-off.
It was clear to all that he was a toff.
High-born, a descendant of Marlborough
(Whom he worshipped), it would never occur
To the great man to take the underground.

How do you imagine he got around?
By taxi, or by private conveyance.
Public transport was kept in abeyance!
Nor had he ever set foot on a bus,
In his life. He was hardly 'one of us'.
Indeed, his wife told his doctor (no joke)
That he knew nothing of ordinary folk.
Yet Churchill appeared a decent sort of bloke,
A man of the people, with the common touch.
His background, it seems, didn't trouble them much.

His great set-piece speeches, without a doubt,
Weighty and grandiloquent, bear this out.
He'd spend hours in preparation
And rehearsal for each oration.

Churchill had a unique ability,
The most astonishing facility,
To say to people what they'd "like to say
"For themselves if they knew how".* To this day,
Listening to his words, they strike a chord.
They inspire. People were overawed.

Never forget, he was a man of war.
As a boy, he would marshal, on the floor,
His soldiers, fifteen hundred or more.
These toys were his passion. His escape
From a POW camp (some scrape!)
During the Boer War electrified
The press. He did not take long to decide,
When he fell from office in World War One,
To volunteer. It might even be fun.
Destiny beckoned. He would take his chance.
So Churchill served in the trenches in France,
As a Major. "A jolly life," he wrote,
"With nice people." You wonder why I quote?
How else would readers credit it? Jolly?
The trenches? This smacks to me of folly.

His temper was mercurial. His mood
Could change rapidly. He was prone to brood,
Apparently completely unaware
Of folk around him. Then he would be there:
Active, alert, challenging, arguing,
A hard taskmaster – even bullying,
For Churchill could be abusive and rude,
As well as sensitive, subtle and shrewd.
His staff were devoted, nevertheless,
More than he sometimes deserved, I confess.

---

*Lord Moran this was. Take it as read,
His doctor hit the nail on the head.

Most days he would take an afternoon nap,
Then work through the night (peculiar chap).

This eccentric timetable, Churchill swore,
Enabled the old man, throughout the war,
To work, over the course of seven days,
One hundred and twenty-two hours! These ways,
Of course, were a considerable pain
For civil servants who, time and again,
Would be dragged into meetings at midnight…
Or later. The Prime Minister was bright
And clear-headed. Until two, even three,
Colleagues marvelled at his capacity
To cram one and a half days' work into one.
Churchill's energy was second to none.

His appearance came to some as a surprise.
You'll probably think I am taking the rise,

But Churchill, far from being six-foot tall
(As many thought), was in fact rather small.
Winston had a slightly delicate air,
Winsome (some called it), with fine, wispy hair.
His face was round, he had artistic hands
And his complexion, one understands,
Was pale. Yet he gave the impression,
With his brooding, bulldog expression,
Of a heavy figure, sullen, morose,
Who could do a man mischief if he chose.

Churchill was a risk. No doubt about that.
He merited more than the odd brickbat
For the Dardanelles, and now for Norway.
But Winston was the one that got away.
It's ironic. Norway was his campaign,
Yet Chamberlain it was who felt the pain.

The King's commission

The King summoned Churchill. Events moved fast.
He would need a government built to last.
Churchill accepted the commission,
Offering, with the King's permission,
To name his War Cabinet before midnight –
Within hours of his appointment, that's right.

Four would serve with him at the top table:
Attlee and Greenwood (willing and able),
Halifax as Foreign Secretary,
With Chamberlain (an astute move, very)
Kept on as his effective deputy,
And Lord President. For Churchill, sadly,
Was far from secure. The Tory Party
Remained in favour, overwhelmingly,
Of the bland, but dangerous, Halifax.
Political rivals must mind their backs.

In the Commons, on the 13th of May –
MPs had been recalled on Whit Monday,
Notwithstanding the spring Bank Holiday –
Chamberlain received a huge ovation
From Tory backbenchers. The occasion
Was less happy for Churchill, it appears,
Who entered, as we've seen, only to cheers
From the Labour and Liberal members.

What History, however, remembers
Is Churchill's speech. An inspiration.
A call to arms. A great oration.
He had "nothing to offer but blood, toil,
"Tears and sweat". Amidst all the turmoil,
He was clear as to "our policy":
To "wage war against a monstrous tyranny"
And to wage that war, he promised, "by sea,
"Land and air, with all our might". Victory
Was the aim, however "hard the road may be".

Chamberlain's loyalty

Unfortunately, party unity
Remained still, for the moment, elusive.
His sternest critics (downright abusive,
In private) were silenced, to some extent,
By the wise and generous compliment
That Churchill paid to the Lord President.
Chamberlain was firm in his commitment
To the Prime Minister, while Halifax,
In Cabinet (also behind their backs),
Launched a series of withering attacks
On his boss. He wanted to negotiate
With Hitler's Nazis before it was too late.

Churchill (it seems almost beyond belief)
Felt an overwhelming sense of relief –

As if "I were walking with destiny".
He alone now had the authority
To direct "the whole scene", as he saw it.
Only Churchill (and few could ignore it)
Had the gravitas, the experience,
The will and the sheer personal presence
To snatch victory from the jaws of defeat.

The fall of Belgium, Holland and France

The PM barely had time to find his feet.
No sooner was his War Cabinet complete,
Than news was confirmed from the Continent.
It was a chilling and solemn moment.
For German forces on the 10th of May –
As he took office, the very same day –
Invaded both Belgium and Holland.

France was soon to follow, you understand.
Hitler's plan for a quick and sure advance
Into an ill-led and complacent France
Had recently changed. Originally,
We are told, the main thrust of his army
Would be from the north (as in World War One).
Belgium (and Holland) would be overrun,
A broad repeat of the *Schlieffen* model.
The surge into France would be a doddle,
Given that Belgium's neutrality
Had caused the latter weak, but proud country
(Too proud, alas) to refuse the presence
Of any allied armies. In essence,
Hitler would enter France by the back door,
As Germany had planned in the Great War.
First blood to the Nazis. Need I say more?

Hitler was sorely tempted, however,
By a bolder plan, fiendishly clever,

And known (in German) as *Sichelschnitt*
(Or 'sickle-cut'). This was the gist of it:
The Germans would score a direct hit
On the Low Countries, but (the cunning bit),
Once this breakthrough had enticed the allies
To move north-east to meet them, a surprise
Would be sprung north of the Maginot Line.*

A second offensive, swift and malign,
Would push through the forest of the Ardennes
And enter France west of Luxembourg. Then,

---

*The Maginot Line, a defensive shield
Along the French border, would never yield
To another German invasion.
Sorry to say, on this occasion
The Germans exposed the Line as nonsense.
This complex, subterranean defence,
Constructed by the French at vast expense,
Could only ever, at best, have made sense
Had it covered the entire distance
Beyond Germany's frontier with France
To the sea. This you could see at a glance.
But it stopped at the Belgian border!
It was considered well out of order
To defend the country from an ally.
The Belgians would play their part. Nice try!
So the French were in a bit of a fix
When Belgium, in 1936,
Declared her neutrality. In some haste,
An effort was made (a terrible waste)
To extend the Maginot Line. Too late.
The French, alas, could only sit and wait.
The Germans broke through, just north of the Line
At Sedan, a dark and ominous sign.

All going well they would head for the sea,
Thus cutting off Belgium completely,
Holland too. What Hitler did not foresee
Was that Britain and France (to his great glee)
Would by then have committed their armies
To a broad defence of the Low Countries.

Yet this is how it played out. Gamelin,
The allied Commander, stuck to his plan.
The General dismissed as plain nonsense
Daily reports from French intelligence

Of Hitler's covert Ardennes strategy.
His brain, in a state of near atrophy,
Could only embrace a German advance
Through the Low Countries. In the name of France,
His troops reached the Belgian frontier –
Along with the brave BEF, I fear –
Shortly before the Dutch threw in the sponge.
Their forces had barely taken the plunge
Before the Germans forced them to fall back.
Rotterdam suffered heavy air attack
From their bombers. By the 15th of May,
Holland had collapsed. The Queen got away.
Wilhelmina and the Dutch government
Fled to England, a glowing testament
To their resolve, along with their navy
(Most of it, at least). It may sound crazy,
But allied forces coming to their aid
Never even reached Holland, I'm afraid.

The gallant Belgians put up a fight.
The German army's superior might,
However, overwhelmed them. The allies
Could do nothing – so easy to be wise
After the event. Too little, too late,
Total collapse was the Belgians' fate.
They surrendered, unconditionally,
Within days. The allies, more's the pity,
Had crossed the frontier: sitting pretty.

The *Luftwaffe* attacked airfields in France,
Holland and Belgium. They took a chance,
But this paid off. The Dutch, without warning,
Lost half their strength in a single morning
And the German *Messerschmitts* destroyed row,
Upon row, of French planes on the ground. Slow,
Ill-prepared and lacking in heart, it seems,
Were the French. Fit for the fray? In your dreams!

The RAF lost some thirteen *per cent*
Of the fighters that the British had sent
To provide air cover for their allies.

One salient fact that no one denies
Is that the RAF did their bit. No,
That's not true. The French (including Reynaud)
Criticised the Brits for not doing more.
What, their argument ran, were allies for
If not to throw their all into the war,
Whatever the cost? The French became sore
(Very) when the British, keen to preserve
Their strength, kept the RAF in reserve
For England's safety. Thank goodness they did.
Imagine the country undefended.
The Battle of Britain? Heaven forbid.

The German advance through France

Time to move on. By the 13th of May,
German infantry, at the break of day,
Were crossing the Meuse. This was terrible.
The Ardennes forest? Impenetrable?
Not so. With Gamelin's eye off the ball,
The enemy had no trouble at all.
They stormed through. German sappers fortified
The only remaining bridge. Terrified,
The French all took to their heels. At Sedan,
Bombarded from the air, they simply ran.
The Germans in their tanks broke through with ease.

Now the French, for all their difficulties,
Had better tanks, but they were thinly spread,
As were their best divisions. Instead,
Alas, of concentrating his forces –
Troops and tanks, guns and other resources –

Gamelin displayed little readiness,
In his areas of greatest weakness,
To deploy his strength to best advantage.

The General had ample foreknowledge
Of the Ardennes attack. He ignored it.
His ten weakest divisions were fit,
He believed, to hold the line at Sedan
Should they ever be needed. Gamelin
Was a fool, complacent and out of touch.
His old-fashioned attitudes were such
That modern methods didn't count for much.

He rarely met his troops and (this is true)
He hardly ever moved from his HQ,
At Vincennes, the ancient edifice
Where Henry the Fifth met his end. It's this,
To me, that appals. He sent messages
By telegram! No radio contact!
He was a dinosaur, to be exact.

Politicians loved him for his tact,
For he never challenged their policies,
Nor they his – just one of many follies
And errors. The General's main concern,
It appears (he certainly didn't learn
From Napoleon), was to keep the war
Defensive. The chief reasoning, therefore,
Behind his campaign in the Low Countries
Was not to bring the Germans to their knees,
But to keep the enemy off French soil.
To prevent the war coming to the boil:
That was Gamelin's top priority.
Why bother harassing the enemy,
By bombing the Ruhr, for example? No.
They might retaliate! As campaigns go,

This policy was decidedly dim.
Gamelin's mistakes came back to bite him.

He made a host of poor decisions,
As forty of his best divisions,
Along with the whole of the BEF,
Pressed on into Belgium. He was deaf,
Alas, to the now desperate voices
Calling from Sedan. The worst of choices,
In his ignorance, the General made.
The French on the Meuse felt badly betrayed.

The German advance was not long delayed.
You need only take a look at the map:
As the French marched right into Hitler's trap,
The allies would be easily cut off
In Belgium and northern France. Don't scoff,
But Gamelin still ignored the danger.
He was now convinced (stranger and stranger)
That the Germans would head straight for Paris.

French defeatism

Poor Reynaud was deeply depressed by this.
He rang Churchill on the 15th of May:
"We are beaten," was all he had to say,
"We have lost the battle." When, the next day,
Churchill flew to France, he asked Gamelin:
"Where's your strategic reserve? What's the plan?"
He just shrugged his shoulders, a broken man.
"Where do you intend to counterattack?"
Asked Churchill. Gamelin was on the rack.
He had no answer. When he got the sack,
Three days later, few were surprised. Why wait?

The elderly General (68)
Was replaced by Weygand (73) –
In the Great War, Marshal Foch's deputy.
Weygand, frankly, was a bit of a bore
And way past it. He thought he knew the score,
But he didn't. Besides, he loathed Reynaud,
Who was desperate. Give Weygand a go!
He could do no worse, the old so-and-so.
Weygand promised Churchill swift action
To push back the Germans. Inaction,
I should call it. For Weygand did nothing.

Churchill himself promised (which was something)
Six air squadrons to support the French. Well,
This was more than generous, truth to tell.
Reynaud originally asked for more –
Ten, I believe. This could lose us the war,
Argued Air Chief Marshal Sir Hugh Dowding.
His objections had a valid ring
And he won the War Cabinet's support.
On the Meuse a bitter battle was fought
To cover the French forces in retreat.
Heavy losses were suffered, in defeat,

By the RAF. How the Meuse was cursed,
Casualty figures the very worst
In its history. Though less than impressed,
Sir Hugh, to his credit, rose to the test.
Embracing the challenge, he did his best,
Despite his gnawing sense of reluctance –
Born out of foresight rather than truculence.
He knew there would be a battle to fight,
Later, for Britain – and boy, was he right!

The French had experienced quite a fright,
As the Battle of Sedan now gave way
To the Battle for France. I have to say,
The French were a-dither. To boost morale –
This at least was Reynaud's rationale –
Marshal Pétain, hero of the Great War,
Joined the government (he was 84),
As deputy PM. Need I say more?

Pétain blamed the Marxists for France's plight.
This time he had no stomach for a fight.
He was the very first (pathetic, this)
To argue for an early Armistice.
The PM opposed him. Make no mistake,
The fate of the Republic was at stake.

The Germans made a quick dash to the coast.
What appeared to concern the French troops most
Was their own safety. Hordes, one understands,
Fell as prisoners into German hands.
Many threw down their arms. All said and done,
They lacked the discipline of World War One.
The Germans advanced some two hundred miles
In under two days. Hitler was all smiles.
Their progress exceeded his wildest dreams:
He had not expected such speed, it seems.

Boulogne fell on the 25th of May.
The 26th was the turn of Calais.
On the 19th, the previous Sunday,
The government of France had called for calm
By holding a service in Notre Dame.
They prayed for divine intervention.
The Lord, it appears, made no mention
Of taking sides or allaying their fears.
The US Ambassador was in tears.
Sad to say, it would be over four years
Before the French could hold their heads up high.
Their horrible fate is hard to deny.

Dunkirk

For the BEF, General Lord Gort –
A solid, unimaginative sort,
But able and practical nonetheless –
Was confronted with the most ghastly mess.

Gort was sure, by the 25th of May,
That France was putting up a poor display
Of resistance. Weygand's counterattack
(Such as it was) was failing to hold back
The Nazi assault. Orders Gort received
To return south left him mightily peeved.
The chances of Arras being relieved,
Or Amiens, come to that, were so slim
That he refused to obey. Good for him!
Instead, the General stuck his neck out.
He knew the BEF without a doubt –
If they sought to do France's dirty work –
Would be massacred. Cut off at Dunkirk,
His sole option was to put to sea
And to evacuate. It seems to me
That the General, single-handedly,
Discharged a rare responsibility.

As early as the 26th of May,
The withdrawal began. We know, today,
That the total number of troops rescued,
And saved from lifelong German servitude
(Or worse), numbered 200,000 Brits
And more than half as many French. Pickets,
Paddle steamers, fishing boats and dinghies
Backed up the Royal Navy. It was these,
And their valiant crews, that pulled it off.
Hermann Göring, for once, incurred the wrath
Of Hitler. Göring had assured his boss
That Gort's forces would be trounced, without loss,
By the *Luftwaffe* alone. Well, not so.

Churchill knew that Dunkirk was touch and go.
Code-named 'Operation Dynamo',
He warned the Commons (and the nation)
Not to have any expectation
That the proposed evacuation
Would bring more than ten thousand to safety.
No one was more realistic than he:
Members should prepare for very bad news.

Dunkirk was the mother of all rescues.
A variety of factors combined
To avert disaster. Hitler, you'll find,
Made a grave error (from his point of view)
In his French campaign, one of very few.
He feared a weakness on his southern flank,
Viz. a challenge from the French, tank for tank,
Should he push further into northern France.
A temporary halt to the advance
Was ordered. Gerd von Rundstedt had seen fit
To press the Führer to sanction it.
Hitler, though it stuck in his throat, agreed.
So, the allied withdrawal could proceed
With greater confidence. The Brits had need

Of a breather and for once they got it.
Hitler, it seems, did little to stop it.
He relied on Göring's reckless promise
That the *Luftwaffe* (optimistic this)
Could wreak havoc on the allied units
Stranded at Dunkirk in north-eastern France.

The BEF now had a fighting chance.
The RAF, flying from home bases,
Put the Nazi bombers through their paces,
Inflicting some heavy casualties.
But the fight was far from being a breeze.
Evacuation came at a cost:
Nearly two hundred fighter planes were lost;
Six Royal Navy destroyers were sunk
And nineteen damaged – a sizeable chunk
Of the British air and naval defence.

Churchill, ever the voice of common sense,
Was of course relieved. He made no pretence,
However, that this was a victory.
Of all the withdrawals in history,
Dunkirk was the boldest, all said and done.
But the PM was clear: "Wars are not won"
(He was right) "by evacuations."

Dunkirk was one of those occasions
When benign forces all came together.
The Channel was a mill-pond. The weather
Was perfect. To their eternal credit,
The brave Belgians fought on with spirit,
Their beleaguered forces doing their bit,
As even Hitler was forced to admit.

The most astonishing aspect of all
Was the way the British answered the call.

An urgent appeal on the BBC
Led to volunteers putting to sea
In any vessel that was fit to float:
Cabin cruisers, yachts, the odd rowing boat,
River launches… The flotilla numbered
(Light craft and the like) over eight hundred.

The Royal Navy too turned up in force
And was largely responsible, of course,
For the majority of those rescued.
But it was the 'weekend sailors' who crewed
This scratch armada, these gallant heroes,
Who, I'm pleased to say, got up Hitler's nose.

The news, as Churchill knew, was less than good.
The BEF, it should be understood,
Left all their guns and vehicles behind.
Many British soldiers were resigned
To a grim life as prisoners of war:
Some 50,000 poor victims or more.
In the early French campaign, as a whole,
Some 68,000, a fearful toll,

From the BEF, were casualties.
It is terrible figures such as these
That remind us of the realities
Of warfare, the sacrifice and the pain.
Pray God it may never happen again.

The disloyalty of Halifax

Churchill came under unexpected strain
In Cabinet. PMs must mind their backs!
That seasoned appeaser, Lord Halifax,
Launched a series of bold, frontal attacks
On Churchill's policy towards Hitler –
Increasingly partisan and bitter.

Poor Halifax, never a big hitter,
Nevertheless considered himself so.
The war, to date, had been a tale of woe.
There was surely more misery to go,
And Halifax used the occasion
To press for an accommodation
With Hitler. The war was as good as lost.
If won, it would be at an awesome cost.
The aim should not be to crush Germany,
But to preserve Britain's integrity
And, in the long term, her independence.

His Lordship was spouting utter nonsense.
Countries that went down fighting rose again –
This was Churchill's view and he made it plain –
But those who yielded tamely were finished.
As all hopes of victory diminished,
Lord Halifax pressed his case with vigour,
Purporting, with more than the odd snigger,
To speak for England. The PM took care
To move slowly, only too well aware

That should Chamberlain side with Halifax
And pursue the issue to its climax,
As sure as eggs he'd be out on his ear –
In office, alas, for under a year.

The Prime Minister played his hand with skill.
He'd treated Chamberlain (good for Churchill)
With courtesy since poor Neville's downfall.
This honest man now had no time at all
For Hitler. He'd trusted him, certainly,
Over Munich. But Nazi Germany,
He now understood, would stop at nothing.
All-out war, for all the pain, suffering
And uncertainty, was the only choice.
So, after a struggle, he lent his voice
To Churchill. Lord Halifax was sidelined.
Had either he or Chamberlain resigned,
Churchill would have been in trouble. Thank God,
I say, for Chamberlain. It may seem odd,
But the 'hero' of Munich saved Churchill.

The Prime Minister, though, had had his fill
Of Halifax. He was shown the door
In December. US Ambassador
Was his new role. He served the nation,
In Washington, with dedication.
Good for him. Anthony Eden became
Foreign Secretary. Remember that name.

The fall of Dunkirk

On June the 4th, Dunkirk fell.* The next day,
A new German assault was under way
Through the heart of France. To Reynaud's dismay,
One of their armies soon reached Brittany,
After sweeping with ease through Normandy;

A second great force stormed into Champagne,
Leaving the Maginot Line in its train;
A third forged on to Lyons in the south.

Reynaud was certainly down in the mouth.
The French government withdrew to Bordeaux.
Pétain wanted a deal. Reynaud said no.
They fled from Paris on the 10th of June –
As events proved, not a moment too soon.

Italy declares war

On the very same day, Mussolini
Declared war on the allies. He, you see,
Saw that Hitler was winning easily.
To partake in the fruits of victory
Was his aim. Rather unrealistic,
But nothing if not opportunistic
Was the glum Benito Mussolini,
The scourge of Europe and of Italy.

He's quoted as saying (more's the pity):
"I shall declare war, but I won't wage it!"
Hitler, had he heard, would have had a fit.
I shall quote, for history's benefit,
Bismarck: Italy, it was his belief,
Had "a hearty appetite, but poor teeth".

Mussolini, for sure, would come to grief.
That, of course, is a different story.
Suffice it to say, the end was gory.

---

*The Führer ordered bells in Germany
To be rung for three days. This victory
Was the finest in German history!

French complacency

The French were hardly covered in glory.
Complacency had ruled the roost for years.
Parisians could not believe their ears
When the news broke. The Nazis on their way?
Impossible, on such a sunny day!

According to Maurice Chevalier,
"*Paris sera toujours Paris!*" The song
Would offer them comfort. How very wrong.
The French government had strung them along:
France was safe behind the Maginot Line,
So no need to panic. All would be fine.

They now fled the capital in despair.
The roads were blocked. Terror everywhere.
Young and old, nuns and priests, all took their chance.
It's calculated that in northern France

Over ten million were on the move.
To keep catastrophe at one remove,
That was their thinking, but what did it prove?

Nothing. Few folk knew where they were going.
What of the future? No way of knowing.
The poor suffered the most, always the case,
While the rich had wheels. A perfect disgrace.
The German fighters strafed them from the air,
Women, with their babes in arms. Cue, despair.

On the 14th, the Nazis occupied
Paris. Five short weeks (you'll be horrified)
It took the German army to achieve
What in the Great War, it's hard to believe,
Had proved impossible in four long years.
Now, tragically, the blood, toil and tears
Of that dreadful conflict had gone to waste.

An Armistice was not to Reynaud's taste.
He resigned his office, a broken man,
And France (*quelle horreur!*) was left to Pétain.
You'd hardly call it a negotiation,
But Pétain agreed to the occupation
Of northern and western France – including the coast
From Belgium round to Spain and, what mattered most,
Paris. The southern part of the country
Would be 'governed' by Pétain from Vichy.
This, in effect, became a puppet state.

Collaboration, at any rate,
Saved Pétain's bacon. The old man was free
To exercise civil authority,
Under Nazi auspices, from Vichy.
All France's colonies, amazingly,
Followed suit. Game, set and match to Germany.

One solitary figure, Charles de Gaulle,
Decamped to England. To the shame of all,
When he urged the French, against all the odds,
To resist, only a handful (ye gods!)
Rallied to his standard. He kept alive
The hopes of the Free French. France would survive.

The French Armistice

An Armistice, on the 22nd,
Was signed. It is generally reckoned
That this was the nadir of Pétain's 'reign'.
The same railway carriage at Compiègne
Where the terms of the German surrender
(On the 11th day of November,
1918) were signed was used again.
The French humiliation was plain.
Hitler rejoiced. He was clearly insane.
Having made his point, orders were issued
To blow up the carriage. Senseless and crude.

To add further insult to injury,
The Nazis celebrated victory
By marching triumphantly through Paris
Along the same route (nauseating, this)
That the victorious French forces had taken
In 1918. Churchill was not mistaken,
As he weighed the odds. How he must have despaired.
"The Battle for France is over," he declared.
"The Battle of Britain is about to begin."
To be sure, Winston Churchill was in it to win.

Among those who fought in France's defence
Were colonial troops. This gave offence,
Tragically, to the racist instincts
Of the Germans. This horrifies. It stinks.

Mass killings of those from the colonies
Took place, massacres and atrocities
Perpetrated upon Senegalese
And others. French combatants such as these,
Some 3,000 victims or more, were shot,
On orders executed on the spot
And out of hand. Nazis: judge and jury,
Motivated by blind, racist fury.

Relations were at an all-time low
Between Britain and France. After Reynaud,
Pétain, the cantankerous so-and-so,
Had no time for Churchill or the British.
The Marshal argued, from start to finish,
That France had been inveigled into war…
By the Brits! He blamed the Marxists before,
But what did that matter? Safe in Vichy,
Pétain now called the shots, more's the pity.
He reckoned he ruled the roost… but did he?

Certainly not. In hock to Germany,
Take the case, lackaday, of the French fleet.
Pétain's shame and dishonour were complete
When the Brits sank most of France's warships,
Hardly a mark of the best of friendships.

Churchill considered the fleet a menace
After France's collapse – obvious, this.
He ordered all her ships to be disarmed
Or scuttled. Marshal Pétain, far from charmed,
Refused. So the fleet in Oran harbour
Was sunk. No choice had ever been harder
For Churchill. The French navy was a risk.
The PM knew that he had to brisk.
Over thirteen hundred French sailors died,
A dreadful tally, it can't be denied.

"Their finest hour"

Churchill was energy personified.
His grand and patriotic rhetoric
In the House of Commons was historic.
One particular radio broadcast,
On the 18th of June, held folk aghast.
"The whole fury and might of the enemy
"Must very soon be turned" (he told the country)
"On us." Hitler knew that he would have "to break
"This island or lose the war". What was at stake
Was "Christian civilisation"
And its survival. Some oration!
"Let us therefore brace ourselves to our duty
"And so bear ourselves" (the speech was a beauty)
"That if the British Commonwealth and Empire
"Last for a thousand years" (Churchill was on fire),
"Men will still say, 'This was their finest hour!'."

It was a speech of monumental power.
The PM's words still echo down the ages.
I urge you, don't just take it from these pages.
Find a recording. Listen to Churchill's stress:
"*This*" (beat) "was their finest hour!" His *finesse,*
His choice of words, his graphic imagery,
His stentorian voice, his delivery –
All combine to make his speeches pitch-perfect.
Churchill saved the nation. That's my verdict.

Britain's defences

The country was woefully ill-prepared
Against attack. Let Hitler, if he dared,
Invade.* Brave words! For the cupboard was bare.
Where were Britain's guns? And her tanks? Nowhere!
The Home Guard (so-called), no rifles to spare,

Drilled with broomsticks. Beaches were protected
By coils of barbed wire. If, as expected,
The Germans were to land in the south-east,
They'd tear their trousers at the very least.

Just one armoured division existed
That could ever hope to have resisted
A full-scale Nazi invasion –
And that (don't laugh) was Canadian.

The Home Guard

The new Secretary of State for War,
Anthony Eden, was quick to explore

---

*Should invasion be imminent,
'Cromwell' was the code word – a strong statement,
This, of the courage, determination
And fortitude of the British nation.

The notion of a volunteer force –
Later known as the Home Guard, of course –
For the urgent defence of the country.
With France up the proverbial gum tree,
He had received many an enquiry
From those not yet in the military –
Or too old for it, unfortunately –
How they might be able to do their bit.

All volunteers, if reasonably fit,
Were welcome to come forward, aged between
(I must say, this sounds far too young) fifteen
And sixty-five. Folk were extremely keen.
Eden decided to make his appeal
On the radio. It hardly seems real,
But before he had finished his broadcast,
Volunteers were enlisting thick and fast.

The Local Defence Volunteers, you see –
Initially called the LDV –
Touched a popular, patriotic nerve.
Throughout the land a burning will to serve
Had been tapped. By the 17th of May,
The LDV were clearly here to stay.
Three days after Eden's appeal (no more),
The men of Kent were in a state of war.
In excess of one thousand LDVs
Lined the white cliffs of Dover, if you please,
And the land round about. Men such as these
Were the backbone of Britain! By mid-June,
The LDV, not a moment too soon,
Numbered one and a half million men.

They were ill-equipped. Only one in ten
(At most) had a rifle. Ammunition
Was at a premium. Their position
Was precarious, but they soldiered on.

From July, 1940 (and thereon),
After Churchill first called the LDV
The 'Home Guard', that name, officially,
Stuck. Their smart new armbands now read 'HG'.
George Orwell called them the 'People's Army'.
So they were. They paraded locally.
There were units, too, in the BBC,
The Post Office, many a factory
And even in Fleet Street – a source of pride.
Hitler would have got a pretty rough ride
Had the Nazis invaded... Or would he?

No one could doubt the pluck and bravery
Of these trusty volunteers. Armed with pikes
(Broomsticks, even), and riding round on bikes,
Not one of them was unprepared to die
For the cause. Hitler invade? Let him try!
Churchill proposed the slogan (this is true,
Spot on): "You can always take one with you!"
They'd fight in the ditches, literally,
These old warriors, for King and country.

At least until the spring of '42,
There was little that the Home Guard could do
But stand firm in readiness. 'Dad's Army',
Written off by some as a tad barmy,
Performed throughout the war a vital role
And were highly respected, on the whole,
By the public at large. They were no fools.
They drilled in earnest and stuck to the rules.

Financed by private donors, training schools
Were established, one at Osterley Park,
In Middlesex. They stepped up to the mark,
These stout volunteers. As the war progressed,
Ministers were increasingly impressed

By their contribution. The Home Guard
Gave critical support, in this regard,
As Hitler's bombs fell. All hands to the pumps!

When Civil Defence were down in the dumps,
Call in the Home Guard! By June, '43,
Overall membership of the HG
Numbered one-point-seven-five million.
Every able male civilian,
It appears, of the appropriate age
Signed up. Volunteering was all the rage.
There was a Home Guard in every town,
Or so it seemed. The 'army' was stood down
On the 3rd of December, '44.*
Abroad the British were winning the war.
Of the heroes at home they could ask no more.

'Operation Sea Lion'

Hitler, strangely, was all of a-dither,
Sure that Churchill would finally swither
And seek terms. He had outline plans, it's true,
For invasion, but the Führer knew,
In his bones, as Germany grew stronger,
That Britain could not hold out much longer.
How wrong he was. He not only lost face
By his delay, but the short breathing space
This gave the British people to rearm,
Re-equip and regroup worked like a charm.
Britain had sixteen divisions in place
In the south-east by September, a case

---

*The embers of the force were kept alive
Until the end of 1945,
When, on December the 31st, finally,
The Home Guard was disbanded officially.

Of factories working at full-throttle.
When the chips were down, the Brits showed bottle.

'Operation Sea Lion', nonetheless,
Was Germany's plan. Yet Hitler cared less
For this than for his other crazy scheme
Of invading Russia, his great dream.
The Führer was still expecting, the dope,
That Churchill would capitulate. Some hope!

No firm invasion plan was in place
Until June. Staring defeat in the face,
As they thought, the British worked at a pace
To mend their fences, blithely unaware
That German commanders were in despair.
The strength of the *Luftwaffe* in the air,
Much vaunted, was dubious, while their fleet
Was reduced, having never found its feet
Since the losses it sustained in Norway.
But the Nazis drew up plans, anyway,
For landing on a broad front between Deal
And Weymouth. This strategy, unreal
And reckless, held little or no appeal.

For invasion was pie in the sky.
There was no co-ordination. Why,
One wonders, did Hitler fail to direct
The campaign himself? He'd come to expect
Complete obedience. His position
Was impregnable: no opposition,
No challenge. Nobody now would have dared.
Those critics he did have were running scared,
But still the German High Command despaired.
Sea Lion, they reckoned, was ill-prepared
And absurdly overambitious.
Indeed, the whole plan was "ridiculous" –
The view of one leading *Luftwaffe* ace.

Yet the Nazi commanders knew their place.
Hitler, relaxed in his mountain retreat,
The *Berghof*, issued the order. Defeat?
Unthinkable. He made one final try –
In a speech on the 19th of July –
To appeal to "reason and common sense".
Britain should sue for peace. Stuff and nonsense,
Retorted Churchill. On the radio,
Halifax added a resounding 'no'
To the PM's rebuff. A subtle choice,
To have an ex-appeaser lend his voice
In arguing the case for resistance –
Presumably at Churchill's insistence.
This was while Halifax, behind the scenes,
Talked peace. Perhaps that's what politics means.

Unconditional German surrender
Was Churchill's sole aim. Britain, remember,
Now stood alone. The 15th of September
Was pencilled in by Hitler as the date
When the British people would know their fate.

Control of the skies

The High Command agreed, at any rate,
That it was the *Luftwaffe*, come the hour,
That would prove indispensable. Air power,
Control of the skies over Britain, was key.
Hermann Göring (folly or naivety?)
Gave the Führer a cast-iron guarantee
That his fighters and bombers could do the job.
Göring, as well as a bully and a slob,
Was a fool. As a simple matter of course,
He ignored the strength of the Royal Air Force.

Churchill's Chiefs of Staff were keenly aware
That superiority in the air

Was vital to their defence strategy.
New planes, as a matter of urgency,
Had to be built. Dozens of pilots, too,
Must be trained. There were currently too few.
One hundred and thirty-six had been lost
(Killed or captured) in France, an awful cost.
As for aircraft, Beaverbrook,* untroubled,
Set the pace. Factory output doubled.
Hundreds of Spitfires and Hurricanes were built,
Per week, workers labouring up to the hilt.

Göring's tactics for his air offensive
Were simple: bombing attacks, intensive
And sustained, on British ports and bases
In south-east England and other places.
The Straits of Dover and the tip of Kent
('Hellfire Corner') suffered bombardment
By the *Luftwaffe* at this early stage,
Though with limited impact. Göring's rage
Was patent: British pilots, the blighters,
Were a strong threat to the Nazi fighters
Escorting his bombers. This he'd ignored,
An oversight the *Luftwaffe* deplored.

For both sides were fairly evenly matched
When it came to fighters. His plans were hatched
On the premise that the Straits of Dover
Could be heavily bombed, a walkover.

---

*Minister of Aircraft Production
From mid-May. A prominent Press Baron,
Proprietor of the *Daily Express*
And Churchill's chum, he made a huge success
Of his new office. The targets he set
Were legendary and were always met.

The British would receive a sound whipping,
Particularly their merchant shipping.

Göring was easily confused, the fool.
It's usually wiser, as a rule,
To do your homework first. He was surprised
At Britain's fighter strength. He now surmised,
In his wisdom, that he should concentrate
On Hurricanes and Spitfires… But wait:
Before these pesky planes could do their worst,
Perhaps he should focus on bombing first…

Air Chief Marshal Sir Hugh Dowding, meanwhile,
Allowed himself the glimmer of a smile.
He knew precisely what he was doing.
Keenly aware of the trouble brewing
From the Nazi fighters (their *Messerschmitts*,
The devils, could blow his pilots to bits),
It was chiefly the German bomber force
He needed to target. For they, of course,
Could do critical damage, on the ground,
To vital airfields. The *Luftwaffe* found,
While the British would have to sacrifice
More fighters, they paid a heavier price,
In lives and planes, when it came to bombers.

The Air Chief Marshal deserves top honours.
He husbanded his resources with care
(Pilots and aircraft), all too well aware
That fourteen hundred men (surely no more)
Could determine the outcome of the war.

The Battle of Britain, fought to a draw,
Would be enough. All the British needed
Was to see Göring off. They succeeded…
By a whisker. It was a close-run thing.

The Battle of Britain

The German assault, code-named by Göring
Adlerangriff (Eagle Attack), began
In good earnest and according to plan
On the 13th of August. The targets
For these Nazi bombers (or 'air pirates',
As some called them) were the great naval base
At Portsmouth (left undamaged, by God's grace)
And RAF airfields. Forty-seven
Enemy aircraft, merciful Heaven,
Were shot down, with eighty-nine Germans killed
Or taken prisoner. Though highly skilled,
Brave and resourceful, three British airmen
Were lost, and thirteen fighters. It was then
That the edge Britain enjoyed became clear.

The south coast was tantalisingly near,
But German bombers could not hang about,
A major drawback, no shadow of doubt.
For only thirty-five minutes, at most,
Could they fly their sorties over the coast.
Any longer, the poor souls would have been toast.

RAF pilots, on the other hand,
For reasons not that hard to understand,
Could land, refuel and be up again
In a trice. It was radar, in the main,
That protected the men and kept them sane.
On permanent standby, the pilots found
They could have a quick kip, or lark around,
Until told the bombers were on their way.
The targets were clear. Radar won the day.

August the 15th brought a fresh onslaught,
The most ferocious battle yet fought.

Squadrons of German bombers, from Norway,
Denmark and France, flew over. Bombs away!
But the British wrought havoc and dismay.
The *Luftwaffe* dubbed this their 'Black Thursday',
For their losses were truly terrible.

The RAF's were hardly less dreadful,
For this was a fight to the death indeed.
Göring now saw, if he was to succeed,
That he must bomb airfields, and bomb again.
British pilots were under massive strain
And Air Chief Marshal Dowding shared their pain.

The Germans intensified their attack
On south-east targets, no holding them back.
Losses were almost equal on both sides,
But the British had the roughest of rides
When it came to pilots. More brave men died
Than could be replaced. Folk were horrified.
Dowding was worried. It's said that he cared,
Deeply, for his men. Far too few were spared.
He mourned their loss, but he never despaired.

The *Luftwaffe* bombings were relentless.
For this was survival, no more, no less.
For air attacks it was perfect weather,
Clear blue skies. At the end of their tether
(Almost), the RAF kept on going.
How long could they last? No way of knowing.

The final week of August, and the first
In September, turned out to be the worst –
Five hundred fighters shot down that fortnight.
RAF casualties, at their height,
Numbered a tragic one hundred and three
In a single week (yes, seriously)
Killed in action; those wounded, in excess
Of one hundred and twenty-eight. Success,
Nonetheless, still eluded the enemy.
The British pilots' heroic bravery
Denied Göring air superiority...
Just. Then a minor miracle occurred.
Göring switched tactics. It may sound absurd,
But this was the result of a mistake.

The bombs fall on London

It was quite a simple error to make.
On the 24th of August, at night,
German bombers (a human oversight)
Overshot their targets and bombed London.
There was considerable damage done
And Churchill's patience was wearing thin.
So he ordered the bombing of Berlin
The following night. In this early raid
Innocent Germans were killed, I'm afraid,
First victims of a British air attack.

The Führer was somewhat taken aback.
He had given his word (he had the knack)

That this would never happen. So, in turn,
He retaliated. Let London burn!

Thus were Britain's precious airfields saved.
However deadly, however depraved,
Was Germany's new bombing strategy,
It was (or rather just happened to be)
A life-saver, a key distraction
From the sort of enemy action
That had threatened Britain's security.
Hitler, in a state of brittle fury,
Decided it was time for an onslaught
On British morale. London, so he thought,
Would cave in. So began the final phase
Of the Battle of Britain: better days
For the RAF; worse, regrettably,
For Londoners, as we shall shortly see.

The British still thought that invasion
Was imminent. On this occasion,
As on others, they were wrong. Germany
Had never been ready to put to sea.
So when, on the 7th of September,
The signal went out ('Cromwell', remember,
Was the code word), nothing happened at all.
The Home Guard stood ready, prepared to fall,
If need be, in defence of their country.
Invasion, though, was never to be.

Most German bombers, unfortunately,
Did get through that day. A massive attack
Upon London (well targeted, alack)
Was launched by the *Luftwaffe.* They headed
For the docks. This Londoners had dreaded.
The fearful damage suffered was immense,
The heat from the fire and flames intense.

Over four hundred civilians died,
A terrible toll. Many more beside,
Some sixteen hundred, were injured. Again,
Ten days later, the East End took the strain.
More bombs. But this time fewer planes got through.
Resistance was stronger. This Hitler knew.

The RAF remember, to this day,
The 15th of September, a Sunday.
For this time there was no hesitating:
The Spitfires and Hurricanes were waiting.
As the *Luftwaffe* returned, in full strength,
The RAF went to every length
To stop them. Comprehensively routed,
Their defeat this time could not be doubted.
Göring was livid, never more annoyed.
Up to sixty of his planes were destroyed
And dozens of crew shot down. By contrast,
Fighter Command (who had recovered fast)
Lost twenty-six fighters, but fared badly
With the loss of thirteen pilots, sadly.

Invasion postponed

Hitler's proposed invasion (mark this)
Was now postponed "until further notice".
On October the 12th, he cancelled it
For the winter. They were clearly not fit.
This convinced Churchill, and everyone,
That the Battle of Britain had been won.

Churchill delivered this final verdict:
"Never in the field of human conflict,"
He said, "was so much owed by so many
"To so few." Now, jokes were two-a-penny
Among the heroic pilots. Humour
Kept them going, according to rumour.

As one wag put it, when he heard Churchill,
"He must have been referring to the mess bill!"

On November the 25th, Dowding
Was relieved of his command, a dumb thing
If ever there was one. His strategy
For the battle had not, apparently
(Defensive as it was), been to all tastes.
A travesty! The mother of all wastes!
We'd have lost, had it not been for Sir Hugh.
Folly at the top, though, is nothing new.

The Blitz

So, no invasion until the spring,
If then. This news had an uplifting ring,
Though raids by night continued. This new phase –
The campaign will never cease to amaze –
Lasted seventy-six successive nights.
Despite the paucity of daytime flights,
The *Luftwaffe* returned. Neither the British,
Nor the Germans, could fight to a finish,
For this was a war of attrition.

Both sides were in the same position:
The Germans had failed to invade Britain,
While the British had no force to invade
The Continent. Bombardment and blockade
Were their only weapons. To do nothing
Was unthinkable. Bombing was something,
At least, indiscriminate though it seemed.
While the British remained calm, Hitler dreamed:
Destruction of Britain's cities, by air,
Would drive her population to despair.

We know it didn't happen quite like that.
Although hardly a case of tit-for-tat –

For Britain's offensive had less effect
Than many folk had been led to expect –
The morale of the people remained high.

It is hard, I confess, to see quite why,
For the bombings were sustained and deadly.
Londoners weren't exactly unready,
It's simply (although their nerve held steady)
That they had no proper means of defence,
And they knew it. To panic was nonsense.
People learned to take the rough with the smooth,
As Churchill, of course, was quick to approve.
"Good old Winnie!" He toured the damaged sites,
Cigar in hand. He'd set the world to rights!

Britain's fighter pilots were powerless
Against the night bombers. It was hopeless
To pretend otherwise. During the Blitz,
A citizen could be blown to bits,
And his house, in a matter of minutes.
The *Luftwaffe's* random, but lethal hits
Caused, by the end of this first awful year,
Twenty-three thousand deaths, with more, I fear,
The next, right through to the middle of May.
It was recently I read with dismay
That more civilians died in the war
Than combatants (a lamentable score)
Up to September, 1941.
And for each victim (yes, every one),
Thirty-five, at least, were rendered homeless.
It really was a most terrible mess:
Three and a half million homes destroyed.

Londoners were far from overjoyed
On the 29th of December.
The Great Fire of London, remember,

Was in 1666 – the last one,
That is. Here was another. Poor London!

Incendiaries set the City ablaze.
One image, which will forever amaze,
Was that of St. Paul's in the midst of it,
Missing, by a whisker, a direct hit.
A miracle. Christopher Wren's spirit
Was surely at work here. Good for Sir Kit!

Some fifteen hundred fires blazed that night.
The great conflagration burned so bright,
The glow could be seen sixty miles away.
The fire fighters were fit for the fray,
But ran out of water. The Thames, alas,
Was at its lowest ebb. One fiery mass
Was the City, as it was left to burn.
Arthur Harris was watching with concern,

Or Air Marshal 'Bomber' Harris to you.
"Well, they are sowing the wind" (sadly true),
He observed. The citizens of Dresden,
And of Hamburg, would reap it, as and when.
In excess of twenty-five thousand died
In Dresden. Those who take Harris's side…
Well, I've my view… I'll leave you to decide.

Those poor souls who perished in the City
Numbered just one hundred and sixty-three –
There were so few residences, you see.
For every death we should show pity.
To reduce it to the nitty-gritty,
However, there can be no comparison
Between the sickening bombing of Dresden
And what occurred in the City that night,
Whatever the victims' harrowing plight.

Coventry

Other cities suffered terribly too:
Portsmouth, Bristol, Glasgow, to name a few,
Southampton, Birmingham… One frightful night,
In mid-November, when the moon shone bright
('Bomber's Moon', so-called), Coventry was struck.
The city was sadly down on its luck.
The Germans coined a word: to 'coventrate'
(*Coventrieren*), meaning to devastate,
Reduce to ashes – nay, annihilate.
Coventry suffered a desperate fate.
For ten deadly hours the bombs rained down.
The Cathedral, its medieval crown,
Was destroyed. One third of its housing stock
Was pulverised. A particular shock
Was the damage done to the factories.
Coventry was one of those key cities
That had converted its old industries

In support of the war effort: aircraft,
Tank engines, batteries… How Hitler laughed.
Worse still, over five hundred lost their lives.
Thousands were injured. The record survives.

The Germans did not repeat their attack.
This was foolish. The city, on the rack,
Might never have recovered. As it was,
Coventry got back on its feet because,
And only because, the people refused
To be beaten. Violated, abused
And threatened, they were never downhearted.
Within days the recovery started.

The Morris Motor Engines Works had lost
Most of its roof. Braving ice, snow and frost,
Over five sixths of Morris employees
Turned up for work. Many were on their knees

From exhaustion and stress. Yet all knew
That they had crucial war work to do.
Sometimes working under the open sky,
They laboured on – theirs but to do or die!
Some wore protective tin hats on their heads,
And slept overnight, bringing makeshift beds.

Buckingham Palace bombed

The King visited the very next day.
He sympathised, but had little to say
Of practical value. Yet a visit
From a King is uplifting, isn't it?

His London home too had suffered a bomb,
Buckingham Palace. He dealt with aplomb
With this crisis, as did his wife. "I'm glad,"
Said the Queen, "we have been bombed." She was sad,
But could now "look the East End in the face".
I confess to finding this out of place.
To compare her Palace to the East End!
Farcical! She had no wish to offend,
But this was insensitive and stupid.
Don't say it out loud, though. Heaven forbid!

Londoners were thoroughly exhausted.
The people had taken too many hits.
Then suddenly Hitler called off the Blitz!

This was surprising and far from clever.
After one of London's worst nights ever,
The capital had been close to collapse.
Could its spirit have been broken? Perhaps…
We shall never know. On one awful night,
Seven hundred acres were set alight
And over fourteen hundred poor souls died.

The House of Commons hit

Saturday May the 10th exemplified **1941**
The worst of the war, and the very best –
The spirit of the Blitz. From the far west
(Hammersmith) to the suburb of Romford
In the east, the Nazis set a record:
More deaths and more terrible injuries
Than ever before. Again, if you please,
It was a 'Bomber's Moon'. The War Office,
The Tower of London (imagine this),
Westminster Abbey, the Mint, all were hit –
Vandalism, no other word for it.
Two hundred and fifty thousand books (rare,
Irreplaceable volumes: I despair)
Were lost as a raging fire took hold
At the British Museum. Churchill, we're told,
Wept amid the charred rubble and debris
Of the House of Commons,* the agony
The poor man suffered a pity to see.

The pumps were busy for eleven days,
This long it took to extinguish the blaze.
Just how much more could this great city take?
The spirit was willing, make no mistake,

---

*By a strange co-incidence, the 10th of May
Was the anniversary, the very day,
Of Churchill's appointment as Prime Minister.
There could have been few omens more sinister
Than the bombing of Parliament. His tears
Were genuine. But he had no real fears.
The House of Commons he had cherished for years,
For this was the cradle of democracy.
Hitler would not put him off that easily.

But there must be a limit. There's no doubt
That for Londoners time was running out.

Was Hitler beginning to feel the strain?
The Führer, every now and again,
Made a fatal error. This was one such.
Pretending he didn't care very much,
He called off the bombings. To 'coventrate'
No longer, he resolved to concentrate,
The fool, on Russia. I'm glad he did.
Had he kept on bombing… Heaven forbid!

Lesser raids continued, on the east coast,
In particular. But what mattered most
Was that Hitler now turned his attention
To Russia. So, rather less tension,
Less risk and some much-needed breathing space.
London for now had been spared, by God's grace.

Lord Beaverbrook

What of the government? Let's take a look.
One inspired appointment, in my book,
Was that of Churchill's chum, Lord Beaverbrook,
At the head of a brand new ministry,
That of Aircraft Production. To me,
He was one of the men who held the key,
In those darkest of days, to victory.

According to Churchill, his old crony,
Beaverbrook would be "at his very best
"When things were at their worst". He passed the test
With flying colours. In two months (yes, two),
His Lordship spearheaded a huge breakthrough,
As figures for fighter aircraft doubled.
A fair measure of discontent bubbled

Below the surface: he pushed staff too hard.
Beaverbrook showed a stubborn disregard
For their welfare. To him what mattered most
Were results, of which he was proud to boast.

Between the months of June and September –
With the Battle of Britain, remember,
At its height – the monthly delivery
Stood at over four hundred and fifty.
In April, the month before his arrival,
As the RAF struggled for survival
(Even then), output had been only half.
Göring would surely have had a good laugh,
Had he known. Britain, though, thank Heaven,
Still had one hundred and twenty-seven
Hurricanes and Spitfires in reserve –
Never fewer. Beaverbrook held his nerve.
With total commitment he worked flat out:
His iron resolve was never in doubt.
He distrusted committees. These, he swore,
Wasted time. They took “the punch out of war”.
This message he pinned on his office wall,
Along with another (the best of all
And one to treasure): “Organisation:
“The enemy of improvisation.”

He launched the ‘Great Aluminium Scare’.
This drove his civil servants to despair.
They should have challenged him, but didn’t dare.
Housewives and citizens everywhere
Were invited to hand in pots and pans.
The public obliged. All Beaverbrook fans,
They collected saucepans, shoe trees, kettles,
Provided that the make-up of metals
Comprised at least some aluminium.
From hat pegs to ornaments: all welcome.

"We'll turn your pots and pans," claimed Beaverbrook –
People complied (how on earth did they cook?) –
"Into Spitfires and Hurricanes!" Well,
This was an empty promise, truth to tell.
Much of the stuff was junk and went to scrap.

Yet Beaverbrook, an enterprising chap,
Devised another, more productive scheme.
Most politicians can only dream
Of such 'initiatives'. You could now buy
A Spitfire (or part of one). To apply,
Simply send a cheque! Beaverbrook's ministry
Had received (from Jamaica) an enquiry,
Asking just how much a bomber would cost.
Twenty thousand! Not a moment was lost.
The sum was received by return of post.
So, what price a Spitfire? Five, at most.

Within days the money came rolling in.
The BBC's nightly news bulletin
Would announce the latest donations.

This fostered the best of relations
Between the public and the ministry.
An individual or a city,
A school or a club, could buy their own plane.
The scheme's success is easy to explain:
Public-spirited, it was also fun.
Within a year, by April '41,
Some thirteen million pounds had been raised
To 'purchase' Spitfires, Heaven be praised.

One day a schoolboy sent in a guinea
For a thermometer. Eager, you see.
Lord Beaverbrook saw only too clearly
That this development was just the thing.
Sixpence bought a rivet, while a whole wing
Cost two thousand. He announced (with aplomb)
That twenty-two pounds would buy a small bomb.

Ernest Bevin

One massive asset to the government
Was Ernest Bevin. In temperament,
Background, experience and politics
(Labour), he was a formidable mix.
Bevin, a union man through and through,
Headed the huge TGWU –
The Transport and General Workers'. Few,
If any, could have matched Bevin for weight,
Integrity and strength. The country's fate,
Churchill was aware, depended, in part,
On keeping Britain's workers in good heart.
This was a brilliant, inspired start:

The appointment of a union man
As Minister of Labour. A strong fan
Of his new boss from early in the war,
Bevin had gone out of his way, before,
To support Churchill (First Lord at the time)
On nautical issues. Now in his prime,
Bevin could do no wrong. His loyalty
Was assured. He'd been the first to agree
With Churchill, during the nineteen-thirties,
Over Hitler. Never one to appease,
Bevin advocated armed resistance
To the Nazis and Churchill's persistence
Had impressed him from the very outset.

No finer ally could you hope to get.
Churchill was blessed in Bevin. He began
As a farm boy, with no career plan,
Aged eleven. Working then as a drayman,
At eighteen, in Bristol, Bevin was thirty
Before he joined a union. Certainly
His start in life was slow. Between the wars
He won his spurs, barely stopping to pause,
By creating one organisation
Out of forty – the amalgamation
Of many small unions into one.
This resulted, no sooner planned than done,
In a great super-union, spanking new,
Bevin's very own TGWU.

He was no red revolutionary.
Far from it. Worker solidarity?
Yes, but only if it served the country.
Ernest Bevin would go to any length
To foster and preserve working class strength.
The workers were "my people". Huge power
He wielded in Britain's 'finest hour'.

Some (the Archbishop of Canterbury
For one) had their doubts. Bevin, possibly,
Was a “future Labour dictator”. Well,
Priestley was nearer the mark, truth to tell:
The new Minister was “the other half
“Of the English people”. You have to laugh:
Churchill, the quintessential Tory,
Preparing for his place in history
With the declared support (you get the gist)
Of Britain’s greatest trade unionist.

What a colleague to have! Ernest Bevin
Was perfect if you had a war to win.
After the Emergency Powers Act
Was extended (in May, to be exact,
1940), he understood that tact,
And discretion, were the ways forward –
Steady and measured; nothing untoward.
For the Act, as folk had come to expect,
Gave him unfettered power to direct
Anyone to perform any service
Bevin thought fit! They might not deserve this,
But hours and wages could be set too.
There was nothing that a worker could do,
Given the Act’s powers, but to comply.

Other unions backed Bevin. Here’s why.
The Minister was a strong advocate
Of ‘collective bargaining’. It was that,
Thanks to him, that forestalled many a spat
Between employers and workers. Lockouts
And strikes were illegal. Few harboured doubts
With regard to Bevin’s quest to succeed.
Industrial unrest? Simply no need.
Wages were for negotiation,
Conditions too. Arbitration

Was the answer, should other attempts fail.
In the past, Bevin had fought tooth and nail
For this process. He even, if you please,
Scotched the alarming prospect of a wage freeze,
One of the Treasury's top priorities.
Strife between employers and employees?
Britain would soon have been brought to her knees,
Beset by these kinds of difficulties.
She was saved from this worst of tragedies
By Bevin. Praise be to heroes such as these.

Beaverbrook and Bevin were enemies:
His Lordship was driving workers too hard.
Absurdly long hours, in this regard,

Were inhuman and counterproductive.
Bevin was simply being disruptive,
According to Beaverbrook – destructive,
Even, in the eyes of some. In background,
And temperament, the gulf was profound.

A new Ministry of Production
Precipitated more disruption.
In a nutshell, Beaverbrook was the boss,
But Bevin (his Lordship was at a loss:
Not to mince words, he was very cross)
Had equal status in the government.
They had many an angry argument,
To neither's credit. It was a fair bet
That if Bevin attended Cabinet,
Beaverbrook tended to give it a miss.

Things simply could not continue like this.
Beaverbrook short-circuited the crisis
By resigning. Later on (not nice, this),
On the day after the fall of Tobruk
(In June, 1942) Beaverbrook
Plotted to supplant his old mate Churchill.
The country, he argued, had had its fill.
The PM would certainly have to go!

His Lordship, the canny old so-and-so,
Approached Bevin, of all people. Why not,
He asked (this was as nasty as it got),
Replace Churchill, the two of them? The plot
Received short shrift from Bevin. In public
He denounced it as a dastardly trick.
"Newspaper millionaires" made him sick,
He declared, in the "filthy business"
Of undermining the togetherness,
And unity, of the nation – this
The lowest and "most diabolical thing"
He had ever known. He would be working,
Bevin pledged, with Churchill as his colleague,
Fighting with him to the end: no intrigue,
No plots. The result was never in doubt:
Bevin was in; Lord Beaverbrook was out.

Attlee

Clement Attlee enjoyed enormous clout,
First as Lord Privy Seal and latterly
Combining the role of Churchill's Deputy
With that of Dominions Secretary.
A key member of the War Cabinet
From the start, the PM had thought it fit
To offer Labour two seats (yes, out of five)
At the top table. In a bid to survive,
He included Chamberlain (soon, sadly,
To die) and Halifax. He would gladly
Have excluded the latter. Remember,
However, his weakness. In December,
He shunted him off to America,
As Ambassador. Something of a snob,
Halifax nonetheless did a good job.

Eden succeeded him, the new young Turk.
Churchill's successor? It would never work,
Thought some. Handsome, but rather a lightweight,
Eden, in the event, would have to wait.*

Attlee was Deputy, in case of need.
One might have expected him to succeed,
Should the Prime Minister die in office.
But when Churchill flew to Yalta (mark this),
With Eden, towards the end of the war,
The PM had quite a surprise in store
For the King. Should both he and Eden die,
Assassinated or shot from the sky,
He advised George not to choose Attlee. Why?

---

*After fifteen long years the crown was his.
Eden made a right old mess of Suez,
In '57 – a dismal business.

The Second World War

Sir John Anderson was the better man.
Churchill had long been an Anderson fan.
With no party affiliation,
Nor with ideas above his station,
Sir John had a fine reputation
Not only for sheer native brilliance,
But for political resilience,
Energy and imagination.

Anderson 'organised' the nation,
Overseeing evacuation
And Air Raid Precautions (ARP).*
A dry man, he was the epitome
Of a top civil servant. Most agree,
He was a sterling Home Secretary.
After Chamberlain's premature death, he,
Sir John, took over Home Security:
The 'Home Front Prime Minister' he became –
The PM-in-waiting in all but name.

The very essence of a quiet man,
By the time the Second World War began,
Clem had been Labour leader already
For four years. Understated and steady,
Attlee was a genius. Twenty years
His tenure lasted. Did it end in tears?
Hardly. Attlee's great post-war government
Was a rare triumph of high achievement
And social reform, a testament
To the Prime Minister's progressive zeal –
A figure of principle, for real.
"A modest little man," Churchill dubbed him,
"With much to be modest about." How dim.

---

*An air raid? All would run, helter-skelter,
Into the nearest 'Anderson shelter'.

Genocide

In Germany, the shift from prejudice
To genocide (you may be sure of this)
Was a slippery slope, a subtle slide.
Were the people aware? You can decide.

The background in Germany

Early persecution of the Jews
Was welcomed by most as the best of news.
When faced with overt racism, you choose –
Or rather, you should. You express your views
And if you don't, either through cowardice
Or apathy, you feed the prejudice.

Never plead ignorance. Hitler's success,
Supported by the sinister SS,
His elite bodyguard, epitomised
The will of the people. For they despised
The Jews, more than perhaps they realised.
Concentration camps? Few were surprised
When the Bolsheviks and the dissidents,
The Führer's political opponents,
Were despatched to the camps for 'correction'.
Homosexuals... Gypsies... Perfection!
Jews, naturally, followed in their wake.
These people were 'vermin', for Heaven's sake.

Well, it was an 'easy' error to make.
Germany had strong leadership at last.
A Nazi government, rearming fast,
Would show its enemies a thing or two.
Nazi philosophy, a lethal brew:
A resurgent nationalism,
Twinned with a perverse idealism

That had its pseudo-scientific base
In dreams of an Aryan master race.
The SS reflected this ideal:
Survival of the fittest made real.
They all took an oath of obedience
To Adolf Hitler. To them it made sense.

Now, under the Führer, the time had come
For a new Germany. All right for some,
But those poor souls who failed to make the grade –
Mental cases included, I'm afraid –
Were destined in time to go to the wall.
Some Germans, it seems, hardly cared at all.

'*Arbeit Macht Frei*'

Once Hitler was installed as Chancellor –
Or had staged his great *coup*, if you prefer –
The pace of change was rapid. This we'll see.

Hitler's Nazis took over Germany
On the 30th of January,
'33. The age of brutality
Had begun. Within two months, near Munich,
The first 'model' camp (prepare to be sick)
Was set up at Dachau. '*Arbeit Macht Frei*' –
An awful irony, hard to deny –
Was the 'moral' message above the gate
Through which thousands would pass to meet their fate.
'Work Sets You Free'. Ugly cynicism,
Beneath contempt: the cult of Nazism.

Anti-semitic laws

The campaign against the Jews gathered pace.
Inhuman laws, insulting to their race,
Deprived them gradually of their place
In German society. Professors
And teachers were fired – their successors
'Pure' German. Schoolchildren were singled out
As Jewish. They were left in little doubt
Of their inferiority. The class
Would be told by their teacher, bold as brass,
That "the Jew is our greatest enemy.
"Beware of the Jew!" There, for all to see,
Was an example: a poor little lad,
Hanging his head in shame, cruel and sad.

Jewish shops were boycotted by the Nazis,
As traders struggled to keep their businesses.
Books were burned, including those by Sigmund Freud
And other Jewish writers. These were destroyed
By order of the Führer. To wild applause
In the Reichstag, the corrupt Nuremberg Laws
Were proclaimed by Göring. The laws forbade
Intermarriage between the Jew (bad)
And the Aryan (good). Pure must not mix
With impure. For Nazi politics
Distinguished the 'dirty Jew', the scheming,
Dishonest, money-lending, double-dealing
Capitalist (I am sure you get the gist)
Or (take your pick) the subversive Communist.

Anti-semitism was based on fear,
Pure and simple. "Jews are not wanted here" –
This was the message. Benches were reserved
For non-Jews. Well, no more than they deserved,
Such was the view of most. The Jews, of course,
Were scapegoats, pilloried without remorse.

A large number of Jews emigrated.
Well over half, it's been estimated,
Fled to neighbouring countries such as France,
Holland and Belgium. They took their chance,
Though most were impoverished when they left.
They paid a heavy price: friendless, bereft
And subject to punitive taxes. Yes,
The Nazis milked them dry. Nevertheless,
These refugees escaped persecution
In Germany. The 'Final Solution'
Engulfed the majority in the end,
A tragedy it's hard to comprehend.

Kristallnacht

It was Hitler's aim initially,
Hateful though this was as a policy,
'Simply' to rid the Fatherland of Jews.
Of the detail there are very few clues,
But after *Kristallnacht*, in '38,
It was clear the Nazi campaign of hate
Was calculated to drive the Jews out.
Of that there can be not the slightest doubt.

On the 9th of November, overnight,
Not only were synagogues set alight,
But shop windows smashed and businesses wrecked.
Was this the worst that the Jews could expect?
Alas, not. The Jewish community
Had to pay for the damage – cruelty
And malevolence on an untold scale.
Resistance sadly was to no avail.
Kristallnacht was followed by a decree:
Jews must cease trading forthwith. Now, to me,
That said it all. No trade, no livelihood.
The Jews should get out as fast as they could.

Easier said than done. Europe was slow
To take refugees. Britain, you should know,
Was hesitant. Chamberlain, "horrified"
By *Kristallnacht*, was strangely starry-eyed
When it came to Hitler. Another year
Of appeasement still lay ahead, I fear.
This was despite the despicable fact
That one thousand Jews, after *Kristallnacht*,
Were murdered and some 30,000 (yes,
That's thirty thousand, certainly no less)
Sent to the camps. This is how it began.
Whether or not the original plan
Was to deport the Jews *en masse*, I fear,
In time, it became abundantly clear
That repatriation was not enough.
There must be other ways. Horrifying stuff.

Hitler's open policy

In January, 1939,
Hitler spelt out the official line
In a major speech in the Reichstag. Fine:
If Germany was "pushed into a war",
Then "annihilation" (this he swore)
Would be the result "of the Jewish race
"In Europe". The Führer laughed in the face
Of objections voiced from overseas –
The United States and other countries.
The President, with no apologies,
Urged Britain to offer territories
To facilitate the resettlement
Of Jews. Roosevelt was far from content
To take a lead.* There was flannel and fudge.
The Australians too refused to budge.
Jewish refugees? They didn't want 'em.
Having themselves "no racial problem",

They had “no desire to import one”.
The world turned a blind eye, all said and done.

Polish Jews

Germany’s invasion of Poland,
In September, strengthened the Führer’s hand.
“Annihilation”, you understand,
May only have involved resettlement
When Hitler made his seminal statement
In the Reichstag. The limited extent
Of this relocation project meant,
Initially, the deportation,
Of Jews from the ‘pure’ Aryan nation
(Germany) to Nisko (south-east Poland).
All non-Jewish Poles were turfed off the land
To make room for them. The death rate was high,
Some 95,000 Jews left to die.
Few were to survive: no shelter, no food,
Reduced to misery, decrepitude
And disease. In terms of resettlement,
The policy failed, as far as it went.
Chaotic, crude, the process was halted.
As a concept, it could not be faulted
By the powers-that-be. Himmler preferred
Madagascar as a ‘homeland’. Absurd?

---

*There is startling evidence of this.
Bound for America, the *St. Louis*,
Carrying nine hundred Jewish refugees,
Was forced to turn back (of all obscenities),
Having been refused permission to berth
In Cuba or in the US. Where on earth,
One wonders, if not in the land of the free,
Could the helpless seek shelter? Democracy?
No. Freedom? The rule of law? Hypocrisy.

Well, yes. This idea was abandoned too,
Which left Himmler with a problem: what to do?

Invasion of Poland was a curse
In this respect. Things went from bad to worse,
With suddenly three million more Jews
To be 'accommodated': deported
Or 'annihilated'. Problem sorted?
Hardly. Soon all Poland was on the move.

'*Echt*' Germans (Hitler was quick to approve)
Returned to Germany. Within Poland
The 'non-Aryans' – Slavs, you understand,
And Jews (ever the bottom of the heap)
Were 'relocated'. The hatred ran deep.
Jews were beaten up in broad daylight
In the street. Those who put up a fight
Would be executed on the spot,
Brutally battered to death or shot.
Thousands of others went to the gallows.

The ghettos

All Jews were herded into large ghettos.
Overcrowding was rife, food in short supply,
No sanitation… Thousands were to die
Of hunger and disease. As a badge of scorn,
A yellow star was ordered to be worn
By all Jews aged over ten, if you please.
There was nowhere to hide. The penalties
For failure to do so were severe.
The Jewish ghettos were places of fear –
Nay, of terror. From 1941
(September), German Jews, every one,
Were obliged to be identified too
By the yellow Star of David. Too few,

Alas, survived the persecution.
The path to the Final Solution
Was gradual, but monstrous nonetheless –
The ultimate in human wickedness.

The Battle of the Atlantic

In the Atlantic, U-boats stalked the night.
Consider the dismal and dire plight
Of Britain's merchant seamen. One third died –
One in three brave souls, you'll be horrified –
In the great Battle of the Atlantic,
So-called. The powers-that-be were frantic,
For the ocean was Britain's lifeline.

Her best hopes would have withered on the vine,
Had a well-targeted naval blockade,
By the Germans, been successful. Her trade
Would grind to a halt, her vital imports
Stop. The country, already out of sorts,
Would suffer a slow, terminal defeat:
Supplies of raw materials, grain, meat,
Oil, weaponry… The list was complete.
According to Churchill, the U-boat threat
Was the only worry that made him sweat.
It kept him awake at night, this alone.

For Atlantic shipping was on its own.
The Royal Navy, in these early days,
Did provide escorts. They won little praise,
However. They could only cover, at most,
An area three hundred miles from the coast.
Moreover, they had young and ill-trained crews.
These were too few in number (still worse news)
And, while air cover was all-important,
There was a shortage of planes. Equipment,

Besides, was poor. Navigation aids
Were lacking, so aerial bombing raids
On U-boats were largely ineffective.

Also, there was no lack of invective
Between the RAF and the RN.
Whitehall mandarins scored nought out of ten
When it came to co-operation
And planning, to the great frustration
Of the Merchant Navy. Lamentable.

German U-boat strength (was this sensible?)
Was weak at the beginning of the war.
This Admiral Dönitz came to deplore,
Head of *Kriegsmarine*'s U-boat command.
Three hundred submarines was his 'demand',
But the Führer proved to be half-hearted
In the case of U-boats. When war started,
Dönitz could muster thirty-six at most.
Three hundred, the British would have been toast.

Major losses at sea

Even so, in the first nine months alone,
Ships torpedoed in the Atlantic zone
Amounted to two million tons lost.
Meeting with little by way of riposte,
In the next six months (after France's fall)
This figure, calculated to appal,
Was two and a half million. The use
Of French Atlantic ports tightened the noose:
The U-boats could now range far further out.

There was not the faintest shadow of doubt
That the Germans had the Brits on the run.
Over two short months, in spring '41,
Thirty-six ships were sunk. All said and done,

This was unsustainable. No one knew,
At the time, as the great tornado blew,
That the Germans had broken British codes,
Thereby making significant inroads
With respect to times of ships leaving ports,
The number of vessels and their escorts,
And how many ships made up each convoy.

They were sitting targets, ripe to destroy.
This was a “happy time” for U-boat crews
(Their phrase). It was certainly less good news
For the British. U-boats launched their attacks
In organised groups, known as ‘wolf packs’.
These ‘sea-wolves’ were Germany’s new heroes –
To Britain, the most dangerous of foes.

The picture became increasingly bleak.
Sinking of merchant vessels reached its peak
In April, 1941 – the worst,
The most deadly of times, for ever cursed.
700,000 tons of shipping
Were lost that month, a most painful whipping.
One hundred and forty-two ships, in May,
Were sunk by U-boats to widespread dismay
And one hundred and seventy-nine more
Were lost in air attacks, a fearful score.
The British came close to losing the war
In the spring and summer of ’41.
It was crystal clear to everyone
That if ships went down at a faster rate
Than they could be replaced, then Britain’s fate
Was sealed. Several factors turned the tide.

It did not take Hitler long to decide
To overrule Dönitz, who was pressing
For an increase in U-boats, distressing
For the Admiral, deeply depressing.

At the same time, happily, the US
Gave the Germans extra cause for distress,
By offering to protect any ship,
Allied or neutral (this was true friendship),
In open waters between her own shores
And the coast of Iceland. Hitler had cause,
By now, for some concern. You may ask why
The Führer opted to turn a blind eye
To American involvement. His fear,
I reckon, was that it would cost him dear
To antagonise the States at this stage.
No doubt in private he vented his rage,
But in public, for once, he kept his cool.
Monster though he was, the man was no fool.

The convoy system was also improved.
The Canadians (this Churchill approved –
Nay, welcomed) took responsibility
For half of convoy escorts (well, nearly).
At long last the RAF extended
Air cover. While nobody pretended
They could provide anything like enough,
This at least was more encouraging stuff.

In May, an Enigma cipher machine
Fell into British hands, which was to mean
Better intelligence, once Bletchley Park
Had cracked the code. No longer in the dark,
Convoys were safer, and U-boats at risk.
Dönitz was suspicious. He was brisk
(As ever) and, early in '42,
Issued orders, without further ado,
For a fourth rotor to be added. 'Shark'
This new Enigma was called. Bletchley Park
Was slow to break it. 'Naval Cipher 3',
Meanwhile, the code of the Admiralty,
Had been cracked by the Germans. The Navy

Still used it for the next ten months or more,
Folly, sadly, that it's hard to ignore.
This gave rise to further trouble in store.

Eleven hundred ships, in '42,
Were destroyed. What more could the British do?
Then another Enigma code machine
Was seized in October. This set the scene
For manic activity at Bletchley.
The boffins were into Shark, already,
By December. Progress was then steady
Right through until May, 1943.

American support

The Americans (now allies, of course,
Also at war) were quick to move, in force,
Against the U-boats themselves (as opposed,
Simply, to reporting them). They supposed,
Correctly, that with new technology –
While Hitler slumbered, astonishingly –
They could finish off the job properly.

Grossadmiral Dönitz (as he now was)
Had a new air of confidence because,
At last, he was in a strong position
To build up his forces and commission
More U-boats. By the spring of '43,
He had four hundred. This, believe you me,
Was a stunning total. He met his fate,
Though, off Iceland. He had left it too late.
Escort ships could now pick up submarines
By surface radio and other means,
Often before the U-boats tracked them. Thus,
There were fewer losses. Another plus
Was the so-called 'Hedgehog', a new device
For which the Germans paid a heavy price.

It was hard to give a Hedgehog the slip,
Which fired charges ahead of a ship,
Rather than dropping them off her stern. Well,
These systems turned the tables, truth to tell.

Some thirty-three U-boats were sunk in May.
Dönitz's younger son, I'm sad to say,
Died in one attack.* He was twenty-one.
The wolf pack strategy, all said and done,
Had shot its bolt. Dönitz had to withdraw.
This, some felt, was the crisis of the war
For the Germans. Churchill could now be sure
That his Atlantic lifeline was secure.

Rationing

Rationing had been a necessity
During the Great War. Anybody could see,
From the very start of the current conflict,
That the rules would need to be equally strict.
Ration books had been ready, in fact,
Since 1938. All that they lacked
Was a war! Most folk, believe it or not,
Supported the ration. What they got
Might be meagre, but at least it was fair.
People were on precisely the same share,
Rich and poor alike, with no need to queue.
Perfectly simple. All you had to do
Was take your new ration book along
To the grocer and you couldn't go wrong.

---

*Eight in every ten U-boat crewmen
Perished in action. No surprise, then,
That they called these hideous submarines
'Iron coffins'. This is what sick humour means.

When rationing of food first began,
In 1940 (on the 9th of Jan.),
A person's monthly allocation
Was just four ounces of ham (or bacon),
Twelve of sugar and four of butter. Tea
Was added in July. Take it from me,
Two ounces of tea do not go far! Cheese
Joined the list in '41, if you please,
Along with jam, treacle and margarine.

The meat ration (this seemed rather mean,
But could not be helped) fell dramatically
To one shilling and tuppence-worth – that's 6p.
Meat was seriously scarce: by '43,
Some four million acres of grazing land
Had been put to the plough. This, you understand,

Guaranteed that bread, for the whole of the war,
Would stay off ration. Grumbles, to be sure,
There were many. The quality was rough.
Bevin claimed he couldn't digest the stuff.*

By '42, there was more austerity.
Imports of food (this was now getting scary)
Stood at less than half their pre-war level – yes,
Half. A new points system proved a success
(Offering more choice), controlling access
To canned foods: vegetables, meat and fish.
The more affluent customers, peckish
For tinned salmon, would have to wait their turn –
An uncomfortable lesson to learn
For some of the rich, but fair nonetheless.

A measure of Japan's awesome success
In the Far East was the dearth of tea, rice
And sugar. The allies paid a high price
For their losses. Also hit were oil, tin
And rubber. More edicts came flooding in:
Rationing (on points) of rice, sago
And pulses. With still a long way to go,
Condensed milk and cereals joined the list,
Followed by chocolate. I shall be brisk.

With more foodstuffs coming onto ration,
The humble spud found itself in fashion.
Unrationed, "that puckish vegetable"
(Beveridge) was to grace many a table.

---

*Although not to everybody's taste,
The law imposed strict penalties for waste.
Feeding bread to the birds? Well out of line.
This could now attract a sizeable fine.

"Potatoes," the *Manchester Guardian* cried,
"Are available for everyone" – fried,
Baked, roasted, steamed… You could even grow your own.
Tasty with scraps of meat or any old bone,
The potato was king! Jacket spuds were best.

The Minister of Food set people a test:
"DIG FOR VICTORY!" Lord Woolton, in essence,
Was 'Britain's grocer'. A comforting presence,
His Lordship, with a whole nation to feed,
Exhorted folk to eat "only what you need,
"Not what you like". That way they would win the war!

Indeed, there were opportunities galore
To take pressure off imports by growing more.
Or support the war effort and "KEEP A PIG!"
There was never any harm in thinking big…
Or small. Need the country be undernourished?
No! A vegetable allotment flourished
Round the Albert Memorial, in London,
In the select Borough of South Kensington.

Clothes rationing? No sooner said than done.
The clothing industry was on its knees.
A low-paid force of ageing employees,
Shortage of cloth and poor facilities
Meant that allowances had to be cut.
Did this cause an uproar? Anything but.
For again it was fair. From '42,
The average adult had to make do
On forty-eight clothing coupons a year.

'Spreading' this allowance, it would appear
That a man could afford one pair of socks
Every four months (one of many shocks);
One shirt every twenty months; one vest
And just one pair of underpants (at best)

Every two years; and one pullover
Every five. Anything left over?
Well, an overcoat every seven
(Yes, years!), by which time, merciful Heaven,
The war might be over. There were rules, too,
For women: four plain pleats would have to do
In skirts. Ribbons and flounces had to go.
"MAKE DO AND MEND, SAYS MRS. SEW-AND-SEW" –
Another 'advertising' slogan. Waste,
In a nutshell, was to nobody's taste.
Turn-ups on trousers, too, were banned for men.
Nevertheless, more than seven in ten
Favoured these constraints. All in a good cause.
The people of Britain deserve applause.

Soap was strictly rationed; petrol, too.
As early as March, 1942,
The petrol ration was suspended
For all private motoring. This ended
Pleasure jaunts and family holidays.

The black market

Some, alas, were adept at finding ways
Of evading the regulations.
Such folk resented the privations
They were made to suffer, asking, "why me?"
Not for them the curse of austerity.
'Racketeering' this practice was often called,
Or the 'black market'. Lord Woolton was appalled.
"WANTED FOR SABOTAGE!" the posters read.
These food and petrol cheats, his Lordship said,
Were "enemies of the people". His bluff
Was called. Many simply thought, "fair enough"
If offered some under-the-counter stuff,
Whatever the cost. A nudge and a wink
Would suffice. Who cared what others might think?

There were penalties, of course. You'd cop it,
If caught. But little was done to stop it.

There was a shortage of commodities
At all levels. Among such rarities
Were razor blades. Most other luxuries
Were unobtainable, or at a price.

To conclude, one anecdote should suffice
To demonstrate how all were affected
By austerity. Folk were expected
To knuckle down. Who would have suspected,
When the wife of the US President
Sojourned as an overnight resident
At Buckingham Palace (on a visit),
That even she would have been asked to sit
In a bath with a black ring drawn round it,
To show her how much water she could use?
Poor Eleanor! She could hardly refuse.

'Careless Talk Costs Lives'

While 'racketeers' posed a serious threat,
It was fear of 'fifth columnists', you bet,
That gave rise to graver concern. The scare
Was that any stray person, anywhere,
Might be an enemy sympathiser.
Friend or foe? People were none the wiser.
How could they tell? They couldn't. Yet again,
This inspired a government campaign.

Under a pair of gossiping housewives
You can read the words, "CARELESS TALK COSTS LIVES".
One's tempted to wonder, why all the fuss? –
Until sitting behind them, on the bus,
You notice Hitler and Göring. "KEEP MUM",
Read another slogan, "SHE'S NOT THAT DUMB!"
And, to show which way the wind was blowing,
This: "OF COURSE, THERE'S NO HARM IN *YOUR* KNOWING" –
As a couple of friends discuss the war,
While under the tablecloth, on the floor,
Sits Hitler, hanging on their every word.

Internment

These anxieties were far from absurd.
Early on in the war, invasion
(Or fear of it) was the occasion
For a poisonous campaign in the press
Against 'enemy' aliens. The stress
That this caused is impossible to guess:
Untold affliction, pain and distress.

German nationals, when war broke out,
Numbered some 20,000. There's no doubt
That some among them may have sympathised
With Hitler – if not, I'd be quite surprised.

But all of them? Hardly likely, I'd say.
To lock them up for ever and a day
Was mad. And what of all the refugees,
In excess of 60,000 of these,
From Austria and Germany? They got
A rough ride in the press. "Intern the lot!"
Shouted Fleet Street from the roof tops. At first,
People seemed to agree. They had a thirst,
I'm ashamed to say (the Brits at their worst),
For treating foreigners like criminals.

Soon, though, through a system of tribunals,
The government took a more measured course.
To impound all these 'aliens', by force,
Was repugnant to natural justice.

By early June, 1940 (mark this),
Two thirds of German and Austrian men
Were interned, soon rising to eight in ten.
The complaints being received from MPs
Concerning the plight of all refugees
Caused the hard-pressed British authorities
To soften their line. New 'categories'
Of aliens were established. Of these,
By 1943, ninety *per cent*
Were free and gainfully employed – decent,
Generous and fair. This was better news
For the refugees (not excluding Jews)
Who had been interned, in the early days,
In 'housing' calculated to amaze –
Nay, appal. There were horrific stories
Of run-down, rat-infested factories
Being commissioned for the purpose.

Some lived in tents (significantly worse),
On the cold, damp ground, with no mattresses.
Of the many bureaucratic messes

Of the war, this was certainly the worst.
Seeking a better life, victims were cursed
With living conditions barely fit
For animals. Food was inadequate.
Husbands, by order, were kept separate
From their wives. Families were desperate,
Often unaware of the whereabouts
Of members. Some began to harbour doubts
Whether life was really better here
Than in Germany or Austria. Fear
Had driven them away. It would appear,
Alas, that their future as refugees
Would be plagued with similar miseries.

The long-term aim of the authorities
Had been to ship 'prisoners' overseas,
To the Dominions. This was revised
After German U-boats (few were surprised)
Sank the British liner, *Arandora Star*,
On her way to Canada. She'd not gone far,
Torpedoed off the west coast of Ireland.
Hundreds drowned, not all fascists, you understand.
Many of the innocent internees
Had been Hitler's opponents, refugees
From murder and torture in Germany.

The government reversed its policy
Following this dreadful catastrophe.
A number of outraged backbench MPs
From both sides of the House, of all parties,
Railed against these "horrible tragedies"
Suffered at the hands of the British state.

Matters improved. I'm happy to relate
That on the Isle of Man, at any rate,
In the camp, a more relaxed atmosphere
Took hold. Conditions, it would appear,

For the inmates were humane and friendly.
No longer despised as the enemy,
They set up their own university
(I kid you not): literature, drama
And music, a mini-panorama
Of culture and civilisation.

That post-war classical sensation,
The famous Amadeus String Quartet,
Established in '47, first met
(Three of them, at least) on the Isle of Man.

Many a worthwhile career began
In internment. Rescued from the abyss,
These three friends, with ample time to practise,
Thrived on the island. We're fortunate in this.
The Amadeus Quartet: too good to miss.

What was likely to be the destiny
Of political prisoner Mosley
And other declared fascists such as he?

All were imprisoned (no judge, no jury).
Widespread consternation, and fury,
Were expressed at Mosley's early release –
Under the watchful eye of the police,
It's true, but unpopular nonetheless,
Even with the right-wing *Daily Express.*

Censorship

There was censorship of overseas mail
And phone-tapping on an extensive scale.
The British press barons fought tooth and nail
To preserve their freedoms, to no avail.
The Communist *Daily Worker* was banned:
Unsafe and subversive, you understand.
This ban, under Regulation 2D –
Draconian out of sheer necessity –
Was quickly lifted when Nazi Germany
Invaded Russia. Selective, you see.

The war economy

Unemployment fell. In the war economy
There was a job for almost everybody.
At the outbreak of the war, unemployment stood
At one and a quarter million. This looked good,
From the standpoint of the armaments industries.
Yet, in one of those statistical mysteries,
Unemployment for a time actually rose –
Owing in part to the hard winter, I suppose,
Of 1940, but also to a backlog
Of training. It was going to be a long slog.

Moving forward to the summer of '41,
There was employment for nearly everyone,
With fewer than two hundred thousand unemployed.
The government, of course, was far from overjoyed:

There was soon a shortage of labour! Now, to me,
This trend was positive, dynamic and healthy.
Unemployment, indeed, by 1943,
Had virtually ceased to exist. Industry
Was crying out for manpower. No surprise there:
Four-point-five million (a thirty *per cent* share
Of available working males), by '44,
Were serving in Britain's armed forces. Furthermore,
The proportion of younger women employed –
And naturally the wages that they enjoyed –
Rose steadily. Total numbers of employees
At work in the essential war industries
Increased from three million in 1940
To some five million by 1943.

There was still a dearth, as early as '41,
Of key workers such as these. What was to be done?
Well, Bevin put out a call for volunteers
In March – with limited success, from what one hears.
So, in December, conscription was brought in
(A first for any country) for single women
Aged between twenty and thirty. Good for Bevin.
He understood that Britain had a war to win!
These women had a choice: to work in industry,
Or opt for one of the services. Sensibly,
Bevin was in favour of flexibility.
Employment received a boost. Bevin's strategy
Was vindicated although, astonishingly,
Shortages continued, chiefly at the expense
Of those industries not critical to defence
Or other essential war work – like textiles,
And food distribution. Bevin was all smiles…

Or was he? It will come as no surprise
That the continuance of coal supplies
Was crucial. Yet productivity
Was in decline. By 1943,

The mines were in deep crisis. The process
Had been gradual. There was bitterness,
Spread over years, at lack of investment,
Outdated practice and bad management.
Conditions, in short, were appalling.
The owners were adept at stonewalling,
Yet something, it was clear, would have to give.
Management showed no initiative.
Profit, pure and simple, was their motive.

Other industries proved more attractive.
Many miners moved into armaments.
The work was far better paid. It made sense.
Others, tired of being workhorses
Down the pit, preferred to join the forces.
These were likely to be the fittest, too.
Some 80,000, by March, '42,
Of the "strongest men in the industry" –
The words of the Mining Secretary,
David Grenfell – had entered the army
And 60,000, of their own accord,
Had left to take other work. Their reward?
Better conditions and higher pay.

Strikes

This was greeted with undisguised dismay
By Bevin. He came up, as was his way,
With a scheme: miners now employed elsewhere
Were ordered back. Imagine the despair,
The resentment. Labour relations
Had ever been poor. Their frustrations
Now boiled over, with walk-outs in the mines.
Over one thousand miners received fines
After striking at Betteshanger, in Kent,
Over wages. The rising discontent

Was patent. The chairman, secretary
And a third member of the committee
Were imprisoned, but refused to back down.
The Betteshanger strike, the talk of the town,
Was settled, after a tough nineteen days,
In the miners' favour. They had found ways
Of wrong-footing the government. Few paid
Their fines. An important point had been made.
Output improved, but only for a time.
Striking in theory remained a crime,
But the government's softly-softly approach,
Though a fudge, made sense and was beyond reproach.

The 'Bevin Boys', so-called, made little impact –
An entertaining sideshow, to be exact.

The extraordinary system worked like this.
When of an age for National Service,

A ballot picked out the unlucky young men –
For every ID number, one in ten –
For service in the mines. It was quite absurd.

Few showed any aptitude (less than a third).
Between 1944 and '45,
As Bevin's campaign went into overdrive,
21,000 reluctant 'ballotees'
Were sent down the mines. Few had strong enough knees,
Legs or shoulders for the back-breaking labour.
An inspiration? Do me a favour.
It took more to train a Bevin Boy, some said,
Than to do the work themselves. Some stayed in bed,
Others deserted or turned up at the wrong pit.
Bevin Boys and mining proved a pretty poor fit.

Egypt and the Mediterranean

Hitler showed unusual loyalty
To Mussolini – initially,
At least. The summer of 1940
Saw Britain in peril. Mussolini
Believed that the war was as good as won.

Fearful of losing his place in the sun,
He declared war, not a moment too soon,
On Britain and France on the 10th of June.
Italy was seen as a firm ally
By Hitler (I have no idea why),
Though the Führer would quickly change his tune.
Far from the alliance proving a boon,
Hitler soon realised that Italy
Was a burdensome liability.

Be that as it may. The British, for years,
Had been a force in Egypt. There were fears,

Once Mussolini had entered the war,
That their presence was no longer secure.
The Mediterranean was now closed
To British merchant ships. It was supposed,
By many, that Great Britain's naval fleet,
In Alexandria, could face defeat
From bombardment by Italian planes.

This was a worry and perhaps explains
Why the three local Commanders-in-Chief
Were united, for once, in their belief
That British forces in Egypt needed
Reinforcements. Their requests were heeded.
Short of resources early in the war,
This was still a tall order. To withdraw?
Unthinkable. For prestige was at stake.
To abandon Egypt? A big mistake,
And not one Churchill was prepared to make.

The Cabinet were duly consulted.
They agreed. Their strong resolve resulted
In a tank force being sent to Egypt –
One third of Britain's strength. Better equipped,
The Army had a chance of holding out
Against the Italians. There's no doubt,
However, that air cover was still weak.
The overall outlook, frankly, was bleak.

An Italian campaign

Though this had echoes of Gallipoli,
Churchill in the long term saw Italy
As the back door into Europe. Silly?
Well, we shall see. Another reason, too,
For an African presence, in his view,
Were the Italians in Libya,
And their *régime* in Abyssinia.

If the British could make some headway here,
Their success would offer much-needed cheer
To folk at home in a terrible year.

But the blunt truth of the matter was this:
Egypt was none of Britain's business,
Nor Libya. The Brits were in the Med…
Well… because they were. This has to be said.

Success in Libya

The British were outnumbered five to one
By the Italians. Soon on the run,
Nonetheless, were the enemy. With ease,
The Navy saw them off on the high seas,
While Wavell scored an outstanding success
On land. (Churchill was the first to confess
To never having been a Wavell fan:
The General was a cautious man,
Thoughtful and taciturn, unlike his boss –
Well, that's how Sir Archibald came across).
His field commander, Richard O'Connor,
A capital fellow of high honour,
Crossed the eastern Libyan frontier,
Taking the Italians in the rear.
He had fewer than three hundred tanks, a force
Of 35,000 and courage (of course).

The number of prisoners that he took
Was astonishing – if I'm not mistook,
130,000! Tobruk,
Benghazi, Beda Fomm, all quickly fell,
Till all of Cyrenaica, truth to tell
(Northern Libya), was in British hands.
He wanted to press on, one understands –
By now we are into February,
1941 – through to Tripoli.

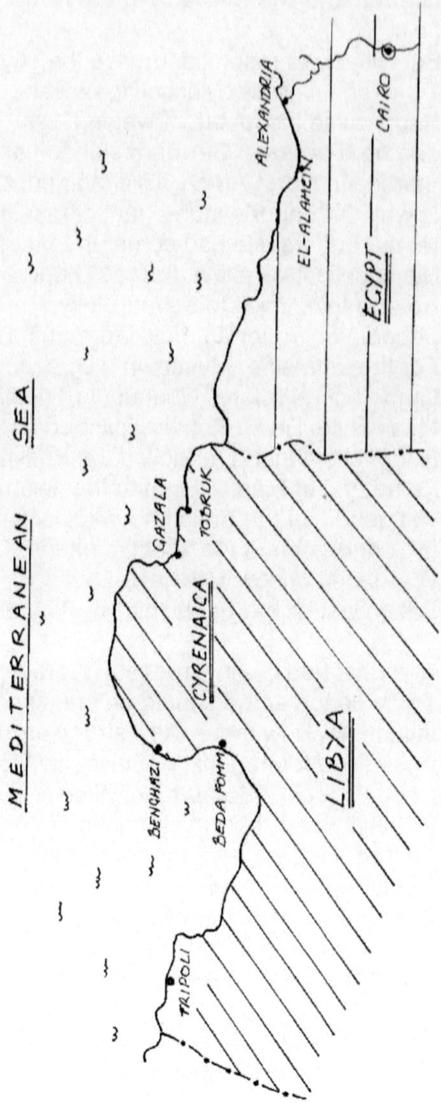
MEDITERRANEAN SEA
ALEXANDRIA
EL-ALAMEIN
CAIRO
EGYPT
GAZALA
TOBRUK
CYRENAICA
LIBYA
BENGHAZI
BEDA FOMM
TRIPOLI

Greece and the setback in Libya

But Hitler had resolved, more's the pity,
To invade Greece. Mussolini, he saw,
Had proved incapable of waging war.
The hard-pressed Germans had to bail him out,
Starting in North Africa. This, no doubt,
Is why O'Connor's triumphant campaign
Hit the buffers. He had come under strain.
His supplies were low. Forget Tripoli,
He was told. Back to Egypt! Sicily
Became an important new German base
For the *Luftwaffe*. Musso, in disgrace,
Limped off to lick his wounds. In Tripoli,
Meanwhile, Erwin Rommel pitched up and he,
Rommel of legend, attacked the British
At the end of March. Fight to the finish?
Not quite, but the British advance collapsed.
O'Connor, one of the finest of chaps,
Was taken prisoner. What an outlook!
Britain lost all her gains, barring Tobruk.

The Brits had given Greece a guarantee
To come to her aid should an enemy
Invade. By now there were strong arguments
Against honouring this promise. Nonsense,
Cried Churchill! Some humiliation
It would be for the British nation
To turn her back on such trusted allies.
Catastrophe beckoned – surprise, surprise.
It is hard not to admire Churchill,
A man of honour and of iron will.
Oh, that we were blessed with such leaders still.

He would stand by the Greeks, for good or ill.
Sadly, it was the latter. In April,

62,000 British were sent out.
The result, predictably, was a rout.
By the time they arrived, the enemy
Had occupied the entire country.
The troops, up the proverbial gum tree,
Were rescued, 50,000 taken off,
Before facing any Germans – don't scoff:
A lesser Dunkirk, yet more of the same,
A tale of dither, disaster and shame.

Catastrophe in Crete

What possessed the PM, in Heaven's name,
To think after this that he could hold Crete?
The calamity was swift and complete.
Churchill declared it was "essential"
To keep Crete. I reckon it was mental.
The RN still controlled the eastern Med,
But only, alas, from what I have read,
If marine power alone was the test.

Yet the British in Crete were past their best
In the air. They had seven fighters left –
Yes, seven! Our forces were bereft.
The *Luftwaffe* won the battle for Crete:
Some seven hundred aircraft, pretty neat.
So, the Germans dominated the sea
During daylight, as the Royal Navy,
Kicking its heels, could only wring its hands
(Mixed metaphors, sorry). In foreign lands,
Military adventures are a risk.

Evacuation was less than brisk.
18,000 allied troops got away,
But some 13,000 were there to stay,
Prisoners of war, sadly the losers.
Destroyed in the campaign were three cruisers

And six destroyers. Britain had lost control
Of the Aegean. Hitler was on a roll…

Or perhaps not. He lost two hundred planes
(Possibly more), which probably explains
Why he dropped plans for more airborne assaults –
Parachutists performing somersaults,
As happened over Crete, with many lost –
On Suez and Malta. A heavy cost
Hitler incurred over Crete: a "sprained wrist,"
In one colourful phrase. You get the gist.

'Operation Battle Axe'

But he could add one more hit to his list.
The Brits launched 'Operation Battle Axe'
In Libya, the mother of all attacks,
Designed to relieve Tobruk and drive out
Rommel from Cyrenaica. A short bout
(A mere three days) saw Wavell off. He failed,
Comprehensively, to get Rommel nailed.

Churchill lost patience. Wavell was sent
To India (which he didn't resent*)
As Commander-in-Chief. Claude Auchinleck,
His predecessor, in turn made the trek
From India to take his place. Success
Eluded him too. He failed to impress.
He never measured up, in Churchill's eyes,
But when he was sacked it caused some surprise.

For Sir Claude showed flair and ability
In the field and a rare agility
In terms of strategy. It's a pity
That Churchill failed to recognise his worth,
For Auchinleck was the salt of the earth.

Better news from Abyssinia

One single victory to celebrate,
At this time, was that of our old mate,
Haile Selassie. On the 5th of May,
1941, in a rare display
Of triumph, the Emperor was restored.

---

*Indeed, Wavell was promoted to Viceroy
In 1943. A pleasant old boy,
He was cultured too. He would read for hours –
Poetry, in the main. *Other Men's Flowers*,
An anthology of his favourite verse,
He published in 1944. Averse,
As Sir Archibald was, to publicity,
He published few poems himself – a pity,
Since the final verse to appear in his book
Is one of Wavell's. It is well worth a look.
"A little wayside dandelion" (that's modest)
"Of my own," he called it. He was one of the best.

One irony that is often ignored
Is that Italian occupation
Had provided his benighted nation
With higher standards of education
And health, contrary to expectation.
This Haile Selassie had never done.

Be that as it may, the battle was won.
The Emperor returned. Mussolini
Felt Abyssinia's loss most keenly.

As a victory, it was the merest blip
In Britain's misfortunes. Yet to show friendship
Towards an ally was worth its weight in gold.
It revived Churchill's spirits a hundredfold.

Hitler invades Russia

Sir Claude Auchinleck took over, by the way,
On June the 21st. The very next day,
The Germans invaded Russia. Stalin
Was ill-prepared. Hitler expected to win
Within weeks. Stalin, from numerous sources,
Had learned of the build-up of German forces
On the frontier. Hitler had assured him –
And this he had swallowed, decidedly dim –
That he was moving his troops east, out of range
Of British bombing! What is even more strange
Is that Hitler's Ambassador to Moscow
Tipped Stalin off too – an intriguing fellow,
Anti-Nazi. Richard Sorge, in Tokyo,
Stalin's 'mole' and a 'Nazi' journalist there,
Had warned him, in terms of increasing despair,
That an attack was imminent. Britain, too,
Confirmed the intelligence. Uncle Joe knew,
However, that the opposite must be true

If the British said it. Stalin had a pact,
Besides, with Hitler. It's an amazing fact
That up to the hour the Germans attacked,
Key supplies were still on their way to the Reich.

The Germans' three-pronged attack

The Germans had three armies poised to strike.
Army Group North would head for Leningrad,
After assaults on the way, I should add,
On the Baltic States. Focused on Moscow,
Army Group Centre would take Minsk (a side-show),
Before making for the capital. This,
Of course, was the prize and too good to miss.
Army Group South would move, with all due speed,
To the Ukraine. They were sure to succeed.
There was never a doubt in Hitler's mind.

Rather too cocky I think you will find,
But Hitler foresaw the simplest of wins.
He recalled Stalin's first brush with the Finns.
The Red Army had proved itself unfit
For battle, that was the bald truth of it.
Soviet Russia was a ruin,
Rotten to the core. They'd kick the door in.
The building would collapse. End of Stalin.

The campaign would be ruthless. To succeed,
Hitler devised a strategy to feed
His huge army. A simple case of greed:
"We take from the country the things we need" –
This a quote from an army directive.

Viewed from a Russian perspective,
This spelt disaster. "There is no doubt
"That millions" (it's best to have it out)

"Of people will starve to death." So? Who cared?
Not the Nazis, for sure. Nobody dared
Challenge the Führer. They were all too scared.

The object of the Russian campaign
Was conquest. For Hitler had made it plain
That victory alone was not enough.
The Germans craved space (insidious stuff),
Lebensraum, he called it: room to expand.

Hitler never sought to conceal his hand.
He was quite honest about it. The Slavs
Were mere vermin (he did nothing by halves).
Through terror and extermination,
The future of the German nation
Would be guaranteed. For a thousand years
The Reich would live on. To the people's cheers –
Nay, their hysteria – the dictator
Looked invincible. More of that later.

Two million Russian prisoners of war
Were murdered by the Germans. Ten million more
(Civilians) were shot, or hanged, or starved to death.
The horror speaks for itself. I shall save my breath.

In terms of numbers, Russia was strong.
The Führer must have known all along
That both sides' armies were pretty well matched.
Yet Russia's air force was soon despatched:
Over eighteen hundred fighters were found
And bombed to pieces, lined up on the ground.
I told you that Stalin was unprepared.

The German *Luftwaffe* (they hardly cared)
Lost a total of thirty-five aircraft.
Now master of the skies, how Göring laughed.

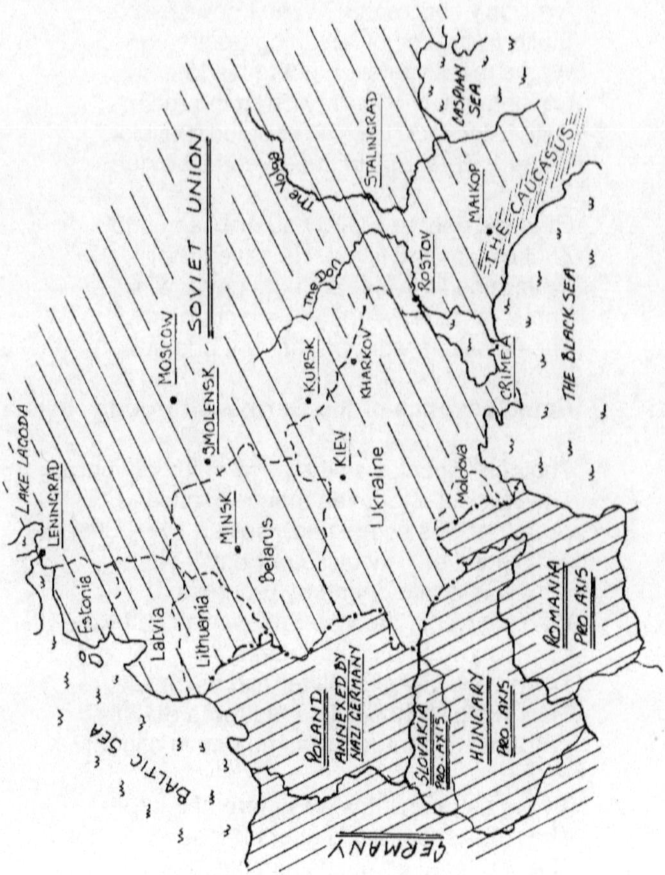

Stalin's purge of the Red Army

In the 1930s, the Red Army
Had been purged. This was completely barmy.
Stalin left himself with just ten *per cent*
Of his generals. Was it his intent
To boost his own ego, or to prevent

A military *coup d'état*? Who knows?
Stalin's strategy of 'anything goes'
Was a massive risk, a gift to his foes.
He 'beheaded' his army. Stop the rot?
Rather too late. He was saddled, the clot,
With the B-team. He deserved all he got.

Of those generals who had not been shot,
Zhukov was the finest. He saved Stalin,
Determined the Nazis would never win.
That's for later. What of the picture now?
The Russians were on the run, and how.

Rapid advance of the Germans through Russia

Their first shock was the pace of the advance.
The Nazis, faster even than in France
(And that was something), seized every chance.
A distance of sixty miles per day – yes,
That was a rate of enemy progress.
Within a week, the *Wehrmacht* was half way
To Moscow, impatient of delay.
Towns and villages, all fell like ninepins.
They hadn't a hope. The fault was Stalin's.
Who was in charge? Was no one in control?

To the Germans this was more of a stroll.
The Russians were in utter chaos.
They suffered an unsustainable loss
In tanks: some 6,000 lost in July
At Minsk and Smolensk. Folk were asking why
Stalin was still failing to take a lead.
His absence was noted. Odd indeed.

His forces simply weren't up to the fight:
500,000 killed in a fortnight,

With one million prisoners of war.
A sobering truth that one can't ignore
Is that few of the latter survived. Shot
(Or worse) or left to starve to death, their lot
Was hideous. Yet the men showed no fear.

Stalin finally roused himself, we hear,
With a speech on Soviet radio,
Read by Molotov (which was strange, I know):
"Victory," he declared, "will be ours,
"The enemy shattered." Within hours,
There were long queues of hopeful volunteers,
Eager to enlist. Also, it appears,
There was a certain feeling of relief
That the pact with Hitler had come to grief.
Russians had never thought much of it
And this now worked to Stalin's benefit.

Stalin's determination

Although they were manifestly unfit,
In terms of training, arms and equipment,
They kept on coming. That's what courage meant.
For the tide would turn. On July the 1st,
Stalin returned to Moscow. He'd been cursed
For staying away. Another broadcast,
This time from the Kremlin: Stalin, at last,
Addressed his people. Many were surprised
By his Georgian accent. How he prized
Their patriotism! The Motherland
Must be defended with all means at hand!
A scorched earth policy! Total warfare!

The Germans were increasingly aware
That there were Russians everywhere.
Some combatants were driven to despair

By the vastness of the country. Defeat
Of the enemy would appear complete,
Only for more to be up on their feet.

In the fall of Kiev, in September –
Three months into the campaign, remember –
Seven hundred and fifty thousand men
Were taken as prisoners of war. When,
The Germans wondered, would the foe give in?
Was this a war that they could ever win?

Heavy Russian casualties

Three in a hundred prisoners survived,
While the triumphant Nazi armies thrived.
Over the same period, countrywide,
More than three million Russians died.

Their resilience was astonishing.
The Germans had been taught (a foolish thing)
That their enemy was subhuman. Well,
Soon they knew better. The campaign was hell,
But they rarely heard them scream or cry out.
This was true courage, no shadow of doubt.

What of the German armies in the field?
To the north, Leningrad refused to yield.
It was a close call. The forlorn city
Was surrounded, cut off, more's the pity,
In November. One million would die,
Starved to death. Their only means of supply
Was across Lake Ladoga (when it froze).

The long siege, as everybody knows,
Was one of the great horrors of the war,
Not lifted until 1944.

The campaign in the south

The northern army was tied up, therefore,
At Leningrad. Rather more successful
Was the southern army. Times were stressful
For the Russians, who were poorly led.
One commander there, Budyonny, it's said,
Was an old drinking buddy of Stalin's,
A great buffoon, unsteady on his pins.

The upshot? A comprehensive defeat
For his forces, who were feeling the heat.
Control was being lost of the Ukraine.
Over a thousand tanks went down the drain,
8,000 guns and (the constant refrain)
Up to one million prisoners. This,
Though, was an illusion. In practice,
The prize on which Hitler had set his heart
Proved worthless. Prisoners of war apart,
The great Ukraine cradle of industry
Was trashed: Stalin's scorched earth policy.

The Red Army, though trounced, had the last laugh.
Russia's farming land (well over half)
Was in the south. Most of this they destroyed,
Burned (the Nazis were extremely annoyed),
Along with a hydroelectric dam.
The Germans were in a bit of a jam:
River and railway bridges blown up…
Perfect for *Lebensraum*? Anything but.

The Russians move their industry to the east

The Russians, casualties apart,
Made, it appears, a remarkable start
In moving their industries further east.
In due course famine would give way to feast.
The bulk of the republic's industry,
Many a workshop, forge and factory,
Had already been evacuated,
On Stalin's orders. This move created
Renewed capacity, essential
For fulfilling the state's potential
As a well-equipped, fighting nation.
Stalin displayed imagination
And rare foresight. An inspiration.

Moscow

Hitler then made a critical mistake.
He gave orders (what an error to make)
For Army Group Centre, bound for Moscow,
To stop in its tracks. While progress was slow
In the south (Kiev) and the north (Leningrad),
There was no present advantage to be had
In pressing forward. He feared his southern flank
Would be exposed. Well, to be perfectly frank,
Stalin had Hitler's decision to thank

For Moscow's salvation. For the delay
Enabled the Muscovites (every day
Counted) to rally all hands to the defence
Of the city. The policy made no sense.
So, while his other forces would concentrate
On Kiev and Leningrad, Moscow could wait...

Or could it? By the time Hitler was ready,
It was late September. His nerve held steady,
But he ignored the omens. Only equipped
For summer weather, his armies would be whipped
By the Russian winter and they knew it.
His generals were appalled. Hitler blew it.

The first phase of 'Operation Typhoon',
So-called, began, not a moment too soon,
On September the 30th. Panic
Gripped the Soviets. The mood was manic.
A huge 'tank trap' had been dug round Moscow –
Women, children, old folk, all had a go.

This was the spirit of Borodino.*
With Leningrad all but surrounded, though,
And the Ukraine subdued, the German forces –
Millions of men and as many horses –
Could finally launch a direct assault.
The hard-pressed Russians (hardly their fault)
Were taken prisoner in their thousands –
700,000. Bad as this sounds
(And few survived), the rain, and then the snow,
Were the curse of the Germans. Even so,
Towards the end of November, Moscow
Was well within their reach. How far to go?

---

*The famous battle of Borodino,
Fought some seventy miles west of Moscow,
Was a win for the French. A triumph? No.
Although the Russians were badly mauled,
Napoleon's army suddenly stalled.
A 'Pyrrhic' victory it's often called.
The conquerors entered Moscow, it's true,
Just one week later. But credit is due
To the Russians. The French were bereft,
As Moscow burned! Its citizens had left;
The place was in ruins; winter set in:
Certainly less than a convincing win.
As the world at large was soon to find out,
There followed an ignominious rout.
Exit the French, gone by mid-December.
Napoleon would ever remember
The winter of 1812. The big freeze –
We're talking minus 38 degrees,
Centigrade – saw thousands of poor souls dead,
Hundreds of thousands. The spirit, it's said,
That saved Russia after Borodino
Was the same that inspired Stalin's Moscow.

Thirty miles at the very most! Stalin
Showed courage. He had stayed in the Kremlin.
Even as the winter weather set in,
With a vengeance, the Germans rolled on,
But by mid-December all hope had gone.

The Russian winter

At minus 20 degrees centigrade,
Nazi soldiers were feeling afraid.
Their oil solidified, radios
Stopped working, machine guns and rifles froze.
Their horses lacked forage and the troops found
Digging trenches in the iron-hard ground
Was impossible. Frostbite was a curse,
Numbers of serious cases far worse
Than those who were wounded in battle. Still,
The determined Germans pressed on until,
Finally, they had to admit defeat.

The Nazi retreat

The Russians, meanwhile, had found their feet
And forced the enemy into retreat.
Zhukov, who had been transferred to Moscow
From Leningrad, took comfort from the snow.
He launched an offensive. First to arrive
Were new ski battalions (twenty-five)
From Siberia. Stalin had been told –
It's remarkable how these things unfold –
That another of his arch-enemies
On the Chinese border, the Japanese,
Were now focused on the Pacific (yes,
The US fleet in Pearl Harbour, no less),
So Russia could afford to withdraw
Her ski troops from this theatre of war.

The Germans were in for a shock, therefore,
When they found themselves harried and pursued
By these ace ski warriors. It was crude,
To put it mildly, how they were treated
(The Germans, that is) as they retreated.

For the Russians for the first time saw
How Nazis punished prisoners of war.
The climate sadly was ripe for revenge:
Multitudes of crimes there were to avenge.
The Germans suffered a nervous collapse.
A handful no doubt were sensitive chaps,
But should we show sympathy? Not a lot.
Any rebels, of course, would have been shot,
Had they objected. Hitler wrote the plot,
But they signed up to it, like it or not.

300,000 were captured or killed
In the German retreat. Voices were stilled
In Berlin and the *Reichstag.* Victory,
For the first time in recent history,
Had eluded the triumphant Nazis.
Yet Hitler's armies, though brought to their knees,
Would live, poor souls, to fight another day.
More blood. More ruin. More death and decay.
More agony. Such was the Führer's way.

Russia: Britain's new ally

Churchill had never made any secret
Of his loathing, in public or private,
Of Bolshevism. But he now saw fit,
Without denying this one little bit,
To pledge immediate allegiance
To Soviet Russia. No grievance,
However strong, could outweigh the present.
Hitler's folly, indeed, was Heaven-sent.

Britain had won a vital new ally
In Stalin. Few Londoners could deny
Their good fortune. Hitler's attention
Now lay elsewhere. He'd no intention
Of dropping bombs, simultaneously,
On two fronts. The Labour Party, strangely,
Was less enamoured of joining forces
With Stalin (according to some sources),
But the PM's determination
Was total. His justification?
Self-evident. There was a war to win.
Short of the Americans coming in
(Watch this space), an alliance with Stalin
Was a good second best. As he broadcast
On radio: the crisis had not passed,
But this was a partnership built to last.
Churchill's resolve and promise were steadfast.

He nailed his colours firmly to the mast.
"One single irrevocable purpose"
He declared: to rid the world of the curse
Of Hitler. He had one aim, only one:
"Any state that fights against Nazidom
"Will have our aid." No Soviet fan,*
He would still "give whatever help we can
"To the Russian people". So began
This strange alliance. Inauspicious
At first (for Stalin was suspicious

---

* "If Hitler invaded hell," said Churchill,
Speaking once in private to John Colville,
His Assistant Private Secretary,
He confessed he would be more than ready
To "make a favourable reference
"To the Devil". Such was his preference!

Of Churchill's motives), a second front *now*
Was what the Russians demanded. How,
They asked, could Britain stand idly by,
While the Motherland suffered? Why, oh why,
Could sea-borne forces not simply invade
Europe? Stalin professed himself dismayed.
Some ally, the British! No case was made,
However, that could have convinced Churchill,
Who held off the invasion until
(Wait for it) the spring of 1944.

Churchill, nonetheless, was loth to ignore
His new ally. He'd only win the war,
This he knew, by keeping Stalin on side –
US President Roosevelt beside
(Keeping all fingers crossed). What did he do?

He diverted supplies (too few, it's true,
Since urgently needed by Britain too)
To the Soviet war effort: some tanks,
For which he received very little thanks,
Inferior to those the Russians had;
Large consignments of steel-studded boots, bad,
I've read, because they encouraged frostbite;
And standard-issue greatcoats, far too light
For Russian winter conditions.

Churchill also offered munitions
And other military equipment.
However useful, every shipment
Meant less for Britain's beleaguered forces.
It was, as they say, horses for courses.
Sending these valuable resources
Was done in the best of faith, to build trust
And goodwill, as Churchill knew he must.
Stalin would hardly have settled for less.

The Jews in Russia

Following the Nazis' early success
In Russia, five million more Jews
Were added to the list, even worse news
For Himmler and his infernal SS.
How to be rid of them all? I confess
To feeling considerable unease,
Recording such broad statistics as these.
Five million? Six million? Who knows?
Seven million…? As the figure grows,
We should never forget: every one
Was a mother or a sister, a son
Or a father, a grandparent, a wife,
A husband, a child… Above all, a life.

Himmler and the SS

With no easy 'solution' at all,
The numbers, calculated to appal
(The SS, that is), gave cause for concern.
The ghettos, Himmler would be quick to learn,
Were a burden. They were already full.
Besides, Himmler had had his bellyful
Of Jews. He and Hitler, never at odds,
Agreed. They'd try execution squads.
Einsatzgruppen these were called. Men, women,
The frail and the old, even small children,
Were marched out into the forests and shot –
Families, friends, neighbours, as like as not,
Often whole communities at a time.
Imagine a more despicable crime.
These *Einsatzgruppen* were mobile units,
Who then threw the bodies into huge pits,
Usually dug by local workers,
Who had little choice. They shot the shirkers.

The SS revelled in their crimes. Who knows
How they lived with themselves. Anything goes,
It seems, in warfare. They sent home photos
Of their unspeakable atrocities.
Yet no one challenged these monstrosities.
Even as the SS celebrated,
The numbers killed, it's been estimated,
Exceeded one-point-four million. Yes,
You read that right – hard, I have to confess,
For a fellow human to comprehend.
When, one had to ask, would the nightmare end?

Himmler visits Minsk

Not yet, was the dismal answer to that.
Heinrich Himmler was feeling rather flat
One sunny day in August, '41.
So he reckoned he'd have a bit of fun
And visit Minsk to see how it was done –
The shooting of those with dissident views
In the camps, above all, of course, the Jews.
For the guards this was most exciting news:
A visit from the boss of the SS,
From *Reichsführer* Himmler himself no less.

They put on a 'magnificent' display
Of mass shooting that particular day.
They stood Himmler at the side of a pit,
The very edge, so he could witness it.
He'd never seen a dead body before,
Or so we are told. There was blood and gore*
In large supply, as corpses by the score
Tumbled into the pit, hundreds and more.
He turned pale. It seems that a bit of brain
Splashed onto his cheek. It's hard to explain,
But Himmler kept his cool. He walked away,

Thrilled, he said, with this "impressive display".
Before he left he stood up in his car
And praised the men: every one a star.
However, "how deeply shaken they are,"
He remarked in private. He felt their pain…

Gas

He sought a method that was "more humane" –
For the executioners, that is.
The main responsibility was his,
Himmler's, for the step-change that now took place.
Not only did the killings gather pace,
Another method of murder, alas,
Superseded the shootings. This was gas.

On the 3rd of September, Zyklon B,
A pesticide, was used, in secrecy,
At Auschwitz. Polish prisoners of war,
Russian dissidents, gypsies and more
(Including Jews again) were gassed. Easy.
Shootings had made the soldiers queasy,
As Himmler had witnessed. Gassing, you see,
Could do the job more efficiently,
With minimal effort, rather less stress
And furthermore (forgive me) far less mess.

Revolting. Horrific. You want to weep.
Hitler was resolved to "make a clean sweep"

---

*This level of detail, I realise,
Is offensive. It will antagonise
Some, but I am loth to apologise.
For however terrible, it is true.
So it's something I think I have to do.

Of Jews in Europe. This was Goebbels' phrase
(In his diary) and, in the grim days
Of 1942, this foul campaign
Slid into top gear. Gas would take the strain.

The Wannsee conference

A conference was convened at Wannsee.
Hitler, in his usual canny way,
Did not attend, but his orders were clear.
European Jews were to 'disappear',
As simple as that. Himmler's deputy,
Reinhart Heydrich, drew up a policy
For the "physical annihilation
"Of the Jews… either by emigration
"Or evacuation". It's my belief,
Once Heydrich had the bit between his teeth,
That this instruction gave the green light
To the Final Solution. Keen, bright
And a fanatical anti-Semite,
Heydrich was the devil. Himmler was right:
The *Obergruppenführer* was the man
To liquidate the Jews. Planning began.

Reinhart Heydrich's list

First and foremost, Heydrich drew up a list
Of Jews by country (they'd never be missed) –
Eleven million the final total.
Much of the evidence was anecdotal:
These were round numbers. But even to think
In these gruesome terms (Heydrich didn't blink)
Was criminal. He included England,
Where the total head count, I understand,
According to the list, numbered no less
Than one third of a million – a guess,
I'm sure, but horrifying nonetheless…

No worse, of course, once the gassing began,
That England should have been part of the plan
Than any other occupied country.

We shall never know, with accuracy,
How many died in the camps, not for sure.
But the terrors that they had to endure
Were horrible. In the occupied east
New camps were specially built. The beast,
Himmler, ensured they had capacity –
Huge gas chambers, supplied with Zyklon B –
To murder on an industrial scale.
Millions were to die. It couldn't fail.

Most of the poor victims travelled by rail.
They were even made to pay their own fare.
Few of them resisted. They did not dare.

The Japanese bombing of Pearl Harbour

The course of history changed when the Japanese
Bombed the American fleet, with apparent ease,
At Pearl Harbour on the 7th of December,
A Sunday the US will ever remember.

Pearl Harbour was open to attack: aircraft
Parked on the runways (how the Japanese laughed);
Battleships in harbour, mostly understaffed,
All sitting targets; the anti-aircraft guns
Locked and unmanned. The fault must have been someone's.
How could a navy have been so unprepared?

The Japanese triumphed. The US despaired.
Terrible carnage. A vision of hell.

More than three and a half thousand personnel
Were killed or seriously injured that day,
Most of them combatants. It's hard to convey
The full extent of the devastation:
Four battleships sunk (an aberration);
Four severely damaged; ten more men-of-war
Put out of action; and (this I deplore)
Three hundred and fifty US aircraft lost.

The disaster was at very little cost
To the Japanese. They lost twenty-nine planes
And not one of their fleet, which perhaps explains
Why Pearl Harbour has gone down in history
As a famous military victory
For the Japanese and a catastrophe,
On an epic scale, for the US navy.

Yet it could have been far worse had it not been
For one fortunate circumstance, unforeseen

By the Japanese. For away, on repair,
Or on exercise (a miracle, I swear),
Were all four aircraft carriers, a nightmare,
Otherwise, for the whole American fleet.

The Japanese success was thus incomplete.
As the US navy got back on its feet,
It was far from business as usual –
But their aircraft carriers proved crucial.

War with Japan

The political response? Nobody felt
The horror more than President Roosevelt.
For this was a declaration of war
By the Japanese. Hitler levelled the score
By declaring war on the United States,
And Mussolini (to show they were best mates)
Joined him. The Soviets kept well out of it.
This was wise. It was to Stalin's benefit

That the Germans had another enemy,
So Uncle Joe acted very sensibly.

President Franklin D. Roosevelt

What of Churchill? He declared war on Japan
The following day. A big Roosevelt fan,
He knew that FDR was a complex man.
The two first met (apart from a brief meeting
In London some years earlier, so fleeting
That Churchill had forgotten it) in August.
The British craved US support (well, needs must),
But Roosevelt stood aloof. As expected,
To Churchill's relief, he'd been re-elected
In 1940, a far stronger ally
Than Wendell Willkie would have been. To deny
The proud Republican spirit, however,
Despite his great win, would not have been clever.
Republicans were isolationist
In spirit. Roosevelt was not, that's the gist.

As early as September, '39,
The President had taken a firm line,
But allowed himself enough wriggle room –
In case of an attack, we may presume,
By some hostile country – to go to war.
FDR gave this assurance therefore:
"I hope the United States will keep out
"Of this war." Indeed, he had little doubt
That it would. This was his steadfast intent.
"Every effort of your government
"Will be directed toward that end." Well,
That was the truth, as far as one can tell,
But Roosevelt entered this *caveat*:
"There will be no blackout of peace" (mark that)
"In the United States" while "it remains
"Within my power to prevent." * The pains,

To his credit, that the President took,
Should this change, to let himself off the hook
Were considerable and, in my book,
Masterly. He went as far as he could,
As any smart politician should.

Lend-Lease

So he moved with caution. His Lend-Lease Bill
Passed Congress by a whisker, a bitter pill
For the Republicans, who had had their fill,
But a lifeline for Britain, whose finances,
By 1941, were in deep crisis.
For "the great arsenal of democracy,"
President Roosevelt argued, "we must be".
Or, as he explained rather less formally,
If you see your neighbour's house is on fire,
You lend him your hose. He sought to aspire
To offer help, while keeping his powder dry.

Lend-Lease was a novel idea, whereby
The United States would provide an 'ally'
With key supplies for prosecuting the war,
Without those exports needing to be paid for
(In cash, at least: the conventional sense).
To 'lend' support – that was the Act, in essence.
It applied to goods "vital to the defense
"Of the United States". So, while the US
Remained neutral, the country, nevertheless,
Could offer a variety of supplies
To its potential warrior allies
On terms they could afford. They were the good guys!

---

*A tad ungrammatical, but never mind.
FDR spoke from the heart I think you'll find.

Tanks, aircraft, weapons, chemicals, food, clothing…
Lend-Lease effectively kept Britain going
Through the darkest days of the war. A high price
Was paid though: near-bankruptcy, to be precise.
The UK had to off-load her gold reserves
And foreign investments. FDR deserves,
At least, a small measure of grudging respect.
For his famed Lend-Lease (what else would you expect?)
Was more in the States' interest than ours.

Sorry, I know… I could go on for hours.
I'll quote the economics guru instead:
"We threw good housekeeping to the winds," Keynes said,
"But we saved ourselves." It may sound funny.
We saved the world, but we ran out of money.

FDR's first meeting with Churchill

The President's courage was hard to deny.
He supported the principle of supply
To Russia, despite dissident voices
In the States. This was the simplest of choices,
Compared to an all-out commitment to war.

At their August meeting FDR, therefore,
Played it pretty cool. The British should withdraw
From the Middle East – a liability!
He also declined to discuss strategy.
To declare war against Nazi Germany
Was a non-starter. They would never buy it
At home. Roosevelt, he could not deny it,
Had to tread warily. At the very least,
Churchill had hoped they could discuss the Far East.

Not so. He was worried about Singapore.
Would the US be prepared to go to war

On behalf of Britain, should the Japanese
Threaten that stronghold? FDR, if you please,
Would not talk about it. One outcome, of sorts,
Was the provision of convoy escorts
West of Iceland and bombers for the campaign
Against Germany. Roosevelt made it plain
That this first meeting at Placentia Bay,
Newfoundland, was to establish trust. Okay,
Not much was accomplished, but that was his way.

His caution was well-justified. Take note:
The first peacetime draft passed by a single vote
Through the House of Representatives. He walked
A tightrope. While Churchill talked (and how he talked),
FDR was bound by practicalities.
Isolationism was one of these.

The US also at war with Japan, Germany and Italy

The attack on Pearl Harbour altered all that.
Placentia Bay, little more than a chat,
Changed nothing. The Japanese action did.
The American people were rock solid
Behind their President as he declared war.
Their way of life was threatened. They knew the score.
With the heaviest of hearts, you understand,
In his dark suit, with a black tie and armband,
He signed the declaration. Germany,
Japan, Mussolini's Italy, all three,
At a stroke, were America's deadly foes.
Was Herr Hitler just a tad nervous? Who knows?

Churchill was jubilant. Pride before a fall?
Far from it. Britain's back was against the wall.
Dark days lay ahead. It was still a close call.
But he wrote later: "So we had won after all."

Background to the war in the Far East

What then of the war in the Pacific?
The Pearl Harbour attack was horrific.
The Hawaiian base, to be specific,
Lay some 4,000 miles east of Japan.
The bombing had gone according to plan,
But the Japanese, belligerent chaps,
Were focused on the south. It's time, perhaps,
To consider the background to this war.

The seeds were sown many years before.
Japan had suffered as much (if not more)
As any struggling economy
In the depression. Her industry

Was outdated, the state of her farming
Primitive. What was still more alarming,
With a million extra mouths to feed,
Year on year, was the overwhelming need
For mineral resources. For Japan
Had none within her own shores. So began
A new age of expansion. Indeed,
There was a common saying: to succeed
Was to conquer. A simple case of greed?
More of necessity, as most folk saw it.

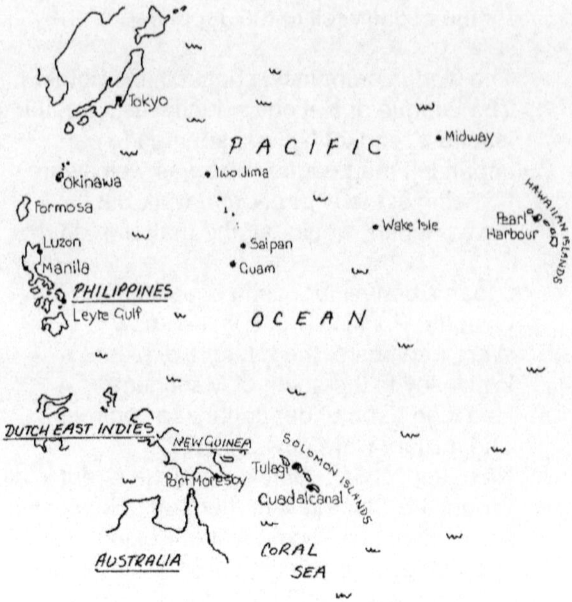

The Japanese were broke. Few could ignore it.
Though the world at large came to deplore it,
They bullied their neighbours as they saw fit.
They plundered Manchuria for profit,
Asserting they had the right. Come off it!

Manchuria in 1931

It was reserves of iron-ore and coal
That they lacked. Manchuria, on the whole,
Supplied their needs. In 1931,
The Japanese went further. One by one,
Their troops occupied industrial sites,
Then towns and cities, demanding their 'rights'.
The people were in no position
To put up any opposition.
Manchuria, alas, was on her knees,
As the country fell to the Japanese.

The world community, shocked, did nothing.
The League of Nations, which was something,
Issued a rebuke! No one seemed to care.
Japan left the League. She was well aware
Of being in the wrong, but a walk-out,
It was hoped, would put the matter in doubt.

Japan's behaviour cast a shadow
Over the Pacific. Those in the know
Were nervous of the future. Korea,
Which lay to the south of Manchuria,
Had long been under Japanese control.
The military were now on a roll.
Next stop, China. Safe behind the Great Wall,
Would the Chinese see them off? Not at all.
An incident just south-west of Peking
Was 'staged' by the Japanese. The thinking,
In Tokyo, was that their victory
Would be short and sharp. It was not to be.

China

Nonetheless, the Japanese overran
Northern China in a week. There began

A campaign of the utmost cruelty,
Not only against the military,
But the common populace. Peking fell –
The pain acute, a veritable hell –
Bombed to smithereens, followed by Shanghai.

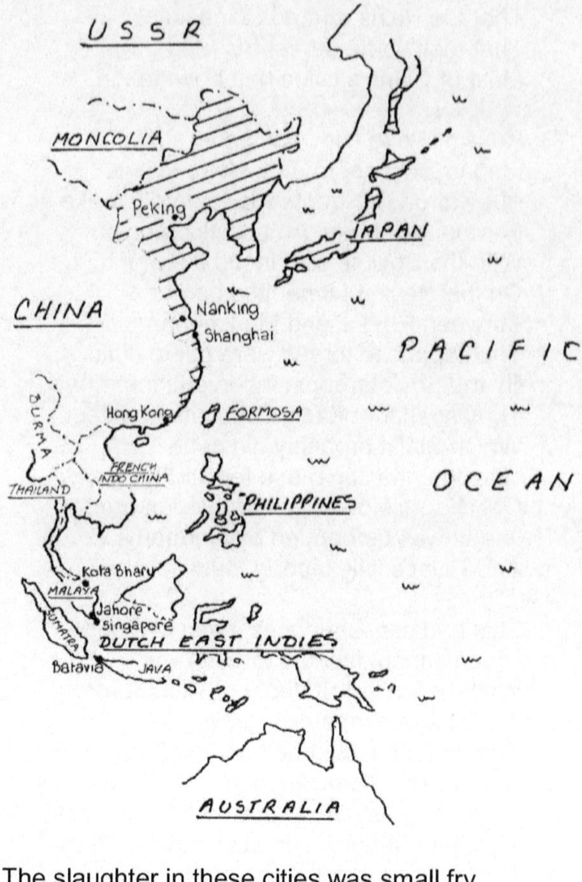

The slaughter in these cities was small fry
Compared to the massacre in Nanking
(Then the Chinese capital). Sickening…

200,000 murdered in cold blood –
A trickle, then a river, then a flood,
Women and children, the young and the old,
Men of all ages… Who could have foretold
That even Hitler would be horrified
(Allegedly). So many poor souls died
That the Nazis offered to mediate.
That took some nerve! By 1938,
Most of China's cities had been taken.

Russia, we're told, was badly shaken
(Japan's old enemy) by these events.
But war on two fronts would hardly make sense
For the Japanese. An unwelcome spat
With the Soviets convinced them of that.
On the bleak, uninhabited border
Between Russia and Manchuria
The Japanese forces were put to flight
By the Soviet troops. It served them right.
They sued for peace. One curious effect,
Which Stalin probably did not expect,
Was that the Japanese fell for the charms
Of Hitler (his own foe). With open arms
Japan was befriended by Germany,
And Hitler's little lapdog, Italy.

This had consequences, most certainly,
When Japan decided to go to war
With the United States. For Hitler swore
To Japan's Emperor Hirohito
That the US would be their common foe
Should Japan declare war. Who is to know
(A good question) what would have occurred
Had the Führer sat on his hands? Absurd?
Far from it. From Germany's point of view,
A campaign on two fronts was nothing new,

But three? Had Herr Hitler stayed out of it,
The United States (little doubt of it)
Would have concentrated on the Far East,
Japan, and ignored that other big beast,
Germany. Britain, without the US,
Would have found herself in a dreadful mess.

All fantasy, however. I digress.
The 'what ifs' of history, I confess,
Are engaging, but ultimately fruitless.

The Tripartite Pact

Japan had been watching with interest
Hitler's successes in Europe. Her quest
For territory continued apace.
The thought of the Empire losing face,
Through sheer timidity, was a disgrace.
If Germany could do it, why not us?
Japan was afraid of missing the bus.

As the mood became ever more warlike,
In 1940 her troops launched a strike
Against French Indochina. It would seem,
Amazingly, that the Vichy *régime*
Offered little or no discouragement.

Within weeks, the Japanese government
Was in total control of the country.
This was too close, for Roosevelt's money,
To US interests in the South Seas.
Would the Philippines, bases such as these,
Be the next to fall to the Japanese?
In particular, the Dutch East Indies,
With their huge oil reserves, were at risk.
The President's reaction was brisk.

In response, too, to the Tripartite Pact
That Japan had signed (a defiant act,
In Roosevelt's view) with both Germany
(Hitler) and Italy (Mussolini),
He placed an embargo on iron-ore
And oil exports. Would it trigger war?
Japan's Imperial Fleet, it was clear,
Would run out of fuel within a year.
Diplomacy? Forget it? A charade.
Both sides made out they were struggling hard
To find a solution, but all knew,
In their hearts, there was little they could do
To avert the impending disaster.

The aftermath of Pearl Harbour

So the Japanese moved, ever faster,
Towards war. To seize the oil they'd need,
It soon became obvious, to succeed,
That they'd have to launch a pre-emptive strike
Against the US. So, calm as you like,
They got in first with their daring attack
On Pearl Harbour. There was no going back.

The loss of Hong Kong

From December, it was 'anything goes'.
Pacific Islands fell like dominoes –
British, Dutch, American… Guam fell
(US) on the 10th; Wake Island, as well,
On the 23rd. But it was Hong Kong,
Which the British had known all along
Was highly vulnerable, come what may,
That was taken by storm on Christmas Day.
Two weeks earlier, to Churchill's dismay,
HMS *Prince of Wales* was torpedoed
And sunk, with heavy losses. This followed

The bombing of HMS *Repulse.* She,
Too, went down, an utter catastrophe.
The loss of the *Prince of Wales*, for Churchill,
Was a particularly bitter pill.
He had sailed in her, just five months before,
To meet the President, a ship, therefore,
With which the PM could identify.
The scale of this loss was hard to deny.

The fall of Singapore

Singapore was one of the star prizes
On Japan's list. There were no surprises.
Bombing began on the very same day
As the Pearl Harbour attack, that's to say
The 7th. It was to aid Singapore
That both the unfortunate men-of-war,
The *Repulse* and the *Prince of Wales,* were bound.

The British, Japanese commanders found,
Were in a state of ill-preparedness –
To put it bluntly, one heck of a mess.
Rich in tin and rubber was Malaya,
Which made the country a major player
In Japan's grandiose plans for conquest.
Arthur Percival was put to the test.
The Lieutenant-General did his best,
The military supremo in charge,
But the wretched fellow's brief, by and large,
Proved next to impossible to discharge.

The British were complacent. Percival,
To be frank, failed to measure up at all.
With a wilful degree of arrogance,
The Singapore residents looked askance
At the Japanese and the risk they posed.
Ignorance, it can only be supposed,

Was bliss. The Japanese were short-sighted
(So made poor pilots!), far from united
And, when the chips were down, cowards to boot.
Why should the hardy old Brits give a hoot?

The truth, of course, was another story.
In Japan there was no greater glory
Than to serve the Emperor to the death –
To fight, indeed, to the very last breath.

The British had a modern naval base
On Singapore Island. What a disgrace.
Why so? Well, despite the impressive space,
There were no ships to speak of. It was built
As a showcase, financed up to the hilt,
But the sad truth was it was undermanned
And could never serve the British as planned.

This part of the world, you should understand,
Was low on the list of priorities.
The Mediterranean, if you please,
And the Atlantic convoys – it was these
That drew focus away from the Far East.
As the danger to Singapore increased,
The Navy woke up. It was far too late.
The Brits, high and dry, were left to their fate.

This was not all that the Far East command
Lacked. There was also an urgent demand
In the Middle East, and Russia too,
For aircraft and tanks. What did Churchill do?
Turn a blind eye to Hong Kong, Singapore
And Burma. It's a truth hard to ignore.

Percival nonetheless, optimistic
To the last, hung on. Unrealistic?

I should say! Misguided to boot. Poor chap,
Master, alas, of many a mishap,
He deserves some sympathy, some credit,
At least for his courage. There, I've said it.

On December the 8th, Kota Bharu
Came under attack. The Japanese knew
That Kota Bharu, at the northern end
Of Malaya, would be hard to defend
Once their troops landed and their planes attacked
The only airfield. For the British lacked
Air cover. After gaining this foothold,
Japanese chances increased fiftyfold
Of advancing right down to Singapore.
It took them a mere seven weeks, no more,
To arrive at the southern tip, Johore,
Of the Malay peninsula. The speed
Of their advance astonished all – indeed,
The Brits were taken wholly by surprise.

Percival had decided (this defies
Belief, but who am I to criticise?)
Not to establish a defensive line
At Johore. It was all roses and wine
On Singapore Island, across the Strait
From Johore. The British, at any rate,
Would enjoy themselves at Raffles Hotel
To keep their spirits up. Why, what the hell!

Percival feared the effect on morale –
Such was his dubious rationale –
If Johore was defended in advance.
He would see off the enemy. Fat chance!

Yet the triumphant Japanese, of course,
Stormed the Malay peninsula, in force,

And by the middle of January,
'42, were in Johore – a pity **1942**
That Percival had not prepared for this!

The 31st saw the final crisis.
After two weeks under sustained attack
The remaining British force was pulled back
(Along with their Australian allies,
Indian too), to nobody's surprise,
To Singapore Island. Well, this was wise.
There was no alternative after all.

The dash across the Strait was a close call.
The causeway was then blown up. Sadly,
Those who failed to make it suffered badly.
There had not been time to ferry across
Some of the wounded. I am at a loss
To comprehend how they were left behind.
Percival's fault? Am I being unkind?

Australians, mainly, and Indians
Were the singularly unlucky ones.
Some two hundred were decapitated
By the Japanese. This crime created
An outburst of outrage. Percival knew,
To his shame, there was nothing he could do.

The assault on Singapore now began.
Rather than defend it to the last man,
As Churchill ordered (had he hoped, perhaps,
For a miracle?), a total collapse
In morale followed. Disappointing chaps,
The British – this was the Japanese view.
It was tragic that the Brits never knew
The actual Japanese position.
A severe shortage of ammunition
Meant they'd only have lasted a few more days.
The irony never ceases to amaze.

The unexpected British surrender
Made this the worst of days to remember:
Sunday the 15th of February –
The most ignoble day (yes, really)
In British colonial history.

130,000 troops, alas –
You read that right, a surrender *en masse* –
Laid down their arms. Elated and surprised,
The Japanese army never surmised
That an enemy could simply cave in.
This was cowardice, the ultimate sin.

The Dutch East Indies and the Philippines

South of Singapore, the Dutch East Indies
Were ripe for conquest by the Japanese.

They took the whole of Sumatra with ease.
The oilfields and Dutch Shell refineries
Were a great prize. The island of Java
Followed. Batavia (now Jakarta)
Had surrendered by March. The Philippines
(US), Manilla smashed to smithereens,
Had fallen earlier... The war dragged on
In isolated outposts. Woebegone,
American troops held out in pockets,
Strafed by artillery, bombs and rockets,
But had to surrender in early May.
The 'Battling Bastards of Bataan' (okay?),
They soldiered on while fit for the fray,
Until finally forced to call it a day.

South-East Asia now lay at the feet
Of the Japanese, a sweeping defeat.
The allied rout had been swift and complete.

Hitler would surely never have risked war
Had Roosevelt made it known before
That Europe was his first priority
Over the Far East. Now it seems to me
That FDR behaved generously
And with vision. For Hitler, he knew,
Must be defeated and this was the view
Of most major figures in the US –
To Churchill's vast relief, I must confess.
He'd feared he might have to settle for less.

So his second visit to the US
He should have approached with optimism.

Yet Pearl Harbour and the barbarism
Of the Japanese attack had been such
That it would not have surprised him that much

Had Roosevelt put war in the Far East
On a par footing, at the very least,
With the war against Nazi Germany.

Britain and America in strong alliance

He arrived, then, with no great certainty
As to the President's line of attack.
Churchill was pleasantly taken aback
By Roosevelt's positive attitude.

He'd no time for flannel or platitude.
Though Pearl Harbour would "live in infamy",
Germany was still the "prime enemy".
Hitler must be beaten first. There had been doubt
In the Prime Minister's mind as he set out
On HMS *Duke of York* (sister ship
To the *Prince of Wales*). For 'many a slip'
He feared, as they say, 'betwixt cup and lip' –
But Roosevelt offered the firm friendship
Of a true ally. Churchill told the King,
Later, that his visit, if anything,
Had cemented a kind of marriage.
This was surely nothing to disparage:
"Britain and America," he declared,
Were "now married" (you wonder how he dared)
"After many months of walking out." Well,
A happy couple? Only time would tell.

'Germany first'

Churchill and Roosevelt were in their prime.
The British Prime Minister lost no time.
He set sail on the 12th of December –
Five days after Pearl Harbour, remember –
And was met in person by Roosevelt.
As for Churchill, you wonder how he felt

As he took hold of Roosevelt's "strong hand,
"With comfort and pleasure". Though far from grand,
The President's manner, you understand,
Was impeccable. Churchill was to stay,
As his guest, at the White House. Some dismay
This caused Churchill at first. What do you think?
The Roosevelts were stingy with the drink –
So at least the Prime Minister had heard.

Imagine anything quite so absurd.
Churchill's needs were fully attended to,
Including his taste for alcohol. Phew!

Both Houses of Congress on Boxing Day –
This was an official holiday;
Who cared? – gave him a rousing reception,
Cheered to the rooftops, without exception.
His anti-German remarks were received,
The ever-sensitive Churchill perceived,
With less enthusiasm, he believed,
Than his anti-Japanese comments. Well,
No matter. They all got along just swell.

So, 'Germany first'. But what did this mean?
Pearl Harbour had been largely unforeseen.
The Pacific was a naval affair.
The army needed a focus, but where?
In due course there would be occasion
For a European invasion
From England across the Channel, you bet,
But that would take time. Certainly not yet.

So the Americans gave the green light
To the North African campaign, a fight
They would join sometime in '42,
Codenamed 'Operation Torch'. Who knew,

At this early stage, what that would lead to?
Roosevelt had to build up his army, too.
But Churchill had won FDR's consent,
In principle, so he was well content.

Next, the Canadian Parliament.
His speech was a corker! Some years before,
The French (who Churchill preferred to ignore)
Predicted that Britain, an utter wreck,
Would collapse within three short weeks, "her neck
"Wrung like a chicken". You wonder they dared.
A lesser orator might have despaired –
Not Churchill. "Some chicken!" (a pregnant pause,
Impeccably timed) "Some neck!" Cue, applause.

Massive US armaments and recruitment

He returned to Britain well satisfied.
Roosevelt, determined to turn the tide,
Was proof the allies would be well supplied.
Churchill was more than pleasantly surprised
At the great recruitment drive publicised

By the President: eight million men
For the army!* With a stroke of his pen,
Roosevelt ordered a massive increase
In war spending. Would wonders never cease?
As aircraft numbers doubled in a year,
Would tanks and weapons lag behind? No fear.
There was a huge growth in production,
While the target for the construction
Of merchant shipping leapt (for '43)
To ten million tons. Take it from me,
This was a full-scale war economy.

One hundred and fifty *billion* – yes,
That was the budget, certainly no less.
Before announcing his plan to Congress,
Roosevelt tore up earlier figures –
Resistant to Republican sniggers –
Increasing most of them by more than half.

Adept at sifting the wheat from the chaff,
FDR knew how to prioritise.
His strategy, to no one's great surprise,
Was vindicated. The best of allies.

Göring, we're told, was scornful of the Yanks.
Merchant shipping, anti-aircraft guns, tanks,
Fighter aircraft... He was far from dismayed.
There was only one thing the US made,
Fit for purpose: a decent razor blade!
He soon knew better. Complacent, or what?
A blinkered, arrogant, pig-headed clot,
Göring, I reckon, deserved all he got.

---

*From a mere 200,000 before.
This was truly America at war.

Dark days for Churchill

There were tough times ahead, like it or not,
For Churchill. The PM was overtaxed,
Despite his success, and far from relaxed.
News from the Far East (Hong Kong, remember,
Fell while he was away in December)
Was uniformly bad. Then Singapore
Surrendered in February. What more,
Churchill asked himself, could the British take?

Then he was blamed for another 'mistake'.
Two German battle cruisers, *Gneisenau*
And *Scharnhorst*, 'escaped' (how, people asked, how?)
In an insolent, so-called 'Channel dash' –
Intrepid, insulting, risky and rash –
From Brest, right through to the Straits of Dover,
Back to German home waters. Game over?
Well, hardly. Royal Navy torpedoes,
Nonetheless, when the pressing need arose,
Proved ineffective. The RAF, too,
Failed to bomb the vessels. Over to you,
Mr. Churchill! What could the PM do,
But take it on the chin? Singapore fell
Two days later. Such blows, in a nutshell,
Sapped British morale. Reverses, as well,
In North Africa added to the gloom,
Contributing to a spirit of doom.

Churchill was never one for loss of sleep,
But in these dark days he had to dig deep.
He won with ease a vote of confidence
In the House of Commons. It made no sense
To rock the boat. Humiliation,
However, had shaken the nation,
As two enemy ships had sailed away
Down the Channel in the clear light of day.

The Prime Minister survived, anyway,
By four hundred and sixty-six to one.
The Independent MP, James Maxton,
Voted against. But did this clear the air?
Not altogether. A whiff of despair
Permeated the Chamber. In the Press
There were mutterings. All rather a mess,
And people knew it. To add to the stress,
Voices were raised for a 'Second Front Now'.

Utter madness, of course. How on earth, how,
Could Britain, with her back against the wall,
Invade Europe? It made no sense at all.

The North Africa campaign

Churchill was pinning his hopes for success
On North Africa. To settle for less
Would be to throw in the sponge. The outlook
Was grim and bleak, though, in anyone's book.

On the 21st of June, '41,
Auchinleck took over. All said and done,
He was a great improvement on Wavell.
A poet, contemplating his navel,
Was possibly not the ideal choice
For a desert command. Auchinleck's voice,
Strong and robust, inspired confidence.
His appointment, in short, made perfect sense.

The besieged port of Tobruk remained key.
This was the focus, inevitably,
Of Rommel's campaign that long, hot summer.
Supply had proved a bit of a bummer
(Forgive me). A lifeline second to none,
Tobruk must fall or Rommel's day was done.

The Brits still ruled the Med. In '41,
The first eight months, they enjoyed a good run,
Sinking at least fifty-two Axis ships
And damaging forty more. Such hardships
Caused the Germans considerable grief.
Rommel was starved of supplies. I'll be brief.

The relief of Tobruk

He planned a second strike against Tobruk
In November. He chose to overlook
(Over-cocky?) reports filtering through
That Auchinleck planned an offensive too.
To Rommel such rumours were nothing new.
Weakened though, there was little he could do
In the face of a British tank attack.
As his Afrika Korps was driven back,
Tobruk was relieved. So, at last, some cheer.
For Auchinleck, early in the New Year,
In a triumph completely unforeseen,
Pushed forward to where the British had been
After O'Connor's strike the year before.

But it's fair to say that the desert war
Brought few rewards. A game of 'to and fro',
Any perceived success was touch and go.
Just when you reckoned you had nailed the foe,
Up he jumped! A breakthrough? Who was to know?

Even this second victory, so-called,
Was hard won. Poor Auchinleck was appalled
At the massive loss he suffered in tanks –
Some two thirds of his force. Rommel gave thanks,
Of course (as 'the Auk' expected), for this,
But any advantage was hit and miss.
For Rommel himself was in deep crisis.

He lost one third of his tanks. His supplies,
Yet again, let him down. So it was wise,
Indeed inevitable, to withdraw,
Though hardly the best way to win a war.

What of casualties? The awful 'score'
Was two and a half thousand (maybe more)
Killed on both sides. Some would call it a draw,
Had not the British gained territory.
Not that this seemed to matter terribly.
The object was the relief of Tobruk,
Top priority in Auchinleck's book.

Desert conditions

Conditions were grim in the desert.
The heat was so oppressive that it hurt.
You could fry an egg (literally true)
On the top of a tank. A lethal brew:
Flies in their millions, flies and more flies,
In the food, in the water, in the eyes,
In the hair – even in the gut, I fear.

Cases of dysentery and diarrhoea
Ranged from 'uncomfortable' to severe.
Bully beef, the essential diet,
Was dished up boiled or fried (care to try it?)
Or cold, with dog biscuits. Fit for a cur?
Hardly, alas. And how would you prefer
Your cup of water a day? To drink it?
To shave in it? Or (don't even think it)
To clean the latrine? Then there was the sand…
A three-day-long sandstorm, you understand,
Was welcome, a blessed relief at first
As a break from manoeuvres. Then the thirst,
The boredom, the stress… The heat was the worst.
Suffice it to say, the soldiers cursed.

Auchinleck's success was temporary.
By the 21st of January
(Yes, just a few weeks later), Rommel took
The Brits by storm. His eye still on Tobruk,
He would take the port by hook or by crook.

Losses in the Mediterranean

In the Mediterranean, sadly,
The Royal Navy had suffered badly.
U-boats had sunk the aircraft carrier,
Ark Royal. There was now no barrier
To the transport of Rommel's key supplies.

He enjoyed, too, strong support from the skies.
To ensure the Afrika Korps survived,
The *Luftwaffe* had recently arrived
In impressive numbers in Sicily
And Libya. Malta, more's the pity,

Was suffering air-raid after air-raid,
To the severe detriment, I'm afraid,
Of British supply lines. So you can see,
Auchinleck's gains, achieved, apparently,
With such ease, proved a grand illusion.
The British fled in some confusion,
Abandoning most of Cyrenaica.

The fall of Tobruk was to come later.
Rommel's troops were exhausted so, for now,
He paused. He'd rattled the Auk anyhow.

Tobruk falls again to Rommel

A counteroffensive was planned for May.
It failed. To considerable dismay,
Rommel won an outstanding victory
At Gazala, some miles (under fifty)
West of Tobruk. The rest is history.

Although an attack had been expected,
Tobruk's defences had been neglected
Since the summer before. Supply by sea
Was too great a burden for the Navy.
Ritchie, commander of the Eighth Army,
Prepared to move back, having lost control
Of the battle. Rommel was on a roll.
Tobruk would be lost, or so it appeared.
Churchill in London, as Auchinleck feared,
Would have none of this. It was a disgrace.
"There is no question in any case,"
He telegraphed, "of giving up Tobruk."

So Ritchie went to take a second look.
He left a large force of men in the port,
Then fell back himself, as he felt he ought.

Was Ritchie being seriously dim?
Rommel was too strong and too quick for him.
He stormed Tobruk and in a single day
It fell to the Germans. What can I say?
35,000 prisoners were taken –
Possibly more, if I am not mistaken –
More than Rommel's entire invading force.

His boss, the Führer, was ecstatic of course.
Tobruk was the pinnacle of Rommel's fame.
A *Generaloberst* Erwin now became,
That's Field Marshal to you. Poor Ritchie was sacked.
He'd been overpromoted and that's a fact.

Impatience was not something Churchill lacked.
Why had Ritchie not opted to advance
And confront Rommel? He'd every chance.
Why had Auchinleck allowed him to stall?
This made no sense to the PM at all.

Churchill received the news of Tobruk's fall
In the White House. With his back to the wall,
This was his second Washington visit.
At first he simply could not believe it,
Even though Roosevelt, without a word,
Handed him a note. The worst had occurred.

"Defeat is one thing," Churchill later wrote,
"Disgrace is another." The dreaded note
Had dealt him "one of the heaviest blows
"I can recall during the war". God knows,
The burden that Churchill bore was immense.
Roosevelt was a model of good sense.
"What can we do to help?" he asked at once.
It was weaponry, in the first instance,
That Britain needed: guns, tanks and more tanks!

Churchill under fire at home

There was much muttering in Tory ranks.
In the Commons the knives were out, and how.
"Now for England, home and an unholy row,"
Predicted Churchill. He hadn't long to wait.
A planned vote of censure could soon seal his fate.
Rommel by now had crossed into Egypt,
His troops more bullish and better equipped.
The Germans had just eighty miles to go,
Credit that, before they would reach Cairo.

Churchill was certainly feeling the strain.
He returned to face the Commons again
On the 1st and 2nd of July. This,
He knew, was the edge of the precipice.
His critics claimed it would make better sense
To appoint a Minister of Defence,
Divorced from the role of Prime Minister.

Churchill thought this move deeply sinister,
Depriving him as it would of control
Of the whole war effort. His dual role
Should be scrapped. This was the suggestion
Of Sir John Wardlaw-Milne. No question,
Sir John was an ass. Who did he propose
For the top job? Well, who do you suppose?
The Duke of Gloucester, the third son, no less,
Of King George the Fifth. The Duke was hopeless –
Well-meaning, but weak. All rather a mess.

Churchill's supporters, I have to confess,
Were relieved. Sir John was laughed out of court,
But Sir Roger Keyes, a loyal old sport
And one of the Prime Minister's allies
(Or so he thought), sprang a nasty surprise

By agreeing to speak out against him.
Yet he ended his speech (signally dim)
By saying it would be "a disaster"
Were the PM to go! A past master
At lambasting a sitting government –
Of which the most eloquent testament
Had been his hatchet job on Chamberlain –
Sir Roger was clear: with a war to win,
Who else but Churchill? He hadn't a clue.
Was he for or against? Nobody knew.
For no one was sure who Sir Roger backed.
He'd muddied the waters and that's a fact.

But the most stringent criticism came
From Aneurin Bevan, who made his name
After the war in Attlee's government.
This was the essence of Bevan's lament:
"The Prime Minister," he said, "wins debate
"After debate" (this true, at any rate)
"And loses battle after battle." Then,
Alas, he put the boot in, asking when,
If ever, the country would see results.
"He fights debates" (this the worst of insults)
"Like a war and the war like a debate."
What should be done? Not one to hesitate,
He proposed foreign generals (French, Czech
Or Polish) for command. Well, what the heck!
They could do no worse than the ones we had
And foreigners wouldn't be half as bad.
Bevan ruined a good case, which was sad,
With this odd proposal. Completely mad!

The Commons, wary of rocking the boat,
Backed the Prime Minister in strength. The vote:
Twenty-five against (this gives a flavour
Of the new mood: all had been in favour,

Bar one, of Churchill just five months before,
Shortly before the fall of Singapore);
Four hundred and seventy-seven for –
A solid vote of confidence, therefore,
In Churchill. But some forty sat it out
(Abstainers), leaving a margin of doubt.

El Alamein

So Churchill badly needed a success,
An overwhelming victory, no less.
He looked to the North Africa campaign.
Rommel pressed forward again and again.
Auchinleck was under enormous strain.
He withdrew, but paused at El Alamein,
Where he established a defensive line.

This new position suited him fine,
With the sea to the north. On his south flank
He'd the Qattara Depression to thank
For shielding his troops from assault by tank.

This broad area of marsh and quicksand
Served as an effective protective band
Against Rommel, who now had to attack
Head-on (no subterfuge). To drive him back
Would be easier than at Gazala,
Where the British had suffered disaster
As a result of being wrong-footed
And outflanked. The Auk's choice to hot-foot it
To El Alamein had been a smart one.

Rommel was still keen not to be outdone.
Hundreds of miles long, his line of supply
Was his worst problem and hard to deny.
As he wrote home on the 3rd of July:
"Our strength is exhausted." Why, oh why,

You ask, did he choose to soldier on,
His chances of victory all but gone?
Well, he knew that British morale was low.
There were a mere sixty short miles to go
To Alexandria. And in Cairo
There were reports of panic, so much so
That preparations were being made
To evacuate. The Brits were afraid.

This gave Rommel increasing confidence.
A new offensive might seem like nonsense,
But he pressed on forward nevertheless.
There was sporadic fighting, quite a mess,
Indecisive… but the British held out.
Rommel's withdrawal was far from a rout,
But it left the Germans in little doubt
The road ahead would be ever more tough.

The PM, meanwhile, was cutting up rough.
Defensive 'action' was not enough.
For Churchill needed a breakthrough, you see.
He knew this, and he needed one quickly.

Auchinleck was performing dismally,
This was the Prime Minister's view. Unfair –
Nay, ignorant. How far was he aware
That the Auk had kept his troops together
In the worst of military weather?
His choice of El Alamein was inspired.
True, his forces were demoralised, tired
And badly in need of a well-earned break.
They'd been fighting for years, for Heaven's sake,
Often against the heaviest of odds.
Politicians, the silly old sods,
What did they know? Well, the PM (ye gods!)
Turned up in person and sacked Auchinleck –
Yes, the Auk himself, who had risked his neck

Against Rommel and had fought to attain
The huge advantage of El Alamein.

A visit from the Prime Minister

Churchill's visit was a great success. Why,
You may ask? Well, he was that kind of guy.

Dressed in his siren suit, with his cigar,
He rallied the troops. He was quite a star.
He even wore ballet pumps on his feet –
Which, for a heavy man, were small and neat –
With the large letters 'W' and 'C'
Embroidered on each! Now it seems to me
That these flashes of eccentricity
Are what endeared the Prime Minister most
To the people. Churchill would rarely boast;
He was far from rich; he never cared much
For status. His secret? The common touch.

Auchinleck's replacement as Commander,
General Sir Harold Alexander,
Was a sound choice. A gentle, but strong man
And not a particular Churchill fan,
He would hold fast to his position,
Unfazed by any politician
Once his mind was made up. His 'deputy',
Lieutenant General Montgomery,
Assumed the place vacated by Ritchie,
Taking command of the Eighth Army. Well,
This paid off. Monty would give Rommel hell.

Montgomery's caution

Yet he took his time. It's quite ironic
That Churchill had expected a tonic,
A fresh offensive, once he'd appointed
Alexander. He was disappointed.
For Monty, with the General's support,
Was a thorough planner, a cautious sort,
Who was loth to move till he was ready.
If anything, the pair were more steady
Than Auchinleck. Neither man would be pushed,
Still less allow himself to be ambushed
By a politician. Nonetheless,
Churchill's dynamic, I have to confess,
Worked wonders. He proceeded to Cairo,
Where his customary 'get up and go'
Bamboozled the wary Ambassador.

The British, he said, would never withdraw.
"There will be no withdrawal," he declared,
"No withdrawal" (no one's blushes were spared)
"No withdrawal." The Ambassador then –
I must say, I give him ten out of ten –
Decided to throw a dinner party
In Churchill's honour, the little smarty.

The Embassy's plans to evacuate
Were shelved. The British would accept their fate,
Should Rommel (too awful to contemplate)
Pitch up unannounced. It was feared he might,
But withdrawal? An earlier oversight.

Monty's character

Monty for his part was up for a fight.
Hyperactive and formidably bright,
And the most brilliant of strategists,
He suffered neither fools nor conformists.

A short man, with a beaky little nose,
Who 'fluffed' his r's (endearing, I suppose),
Abrupt or polite as the need arose,
It was Monty's eccentric little ways
That marked him out. Regimental berets,
With a wide array of badges, he wore;
His informal dress you couldn't ignore –
Floppy pullovers and old corduroys.
For Monty, you see, was one of the boys.

He had a huge ego. He was ruthless
And focused. His energy was boundless.
He was ever brimming with confidence.
His sense of self-importance was immense.
Yet he played the popularity card
For all it was worth and in this regard
He met his men face to face, working hard
To command their respect. This was to prove
Crucial. Morale began to improve,
Within days, under Monty's leadership.
His officers were urged to "get a grip".
Orders were orders. Contingency plans
For withdrawal were burnt, as Monty fans

Outnumbered the cynics by ten to one.
The battle ahead was as good as won.

Yet Montgomery did not hesitate
To watch, until the time was ripe, and wait.
Preparedness was the name of the game
And Monty's 8th Army won lasting fame
Only after achieving victory
Once they were ready. It's no mystery
How this was accomplished. Montgomery
Refused to be drawn by Rommel's attacks.
A cautious response of 'mind your backs',
That was enough. Meanwhile a thousand tanks –
Shermans, for which Alexander gave thanks –
New from America, were on their way.
Monty left nothing to chance. To this day,
We should all salute his thorough approach,
Painstaking, careful and beyond reproach.

Rommel's lines of supply

Meanwhile the *Luftwaffe's* bombing campaign
Against Malta had failed. I'd best explain.
Few German supply ships were getting through.
Should Malta fall, this would be a great *coup*
For the Nazis. But when their efforts failed,
The British had Rommel's supply lines nailed,
At least *via* the Med. He now relied
On his desert army being supplied
From Tripoli, fourteen hundred miles off,
While Monty was a mere spit and a cough,
Sixty miles off, from Alexandria.

So Montgomery had nothing to fear
With respect to supplies. The Med was clear,
Moreover, for RAF air cover.
The Brits, as Rommel was to discover,
Were well-supplied, well-armed, well-protected
And well-prepared. Not what he'd expected.

The defeat of Rommel at El Alamein

October the 23rd, '42:
Eleven hundred tanks (most of them new)
And large numbers of guns (a lethal brew)
Were moved forward into position.
There followed a war of attrition,
Lasting over two weeks. Casualties
Were heavy for both armies.* It was these
That led one commentator to report
That this was a World War One battle, fought
With World War Two weapons. When Rommel sought,
For his sins, permission to withdraw,
The Führer refused. This was all-out war.
When he did retreat, Hitler raged and swore.

He was livid. On November the 3rd,
He demanded that Rommel give his word –
Imagine anything quite so absurd –
That he would stand fast. Victory or death:
Rommel must fight to the very last breath.
This was insanity. Rommel knew it.
He had lost the fight. He'd live to rue it,
But the climax of the desert campaign
Was fought to the death at El Alamein.

---

*Over 13,000 from the allies
Were killed or wounded. The figure defies
Belief, representing some nine *per cent*
Of their army. Equally indecent
Were the large numbers of casualties
From the ranks of the two Axis countries:
10,000 killed or wounded, if you please,
In excess of ten *per cent* of their force,
As this terrible battle ran its course.

By the 6th, Rommel had nowhere to run.
His Afrika Korps was as good as done.

On the 13th, Tobruk was retaken
And Benghazi, if I'm not mistaken,
Changed hands for the fifth and final time. Yes,
The British chalked up a major success.

Egypt was secure for good. The relief
Was palpable. It is my firm belief
This saved Churchill's bacon. Church bells rang out
At home, leaving people in little doubt
That victory was theirs. Heaven forfend,
However, that anyone should pretend
It was all over. "Now this is not the end,"
Said he. "It is not even the beginning
"Of the end" (although he knew who was winning),
"But it is perhaps..." (here he paused for effect)
"The end of the beginning." This you'd expect.
For Churchill knew there was a long way to go.
The road would be rocky. Progress would be slow.

Churchill's meeting with Stalin

The PM, on his visit to Cairo
In August, was on his way to Moscow
To meet Stalin. The news that Churchill brought
Was unwelcome. The war could not be fought
In northern Europe until '43,
At the very earliest. Now to me,
This undertaking (though no guarantee)
Was rash. For Churchill could surely see
That even if allied nerve held steady,
Great Britain would still be far from ready
(Notwithstanding American support)
In one year's time. The atmosphere was fraught,

Nonetheless. The news was hard to digest.
Stalin, disappointed and unimpressed,
Was angry. He saw no reason to wait.

All the allies did was prevaricate,
Dream up excuses and procrastinate,
While Russia suffered. He had a point.
Read on. You'll see. The time was out of joint.

The promise of a second front in 1943

Yet Churchill and Stalin were both agreed
That the pressing and overwhelming need
Was to defeat Hitler and, to succeed,
They had to settle on a strategy.
Hence the PM's 'promise' of '43
For a second front: "A deadly attack
"Upon Hitler next year." No going back?
We shall see. Uncle Joe, surprisingly,
Warmed (well, as 'warm' as he could ever be)
To the allies' North Africa landings.

It was the loosest of understandings,
But Churchill for now got away with it.
He dug himself, true, a very deep pit
For the future. For hospitality,
However, and for camaraderie,
Stalin had no equal. Churchill believed –
Given the stakes, he was greatly relieved –
His visit had gone off splendidly well.
Fast forward to '45… Time would tell.

So, the delay had not been the hard sell
That Churchill had feared. He was soon to learn,
A few days later, upon his return
To Cairo, of a fresh catastrophe.

The raid on Dieppe

A raid ('Operation Jubilee')
Had been made on the northern coast of France,
At Dieppe. The allied force hoped (fat chance)
To gain a foothold on territory
Occupied by the Nazis. From the sea,
Alone, such an assault was pure folly.

Most of the Canadian infantry –
For their troops comprised the majority –
Found themselves trapped by rolls of barbed wire
And strong beach defences. Under fire,
They were sitting ducks. The casualties
Numbered over 3,000, most of these
From Canada. The losses were severe.

There were painful lessons to be learnt here.
An opposed landing, it soon became clear,
Was an awesome challenge. Even a year,
Or two years perhaps, might not be enough
To prepare. Good to know, but sobering stuff.

Monty had been scheduled to lead the raid.
It was Louis Mountbatten, I'm afraid,
In his place, who had to carry the can.
Montgomery was a fortunate man.
For all his brilliance and acumen,
He is sure to have failed – two out of ten,
At best. What of his reputation then?

Hitler's new Russian offensive

Russia was on the ropes. Spring again:
A new offensive (that constant refrain)
Was launched, as Hitler renewed his campaign.

The Nazis had suffered a lethal blow,
Driven back from the outskirts of Moscow.
These were desperate times. But endgame? No.

During Russia's winter offensive,
German commanders, on the defensive,
Advised caution. Something would have to give.
They were rattled. Strategic withdrawal,
However, did not suit Hitler at all.
He himself became Commander-in-Chief
On the Eastern Front, in the fixed belief
That the others had lost their nerve. Attack,
Urged the Führer. There was no going back.

Russia's offensive had petered out
By February. There was little doubt
The Germans again posed a deadly threat.
They appeared to be at their strongest yet,
With nearly a million new recruits,
Even equipped (this time) with better boots.
But these numbers alone masked a weakness.
Older soldiers were suffering stress,
Still, while the new boys were half-trained, unfit
And raw. Some wondered, were they up to it?

The *Luftwaffe* were weaker, moreover,
After the winter. Still no pushover,
They had been worn down by the relief flights
Ordered over successive days and nights
In aid of the troops, frozen and hungry,
In retreat from Moscow. Hitler could see
That he had one more opportunity
To crush the Russians, and one only.

He would make no fresh attempt on Moscow,
Not this time, not yet. But who was to know?

Not the Russians for sure. Stalingrad
Was Hitler's target. Against Leningrad
(Under heavy siege) he launched an attack
To entice the Red Army to hold back
From sending more men to the Caucasus.

The Caucasus

For the south was now the Führer's focus.
Here he would split his main army in two.

The first section (a choice he would rue)
Would take Stalingrad by storm. Hitler knew
This city, named for Stalin, was iconic.
It was therefore suitably ironic
That this precipitated his downfall.
For now, he gave no thought to this at all:
Failure was out of the question.

As for the 'split', the second section
Was to cross the River Don at Rostov.
Communications would be cut off
Between the mineral-rich Caucasus
And the rest of Russia. This bonus
Would be a massive economic plus.

Stalin would kick up a heck of a fuss
When he heard his oil fields in the south
Had been seized by Hitler. Down in the mouth?
I'll say. All three of Stalin's spring campaigns
Had failed: mounting losses; minimal gains.

In the Crimea the enemy took
100,000 captive. In my book,
That's a disaster. Very few survived.
Outside Leningrad 60,000 died

In a pitiless onslaught, while the trough,
The nadir, was an assault on Kharkov.

Up to 100,000 lives were lost,
Though few there were who stopped to count the cost.
240,000, we're told,
Were taken prisoner. For all the cold,
Hunger, misery, death and suffering
Of the winter, the Nazis, in the spring,
Were soon celebrating their survival –
An unexpected German revival –
While on all fronts the Red Army lost ground.
The blow to Soviet morale was profound.

In high summer (the 28th of June),
To Hitler's mind not a moment too soon,
The German advance began. That great prize,
The Caucasus, was to spring a surprise.
Russian troops seemed just to melt away…
At first. By August, to Stalin's dismay,
Hitler's southern army had reached Maikop,
Rich in oil. But there they had to stop
As they approached more treacherous country:
Nothing but mountains, Stalin said smugly!

Up, they found, the proverbial gum tree,
The Nazis encountered (their greatest fear)
Heavy snow, for this fell early that year.
Russian winters offered little cheer,
As they knew from bitter experience.

They were meeting, too, greater resistance
From the Red Army. Stalin, it was clear,
Could rest content. He had nothing to fear
In the Caucasus. Hitler went berserk
(He always did) as winter did its work.

Stalingrad

The Führer's focus was on Stalingrad,
A point of honour. He must have been mad.
Riches in abundance were to be had
In the Caucasus. But Stalingrad? No.
By the end of July, I'll have you know,
Hitler was convinced that the final blow
Had been struck. Confident of victory,
He wrote to Halder,* in near ecstasy,
"The Russian is finished!" We shall see.

For the Nazis were clearly on a roll.
Hunger and bombing were taking their toll.
The German 6th Army, under Paulus,
Had reached the Volga. If they drew a noose
Round the city, Stalingrad was finished.

The Germans' optimism diminished
Once they examined the topography –
Viz. Stalingrad's urban geography.
For the city stretched along sixteen miles
Of the Volga's west bank. Stalin, all smiles,

---

*General Franz Halder, a hard man,
Devoted Nazi and Hitler fan.
Chief of Staff, he always had a plan,
Which he would insist was carried out
To the letter. He had little doubt
That Hitler's Stalingrad strategy
Was ill-judged – crazy, actually.
In private he took it as a sign
Of madness and felt compelled to resign...
Or was he pushed? I'm only curious.
Suffice to say, Hitler was furious.

Was confident that a direct attack
Was all that could drive his own forces back.
An attempt at encirclement? Hopeless!
He was not the only one to know this.
General Hoth was aware of it too
(4th Panzer Army Commander). He knew,
Like Paulus, that to storm the great city
Would be no walkover. Tough and gritty
Were the good citizens of Stalingrad.

Paulus and Hoth were alarmed (just a tad)
At the level of civic resistance.
Stalin was the devil! His insistence
That his people should not evacuate
Was key. With the enemy at the gate,
The army would put up a better fight
For a 'live' city. He was surely right.

The *Luftwaffe* were busy, day and night,
Dropping bombs with all their hideous might.
The Führer, hell-bent on devastation,
Ordered the city's annihilation.
Few there were who thanked him for his trouble,
As Stalingrad was reduced to rubble.

Folk soldiered on. The bombing campaign
Subjected them to overwhelming pain.
It was hatred of the Nazis, perhaps,
That saved the people from total collapse.
So long as they held the Volga's west bank,
The citizens had the river to thank
For fresh reserves of men every night
(Altogether too risky by daylight).

While the good old Volga kept on flowing,
Stalingrad, they hoped, would keep on going.

In early September the first attack,
Head-on, by the Germans began. Alack,
A city in ruins! "Not one step back,"
However, Joseph Stalin commanded,
And this the emergency demanded.
Patriotism and communist zeal,
Before the siege was done, would set the seal
On Hitler's ambition. For now, though,
The assault was swift and resistance slow.
That is not to say that morale was low,
Far from it. For the mood was positive.
People would fight so their city could live.

The Germans held the initiative,
Briefly, but something would soon have to give
And Paulus knew it. There was no breakthrough.
All the brave citizens needed to do
Was hold their own. They could have done worse.
For the Germans, snipers were a curse.

Every building became a fortress,
Every street a battleground. The stress,
The despair, the feeling of wretchedness
Suffered by the Nazis knew no bounds.
Yet their sheer, dogged persistence astounds.
Sniffing out the Soviets like bloodhounds,
They moved from street to street, from door to door,
Hell-bent on destruction. This was war,
Cruel, bloody… Could they take any more,
These brave Russian citizens? Well, yes.
The Nazis were in a most dreadful mess.

Heavy German casualties

At the height of the terror, so I've read,
The toll was 20,000 German dead –
Each week. Yet on the 8th of November,
The Führer, speaking in a beer cellar
In Munich, was buoyant: "Do you know what?
"We are modest. We've got it!" What a clot.
How could anyone have believed that rot?

He got away with it, like it or not.
"No one," he said, "would ever be able
"To get us out now." He was unstable,
Quite clearly. Paulus, on the defensive,
Now dreaded a Soviet offensive.
With winter around the corner again,
He understood there was nothing to gain
From persisting in the German assault.

The General wasn't wholly at fault,
Forced as he was to stay and stick it out.
For Paulus was sadly lacking in clout,
And courage. Permission to withdraw
He sought from Hitler. Press on with the war,

Came the swift reply. Could Paulus ignore
His Führer? A few had dared to before,
But Friedrich von Paulus? He wasn't one.
Utter catastrophe, all said and done,
Was unavoidable. With thousands dead,
Or dying, even the animals fled.

Stalingrad had become one vast furnace,
On fire day and night. Too hot was this
For the dogs. They could bear it no longer,
As they plunged into the Volga. Stronger,
Amazingly, were the people. They knew
Winter was coming. All they had to do
Was sit it out. Nine tenths of the city
Was held by the Germans, more's the pity.
Time was of little or no consequence.
Wait for the weather. It simply made sense.

Soon Stalingrad would be one big deep freeze:
Minus thirty… forty… fifty degrees.
It was frightening figures such as these
That led the General to plead again
With Hitler. If he could only explain…
No matter. The Führer's response was plain:
Fight to the death! He was sending supplies!
Hermann Göring promised (surprise, surprise)
An airlift of five hundred tons a day –
Of food, in the main. To the troops' dismay,
He delivered barely one tenth of it
And much of what he did drop was unfit.
So the army, without enough to eat,
Died at their posts. They faced certain defeat.
Stalingrad was their death. Someone, in fact,
Called it "the mass grave of the *Wehrmacht*".

Fresh Soviet troops were ferried across
The Volga. The Germans were at a loss.

The Russians, too, were better supplied,
Accustomed to winter weather beside.

The enemy took Paulus by surprise
In mid-November. He (and his allies)
Were routed. A German soldier died
Every seven seconds… Suicide
It was to continue. On Christmas Eve
A fake Nazi broadcast, can you believe,
Was still heralding a German success.
The troops were in such a state of distress
They were reduced to eating horse flesh, raw:
The Nazi army, rotten to the core.

It's hard to credit that, two years before,
This was the same proud force that stormed through France.
Now, in the east, they had taken a chance
And failed. On the 8th of January –
We're edging into 1943 –
Surrender terms were offered. Thus began
The final phase. To fight to the last man

Was all the madcap Führer could accept –
And all that Paulus had come to expect.

German surrender at Stalingrad

But, by January the 31st,
The 6th Army was at its very worst.
Hordes of them had surrendered already.
General Paulus himself held steady,
Until Hitler made him a Field Marshal –
Not because he counted him a marvel,
Far from it. For nobody of that rank,
For which we have the record books to thank,
Was ever known to have surrendered.

This he was supposed to have remembered!
Paulus should now shoot himself, to avoid
The ignominy. Hitler was annoyed
(Very) when Paulus declined to do so.
Worse still, in the apparent afterglow
Of defeat, the villain proposed a toast
To the Red Army! What upset him most
(Hitler, that is) was that this symbolised
Germany's shame. The world now realised
That the Nazis were not invincible.
Hitler felt cheated. This was risible.

800,000 casualties
Were suffered by the Axis countries,
Of which most were Nazi Germany's.
These include those killed (a lurid score),
Those wounded and prisoners of war.
Many of the latter sadly died.
Only 6,000, we're told, survived
Of those captured after Stalingrad.
Out of 100,000, that's bad –

A ninety-four *per cent* death rate.
So much for the legacy of hate.

Russian casualties at Stalingrad

Over half a million lost their lives
From the Red Army, the record survives.
The same number were wounded or fell ill.
The figures are gruesome and haunt us still.
40,000 civilians, no less,
Died in Stalingrad. I have to confess,
These statistics could well be wildly out.
In fact, there's significant room for doubt,
For nobody was counting, after all.

Hitler's 'philosophy'

What, though, is calculated to appal
Is Hitler's more than relaxed attitude.
Revealed as a master of platitude,
He summed up Stalingrad thus: "What is life?" –
His *faux* philosophy cuts like a knife –
"Life is the nation." What a thing to say!
"The individual must die anyway.
"Beyond the life of the individual" –
I admit, I've nearly had my bellyful –
"Is the life of the nation." Nazism
In a nutshell. That's why nationalism
Is so dangerous, characterised by schism,
Intolerance and, so often, racism.

Smug as you like, immune from criticism,
Lying through his teeth and, quite frankly, barmy,
The Führer announced that the 6th Army
Had succumbed, by the merest of chances,
To "unfavourable circumstances".

The siege of Leningrad

News of the survival of Stalingrad
Put heart into the folk of Leningrad,
Although it was to be a further year
Before the lifting of the siege, I fear.
Dreadful their pain. Prepare to shed a tear.

By mid-November, 1941,
It appeared that Leningrad's day was done.
The Germans, however, failed to break in.
Hitler had predicted an easy win.
Besides, he never planned to occupy
The city, just to let the people die.
It's true. Once they had succumbed to disease
And starvation and were on their knees,
Leningrad would be bombed, then demolished –
I dare say you'll be shocked and astonished –
Prior to being devolved to the Finns.

The Russians dig in

Well, so much for the simplest of wins.
Stalin's second city proved a tough nut.
A German walkover? Anything but.

Some 500,000 men and women
Were mobilised and ordered to 'dig in'.
Anti-tank defences were constructed
And miles of earthworks. These interrupted –
Nay, foiled – the Nazi advance. Leningrad
Was encircled. With all the strength they had,
However, the citizens resisted.
The more the wretched Germans persisted,
The more tenacious the people became.
Leningrad was deserving of its name,

'Hero City'. Marshal Zhukov was sent
To co-ordinate defences, hell-bent
On restoring morale and discipline.

Leningrad had to take it on the chin
And stick it out. The Marshal was ruthless.
Met with defeatism and drunkenness
In Red Army ranks (this he told Stalin),
He gave no quarter. With a war to win,
Soldiers who surrendered would be shot,
Their families to boot, like it or not.

Stalin approved. Sentimentality
He loathed. He ordered, specifically,
That where Germans used women and old men
As human shields (and even young children),
They should be sacrificed. He didn't care.
Nobody challenged him. They didn't dare.

Everyone was encouraged to fight.
Hard was their lot and desperate their plight.
Heavy bombing destroyed six months' supply
Of food for the city. Folk wondered why
So few of them had been sent to the east
Before the siege began, for this, at least,
Would have eased the pressure on food supplies.
These were running low, to no one's surprise.

For there had been no evacuation,
On any scale, of the population,
Which numbered two and a half million,
Including 400,000 children:
In Leningrad's hour of greatest need,
A colossal number of mouths to feed.
With 500,000 soldiers too,
What could the authorities hope to do?

Cold and starvation

Nothing, was the answer to that. Who knew
Where it would all end? People were dying
In the streets. No one gave up for trying,
But folk were starving. Nothing went to waste.
They were even eating wallpaper paste,
Spread on their tiny ration of bread –
No flour, of course, just sawdust instead.
As desperation mounted, a cat
Would be killed for food, a dog or a rat.
I kid you not, it was as bad as that.

Then the cold. At minus forty degrees,
If they didn't die of hunger, they'd freeze.
Folk would keep warm by any means they could,
Chopping up furniture for firewood,
Or reduced to burning books. A splinter
Was better than nothing that first winter.

When spring arrived (the spring of '42),
There was little the citizens could do,
But bury their dead – for the frozen ground
Had concealed the corpses. Bodies were found
In their thousands, for 4,000 a day
Died that winter, I'm horrified to say.
They were buried with respect and sorrow.

Optimism in the 'Hero City'

Yet Leningrad now looked to the morrow.
A huge vegetable planting programme
Was put in hand. They didn't care a damn
For Hitler's threats. Leningrad would survive.
By fits and starts it began to revive.

A symphony was even broadcast, live,
By Shostakovich. How about that!
One in the eye, or I'll eat my hat,
For the Nazis – the 'Leningrad', so-called,
His 7th Symphony. Hitler was appalled.
For it symbolised the fact his war had stalled.

Now there was the mass evacuation –
Against a similar situation
The following winter – of families
Across Lake Ladoga, designed to ease
The pressure next year during the big freeze
If, as the military expected,
The siege continued. Far from dejected,
The citizens would be better prepared
When the Nazis struck again – if they dared.
The Russians even laid a pipeline
Under Lake Ladoga. They would be fine
This time for fuel, for however long
The gruelling siege lasted. Don't get me wrong,

There was still great hardship, sickness and death,
But folk would fight to their very last breath.

Leningrad, the city, refused to die.
The terror lasted, no word of a lie,
For eight hundred and eighty awful days.

It entered its long-drawn-out final phase
On January the 12th, '43 –
With still a year to go, regrettably,
Before the siege was lifted. Finally,
Led again by Zhukov, the Red Army
Launched 'Operation Spark' and broke the ring.
A so-called 'land-bridge', a wonderful thing,
Was opened up, twelve kilometres wide,
After heavy fighting. Better supplied,
As a railway line was carefully laid
To link with the 'mainland', the people prayed
That the siege at last was nearing its end.

Sadly not. The railway was a godsend,
But was nonetheless within easy range
Of German artillery. It sounds strange,
But even though Zhukov had 'closed the gap',
As it were (a brave and resourceful chap),
There was no radical change to the map
Until late January, '44.

The siege is lifted

Finally pushing at an open door,
The Russians launched a mighty attack
On Army Group North. No holding them back,
The Red Army won the day. Just as well,
After two terrible years. The last shell
Dropped by Hitler in that corner of hell

Fell on Leningrad on the 23rd.
The feeling of relief, you have my word,
Was palpable. A victory salute
Was fired, the only fitting tribute
To all the courageous folk who fell,
And the brave soldiers who fought so well.

During the siege, in the city alone,
Over one million died. It's not known
How many suffered from starvation
Or froze to death. Such speculation
Is redundant. Russia's tragedy
Speaks for itself. Further commentary
Is intrusive and unnecessary –
Impertinent, indeed, from the likes of me.

Burma

Back to the Far East. Before going further
We should first consider the fate of Burma.
The country (British) provided a shield
To protect India. Should Burma yield,
Britain's 'Jewel in the Crown' would suffer –
Nay, fall to the Japanese. A buffer,
Therefore, was Burma. Then there was her oil.
The British were thrown into turmoil
At the prospect of losing this resource.
The Japanese needed oil, of course.
This had been at the heart of their campaign
From the start. The British were under strain.
Burma was defenceless and unprepared
For war. If Japan should dare… Well, she dared.

Burma had been milked of reinforcements,
And officers, for Europe. No offence,
But "only the dull had been left behind,"
In the words of one officer. Unkind?

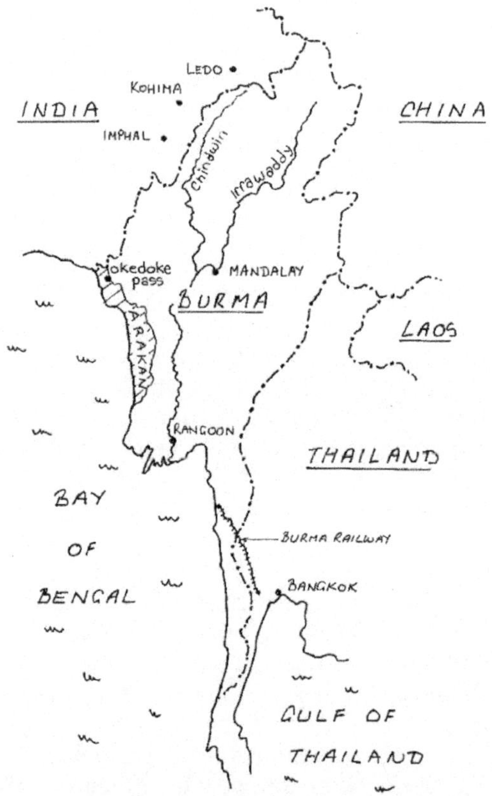

Well, perhaps, but sadly only too true.
There proved little that the British could do,
When, in December, 1941,
The Japanese invaded. On the run,
The British withdrew in confusion.
They would draw one simple conclusion:
Under serious and sustained assault,
Flight was the only option. Whose fault?
Who knows? It was almost beyond belief
That Burma should fall. There was no relief,

However, no air cover. Bombed at will,
The Brits would have collapsed had they stood still.

Their retreat was rapid. All too soon
The enemy had swept through Rangoon
And within five months, by early May,
Had advanced well beyond Mandalay,
Across the Irrawaddy and Chindwin,
Key rivers both. It was the swiftest win.
They reached India's frontier with ease.
Here they paused. First blood to the Japanese.

Jungle warfare

The retreat of thousands of refugees –
Indian, Eurasian and Chinese –
Resulted in hordes of casualties.
Having to hack through jungle, if you please,
Many succumbed to hunger and disease:
Malaria, dengue fever… Plagues like these
Were deadly. There were foul atrocities,
Committed at will by the Japanese.

I'll spare you the details. The enemy
Despised any of the British, you see,
Who surrendered, for it was cowardice.
Their prisoners were made to pay for this.
As for the jungle, the foe relished it.
The Brits didn't like it one little bit.
Damp, dark and dangerous, rife with disease,
The jungle spelt terror. The Japanese
Welcomed it. They foraged for wholesome food,
Bamboo shoots and the like. It may sound crude,
But lizards (if you are in a hurry),
With their heads chopped off, make a great curry.
For the poor British Tommy, though, corned beef,
And more corned beef, was his only relief.

It ran to liquid in the scorching heat.
Sadly, this was all that he had to eat.

The British forces, in short, were dead beat.
That they reached India was quite a feat.
At times they were only one day ahead
Of the Japanese. Their wounded and dead
They were often obliged to leave behind.
The former would suffer… well, never mind –
Suffice it to say, they were far from kind,
Their Japanese tormentors. As they fled,
Though they had no time to bury their dead,
The Brits denied their enemy the prize
Of Burma's oil. Before their very eyes,
The Japanese witnessed one inferno
After another, oil wells, row on row,
Set ablaze in a scorched-earth policy –
The only option quite honestly.

So despite the bloodshed, sweat and toil,
The Japanese were denied their oil.

Wavell's counteroffensive fails

Archibald Wavell, Commander-in-Chief
In India, was firm in his belief
That British forces should make a comeback.
Consequently he went on the attack,
Late in '42. Wavell's offensive,
Daredevil, but focused and intensive,
Was along the Mayu Peninsula,
To forestall an attack on India.

But this uncongenial coastal strip,
Where Wavell proposed his troops should let rip,
Consisted of mangrove swamps, paddy fields
And little creeks – the worst of battlefields.
Before very long he was in retreat,
Another ignominious defeat.

British and Indian casualties
Were more than twice those of the Japanese
In this failed offensive. Deaths (from disease
And hostile action), the wounded and sick
Numbered 3,000 – that's a grim statistic.

Orde Wingate

Japan's conquest of Burma seemed complete.
The Brits, in time, began to find their feet.
Progress was slow. It was a close-run thing.
But in '43, the war in full swing,
The tables began to turn. Britain's fate,
According to Brigadier Orde Wingate,
Was far from sealed. Indeed, to contemplate

Such an outcome filled him with disbelief.
Wingate eventually came to grief
In a fatal air accident. For now,
However, he would prove his worth, and how.

No 'ordinary' man (pardon the pun),
Orde had many a fan. Churchill was one.
For Wingate was a one-off eccentric.

The effect on his men was electric.
For he drove them hard, though no worse, it seems,
Than he drove himself. Defeat? In your dreams.
Scruffy and bearded, his sola topi
Was too big for his head. He strained his tea
Through a sock. He walked around in the nude.
His unconventional attitude
Failed to enamour him, you can be sure,
To his superiors. They could ignore
His personal foibles. His strategy,
However, the irregularity
Of his approach and his insolent air,
His louche demeanour of devil-may-care,
Drove senior officers to despair.

Yet Churchill liked him. Burma needed him.
When the PM spoke, Wavell heeded him
And Burma's high command agreed with him.

Wingate came up with a novel idea:
To launch assaults on the Japanese rear,
Raiding parties, in effect, to surprise
The enemy and attack their supplies
And communications – a huge risk,
But Wingate was authoritative, brisk
And confident. Wavell supported him.
The canny Brigadier was far from dim.

He knew the dangers. Intensively trained
And careless of however hard it rained
(Good show), Wingate's troops, Gurkha and British,
Were all prepared to fight to the finish.
The Chandits, so-called (after the river),
Were bold and committed to deliver.

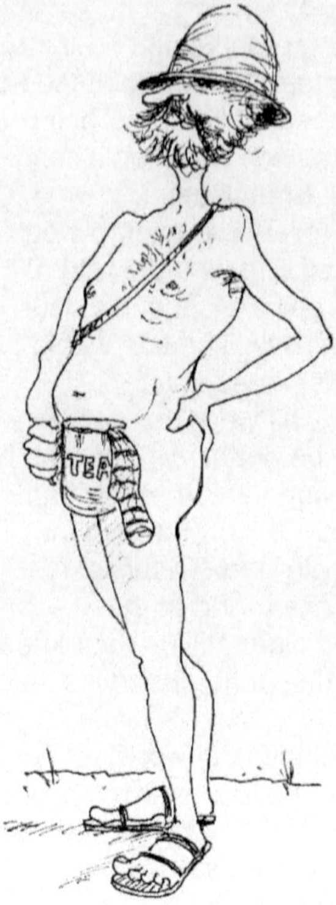

Roll on to February, '43.
Deep into enemy territory
They went. The jungle gave them cause to curse.
The heavy going could not have been worse.

The heat was extreme, drinking water short,
Malaria rampant. If they were caught
And taken prisoner, their cruel lot
Would be torture. They would rather be shot,
But the Japanese troops, like it or not,
Preferred to take their pitiful victims
And break their spirits – one of their little whims.

After four gruelling months, in mid-June,
Wingate's Chindits, not a moment too soon,
Returned from deepest Burma. Their mission,
Sad to say, had failed. The men's condition
Was lamentable. Emaciated
And exhausted, few had contemplated
Such agony. But those who did return
Insisted that there were lessons to learn
From their experience. The tide would turn.
Jungle operations, air supply,
Guerrilla tactics… all were reasons why
Next time would be better. Morale was high,
Despite men having seen their colleagues die
In their hundreds. Of 3,000 who went,
Only two thirds returned. To this extent
The expedition failed. And of these,
Over six hundred were still on their knees
After many months, unfit for service.

What had the Chindits done to deserve this,
Some wondered, those poor wretches left behind,
In particular? Orde, I think you'll find,
Had the answer. Future leaders would bless
Their efforts. The eventual success
Of the Burma campaign, most are agreed,
Was down to Wingate. In her hour of need,
He did Burma proud. He fought tooth and nail,
And failed. But the Brigadier blazed a trail.

Vera Lynn

One 'artiste' prepared to travel as far
As Burma was that perennial star,
The 'Forces' Sweetheart', songbird Vera Lynn.
With the voice of an angel, pencil-thin
And graceful to boot, with a war to win,
She understood that servicemen abroad
Were not only at risk of being bored,
But in danger, too, of feeling ignored.

So Vera did her bit. *We'll Meet Again*,
Her most famous hit, a rousing refrain,
Was recorded in 1939.

It was hard graft, far from roses and wine,
Touring to these remote outposts of war.
To Egypt, India, Burma and more
Vera travelled. Boosting morale, for sure,

Was her mission. Back home (never a chore)
The popular star was happy to tour
To hospitals. Talking to new mothers,
She sent messages to husbands, brothers
And loved ones on her radio programme,
Sincerely Yours. From Cairo to Assam,
They tuned in to listen to Vera Lynn.

ENSA

To ENSA. I'm not sure where to begin.
Battling with gusto through thick and thin,
They toured the world. The money was tight,
The talent 'limited': 'Every Night
Something Awful'! This was a painful slight.
The Entertainments National Service
Association did not deserve this –
Well, not altogether. Stars of top rank
(Vera Lynn herself) had ENSA to thank
For sponsoring their tours. George Formby
Was another, with his ukulele.
Established stars such as Noël Coward
Joined Terry-Thomas and Frankie Howerd
From the ranks of the unknown (to date) –
A famous list of names, at any rate,
Whether current or for another day:
From Gracie Fields to Stanley Holloway;
From Peter Sellers to Kenneth Connor;
And from Jessie Matthews (who, good on her,
Loved to tour) to more lowly riff-raff.

For ENSA suffered (and you have to laff,
As wee Georgie might say) from a small pool
Of talent. Most of the acts, as a rule,
Were cobbled together and of low grade,
And a number quite smutty, I'm afraid.
Even the stars were pretty poorly paid,

But few really cared. Didn't folk know
There was a war on? So, keep on the go,
That was the motto, and go with the flow.

The number of ENSA concerts given
Exceeded two and a half million
By the time the war was over. Not bad.
All in all, I'd say, a good time was had.

The BBC

The BBC for many set the tone.
In wartime 'Auntie' came into her own.
A vital source of information,
The 'voice of Britain' kept the nation
Abreast of the news. When the war began,
The BBC boasted many a fan
Abroad: the Beeb was equipped to broadcast
In eight languages. You'll be aghast
(With wonder), but by 1943
Its foreign output had increased massively.
The fiercely independent BBC
Could broadcast in forty-seven tongues, no less,
A clear sign of its spectacular success.

There was government censorship, of course
(For security), all controlled at source.
The average listener was no fool
And trusted the BBC, as a rule,
To tell it as it was. In their own right,
The newsreaders became 'names' overnight:
Frank Phillips, Bruce Belfrage, Alvar Liddell.
Would Britain win through? Only time would tell.
The worst of tidings and the best alike
Were read by these broadcasters, on the mic,
Without emotion, as calm as you like.

During the summer of 1940,
Popular novelist, J. B. Priestley,
Broadcast on *Postscripts*, a Sunday night slot,
Following the news. Folk liked him a lot.
Man of the people, he was down to earth,
Blunt and plain-spoken. Their six-pennyworth
Listeners enjoyed. Too political?
Well, yes... Conservatives were critical
When Priestley attacked private property
As old-fashioned. He spoke improperly,
According to the Tories. I despair.
The great Priestley was taken off the air.

Then there were the classics: *Vanity Fair*,
Cranford, even (although it overran)
Hamlet. Fine if you were a Shakespeare fan,
But a tad too highbrow? As dry as dust
(Well, according to some) was the *Brains Trust.*
Yet it proved a most popular broadcast.
Its weekly airings were destined to last.

The panel at first was made up of three:
Renowned scientist, Julian Huxley;
C. E. M. Joad, the famed philosopher;
And a retired naval officer,
Commander A. B. Campbell. This trio
Told listeners all they needed to know,
On any subject! People submitted
Questions. A whole range was permitted.
The topics were speculative, moral,
Scientific and philosophical.

Surely this was too intellectual
For the great British populace? Not so.
Families sat glued to the radio.
The following day, at work, very few
Admitted they'd had better things to do

Than listen in. By 1943,
The *Brains Trust* audience, regularly,
Topped ten million. There was a clear thirst
For knowledge. The public were fit to burst.

Radio comedy

There was lighter fare on offer. *ITMA*
(*It's That Man Again*) made an instant star
Of comic, Tommy Handley. For his team,
And the BBC, *ITMA* was a dream:
Brilliant scripts, spot-on performances,
Perfect in the trying circumstances
Of Britain at war. Well-written? Not half.
Timed to a T, there had to be a laugh
Every eight to eleven seconds.

Strong radio comedy, one reckons,
Must be easy. Not so! The very pace –
A quick sprint rather than a steeplechase –
The characters, the catchphrases, the puns,
These require fine artistry. The ones,
However, who made the show were the cast.
Character comedy came thick and fast:
Funf, the blundering German spy; Vera,
Admittedly from another era,
A tad sexist and certainly no frump,
With her suggestive, "Oh, Mr. Handpump!";
The Diver, with his memorable phrase,
"I'm going down now, sir!"; and, beyond praise,
Mrs. Mopp, whose "Can I do you now, sir?"
Raised the roof. There was no forgetting her!

Some sixteen million a week, no less,
Tuned in to *ITMA*. The programme's success
Captured the public imagination.
In Bath, in a rescue operation

Following an air raid, a warden heard
The small voice of a boy (you have my word
This is true, although it may sound absurd),
Piping up plaintively from the debris:
"Can you do me now, sir?" Great comedy,
And a terrific tonic, was *ITMA*.

Cinema

The popularity of cinema
Was also striking. In spite of the Blitz,
Most remained open. Some took direct hits,
But all provided the welcome respite
That people craved. Some stayed open all night:
You could watch several films in a row.
Picture houses were the places to go!
Up to thirty million seats, we're told,
In a single week in Britain were sold.

The magic of film gripped the nation.
Three quarters of the population
Went to 'the pictures'. You want to know why
Attendances grew and remained sky-high?
It's simple. Films helped the people unwind,
Relief and escape from the daily grind.

Hollywood movies were sure-fire hits,
Like *Gone With the Wind,* making huge profits.
Yet Britain's domestic film industry
Shared in the growing popularity
Of cinema. Laurence Olivier
Starred in (and directed, as was his way)
Henry the Fifth, a triumph of its day,
A patriotic epic about war,
With, as it happens, a terrific score
By William Walton. Hard to ignore.

Then there was Noël Coward's *tour de force*,
In Which We Serve, a masterclass, of course,
In writing, acting and direction.

The film was scripted to perfection,
With the 'Master' himself cast in the lead –
Against type, to be sure, a risk indeed –
As a naval officer. David Lean
Made his mark as a director, young, keen
And talented. Other famous names, too,
Were fortunate in making their debut,
Nine-year-old Daniel Massey for one
(Chancing to be Noël Coward's godson),
And Richard Attenborough, aged nineteen.
Other future stars of the silver screen
Were young John Mills and baby Juliet
(His daughter) and Bernard Miles – a full set,
One might say, of British acting talent.

Charlie Chaplin was in his element
In *The Great Dictator*, a Hitler spoof,
Writer, director and star – living proof
Of his comic brilliance: great satire,
Lampooning at will the strutting pariah.
The movie was produced in the US –
British to its fingertips nonetheless.

Literature and theatre

Wartime literature, I must confess,
Was less thrilling. Novels about the war,
Like *Put Out More Flags*, by Evelyn Waugh,
Were few and far between. Poetry, too,
Was thin. Who were the poets? There were few.
Dylan Thomas, Edith Sitwell were two,
But where were the others? Nobody knew.
There were T. S. Eliot's *Four Quartets*...
As for the rest, no one was placing bets.

However, after 1938
Book sales rose at an unexpected rate,
Some fifty *per cent* – amazing, but true.
Sales of the best-loved classics grew and grew:
Jane Austen, as popular as ever,
Dickens, Trollope... It was now or never!
Get cracking! All those books you had meant to read,
But never had the time. Opportune indeed.

Theatre was ailing. *This Happy Breed*
And *Blithe Spirit* (two of Noël Coward's best)
Were wartime products. But where were the rest?
J. B. Priestley's one play, more's the pity,
Was a let-down, *They Came to a City*,
A drama that disappeared without trace.
Apart from these (an abiding disgrace)

There were few additions to the list.
James Bridie, a popular dramatist,
Wrote a number that would never be missed.

Otherwise, productions of Shakespeare
Toured the provinces from year to year –
Nothing wrong with that, but little, I fear,
Of any great originality.
Theatre in London was all at sea,
Owing to the Blitz. In May, '41,
The Old Vic, losing its place in the sun,
Was badly bombed. Theatre continued
Out of town, but (with no wish to be rude)
Much of the product was clumsy and crude.
The public had done nothing to deserve this,
But with actors away on active service
The standard was bound to be variable –
Competent, if not downright terrible.

However, towards the end of the war,
London's New Theatre, in '44,
Presented Olivier's *Richard the Third*,
A legendary staging, you have my word.

Back to the Far East

1942 was a dreadful year.
The Japanese were dominant, I fear,
In the Pacific region by May.
As we have already seen, they held sway
Over Malaya, the Dutch East Indies
And the Philippines. Conquests such as these,
In hindsight, however, would represent
For the Japanese the fullest extent
Of their advance. It was to take three years.
A dark catalogue of bloodshed and tears,

But from 1942, strange to say,
For Japan it was downhill all the way.

US air raids on Tokyo

The first blow came in April, with a raid
By the US on Tokyo. Dismayed?
You bet. For the people had been assured
They were safe. The authorities were floored.
It had been claimed by the military,
In the clearest of terms, repeatedly,
That Japan's skies were impenetrable.

The effect, to be sure, was terrible –
Not in terms of any great damage done,
But the shock suffered by everyone
Was huge. Japan's vulnerability
Was patent. The people, more's the pity,
Were open to attack. Five months after
The unexpected joy of Pearl Harbour,
The war was not so very far away.

The raid gave rise not only to dismay,
But to anger. Bombs were for other folk,
Not their own citizens. This was no joke.

Following the so-called Doolittle raid,
Eight American pilots, I'm afraid,
Were taken prisoner and later tried
In a military court, but denied
Legal representation or justice.
Three were executed (damnable, this).
The fate of the others, be in no doubt,
Was terrible. Their demeanour, throughout,
Was noble. Blindfold, they were paraded
Through the streets, dishonoured and degraded.

Port Moresby

A more bitter shock for the Japanese
Lay in store. They attempted, if you please,
To threaten Australia. Port Moresby,
Down on the south-east coast of New Guinea,
Was their target. Out in the Coral Sea,
To the east, the American navy
And the Japanese engaged. Victory,
By a whisker, was won by the US,
Though, to be blunt, it was a mixed success.

They lost one carrier, the *Lexington*,
While the Japanese lost a lesser one,
The *Shohu.* Another, the *Shokaku*,
Was badly damaged. In my humble view,
The result was an honourable draw.

The Japanese, though, were forced to withdraw
From Port Moresby. This was no easy war.
For the future, Australia's north coast –
Which. after all, was what mattered the most –
Was safe. The Japanese were far from toast,
But they suffered a serious setback.

For Admiral Yamamoto, attack
Was the only option. The sinking
Of the *Shohu*, to his way of thinking,
Confirmed his view that Japan should strike first.
Hold back and the Admiral feared the worst.
The pesky Americans (this he knew)
Could produce more carriers, spanking new,
Than the Japanese could ever afford.
He and High Command were of one accord:
The great American Pacific Fleet
Was a mere hairsbreadth away from defeat.
Attack now, its ruin would be complete;

But allow time for the US navy
To build more carriers... Simply crazy.
The Doolittle raid, too, like it or not,
Had focused minds. Strike while the iron is hot!
That was the tack Yamamoto preferred.
To back off now? Little short of absurd.

The Battle of Midway

To seize the US Island of Midway,
This was the Admiral's plan. Midway lay
North-west of Pearl Harbour, less than half way
To Japan. Yamamoto put to sea
With the largest force in the history
(At least, so I've read) of the Pacific:
Four large carriers (to be specific),
And four smaller ones; twenty-two cruisers
(The Japanese would not be the losers);
Some sixty-five destroyers (quite a list);
Eleven battleships (you get the gist);
And twenty-one submarines. Not half bad!

To face this armada, the US had
Three carriers (these were real bruisers),
Seventeen destroyers and eight cruisers.

But the US had the intelligence.
They'd cracked the Japanese codes. It made sense,
Therefore, to engage the enemy fleet.
With knowledge of the latter's plans complete,
The Yanks would spring them a nasty surprise.
The Japanese could not believe their eyes
As bombs in their thousands rained from the skies.
Within minutes, Japanese dominance
Of the Pacific was over. Mischance,
Miscalculation, call it what you will,
The savage onslaught proved a bitter pill

For Yamamoto. US bombers sank
His four carriers of the finest rank.

It proved to be enough. Forget the rest.
The Japanese navy had failed the test.
It never recovered. The US lost
One carrier, the *Yorktown*, this a cost
Borne with fortitude, given the result.
For the enemy the final insult
Was the loss of over three hundred planes.

The powers-that-be took the greatest pains
To cover up the extent of the rout:
A famous victory, without a doubt,
Japan was told. To have taken a hit…
Unthinkable! Even the Cabinet
(The majority) were kept in the dark.
For those in the know the message was stark:
Midway would prove a fatal turning point.
Japan was doomed. The time was out of joint.

The Burma Railway

Work on the infamous Burma Railway,
By June '42, was well under way.

The Japanese, defeated at Midway
And forced to a draw in the Coral Sea,
Faced an unexpected difficulty
With regard to their prospective campaign
To invade Assam – a coveted gain,
A first foothold in India. Their plan
Was now frustrated before it began.
After Midway, sea-lanes between Japan
And Burma were no longer secure.
Supply lines were weak. Trouble in store.

An overland route was needed to link
Thailand with Burma. So, what do you think?

Two hundred and fifty-eight miles of track
Were laid in sixteen months. The price, alack,
Was hideous. The prisoners of war
Who were 'employed' (60,000 or more),
Along with 200,000 conscripts
(Native Asians), were punished with whips,
Rifle butts, vicious blows to the head
And terrible torture. Better off dead,
Thought some of the wretched victims. Indeed,
They succumbed, as their colleagues watched them bleed.

Malnutrition was a deadly curse.
Malaria, dysentery or worse
Were all hazards. Contaminated food
(With rats' droppings) was one vile ruse: crude,

Abhorrent and cruel. Twenty *per cent*
(At least) died from disease, malnourishment,
Overwork and violent punishment.
Those who survived, the ones who remained sane,
Were scarred for life. Most broke under the strain
And few would ever be the same again.

French North Africa

After El Alamein, as we have seen,
Rommel was driven back. Picture the scene.
Tobruk was retaken, then Benghazi,
Rid once and for all of its last Nazi.
The great port of Tripoli, finally,
On the 23rd of January – **1943**
We are now up to 1943 –
Fell to the 8th Army. Thus the allies,
To their eternal credit, took the prize
That had slipped through the hands of O'Connor
Two years earlier. A point of honour.

The fame of the Desert Army had spread
Throughout the world, the Prime Minister said.

In June '42, Roosevelt agreed
That no landing could possibly succeed
On the French north coast before '43.
Even this, the President would soon see,
Was optimistic. Churchill was relieved.
An earlier strike would be ill-conceived.
Stalin was particularly aggrieved
That the 'Second Front' was so long delayed.

Uncle Joe, in fact, felt badly betrayed,
But his two allies were far from dismayed.
The US forces were hardly ready
For a major campaign. Slow and steady,

These were the watchwords. On the other hand,
The President was quick to understand
That American troops must be deployed…
Somewhere… His critics were highly annoyed
That Roosevelt was focused, stubbornly,
On Europe. What of the South China Sea?
And the Pacific? He stuck to his guns:
The Nazis were the target and the ones
In his sights. The only alternative
To northern France (and something had to give)
Was French North Africa. Planning began.

Should the Germans (so the argument ran)
Defeat Russia and thus take control
Of Europe, a secure allied bolthole
In North Africa would prove critical.

This reasoning (largely political
As well as strategic, given the fact
That Roosevelt was floundering and lacked
Any other sound option) was backed
By another consideration.
The move would be a preparation
For the landings later in northern France.
The allies could also see at a glance
That a full-scale North Africa campaign
Would put the Germans under extra strain
And so divert their much-needed forces
From Russia and France. Their resources,
Stretched and depleted, would be spread too thin.
This was a war that they could never win.

'Operation Torch'

'Operation Torch' began badly.
The simultaneous landings, sadly,

Were a shambles. Patton's US task force
Met initial resistance, of course,
From the colonial French. The allies
Were beaten back, to no one's great surprise,
Before the French command finally broke
With Pétain and his government (the bloke,
Remember, who led the Vichy *régime*
In France) and joined up with the allied team.
Poor Patton had been driven half frantic
When he disembarked from the Atlantic
On the French Moroccan coast at Safi
And Casablanca. I'll tell you for free,
The Americans were totally naive
With respect to what they could hope to achieve,
Faced as they were by French opposition.

The British were in the same position,
Alas, when their troops pitched up in Algiers
And Oran. Their sudden landing, it appears,
Also encountered dogged resistance
From the French colonists. In this instance –
As at Casablanca, I'm pleased to say –
Their opponents simply melted away.
The French were prepared to call it a day.

All this caused a most frustrating delay,
Resulting in allied casualties
Well in excess of two thousand. Of these,
More than a thousand were fatalities.
French losses were half as many again.

All to no purpose. The stress and the strain
Of the early stages of this campaign
Took their toll. Nevertheless, in the main,
The allies made progress, albeit slow.
The US, advancing through Morocco,

Joined up with the British and headed east.
This was the agreed strategy, at least.
Although Eisenhower did his level best
(Allied Supreme Commander), he confessed
That the whole business would take longer
Than he had hoped. The Germans were stronger,
Far stronger, than he'd anticipated.

Yet again the Führer demonstrated
(It sticks in my throat to say it) foresight,
Cunning and iron will. Give up the fight
In North Africa? Never! Once he heard
Of the allied landings, you have my word
He gave strict orders (however absurd)
To defend Tunisia to the hilt.
He poured in extra resources, full-tilt,
And commanded Erwin Rommel (aghast)
To defend North Africa to the last.

In 1942, on Christmas Eve,
General Eisenhower, can you believe,
Suspended the offensive. We assume
It was his intention to resume
Once conditions improved. Heavy rain
Had put his forces under massive strain,
With little hope of immediate gain.

Casablanca

The campaign did not get going again,
In earnest, until late January.
The British 8th Army took Tripoli
(As we've seen) on the 23rd. Meanwhile,
Roosevelt had travelled (hardly in style:
A bumpy passage) to meet with Churchill
In Casablanca. Exuding goodwill,

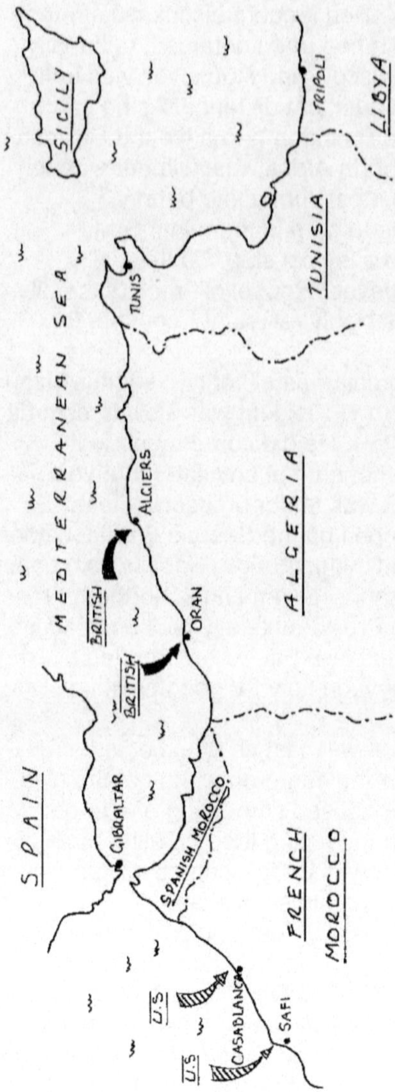
SICILY
TRIPOLI
LIBYA
TUNISIA
TUNIS
MEDITERRANEAN SEA
ALGIERS
ALGERIA
BRITISH
BRITISH
ORAN
SPAIN
GIBRALTAR
SPANISH MOROCCO
FRENCH MOROCCO
U.S
U.S
CASABLANCA
SAFI

The allied leaders discussed strategy.
Stalin had been detained, unhappily,
In Moscow and Roosevelt was unfit
To travel that distance. As he saw it
(The President), to drive the Germans out
Of North Africa was, without a doubt,
The most immediate priority.
Then to pursue them into Sicily
Was a logical step. To Italy,
However? Roosevelt, more's the pity,
Was highly reluctant to go that far.

Churchill was all for it. It sounds bizarre,
But the President was slow to commit
To Italy. He did come round to it
In time, but not until later that year.
FDR was under pressure, I fear,
To open up the Second Front too soon.
The timing, though, was far from opportune
For an allied landing in northern France.
The President finally took a chance,
Off his own bat, when prodded by Churchill,
To invade Italy for good or ill.

Roosevelt cast an unexpected chill
Over the conference. Out of the blue,
FDR caused something of a to-do
By announcing that the allies' sole aim –
What was he thinking of, in Heaven's name,
Declaring this unilaterally? –
Was total defeat of the enemy.

He should have asked Churchill, it seems to me,
And Joseph Stalin. It was not to be.
The words he used (and this they'd remember)
Were "unconditional surrender".

Churchill fell silent. Even Italy,
He wondered? Roosevelt, quite possibly,
Was seeking to offer a guarantee
That neither the British nor the US
Would ever put Stalin under duress
By concluding any compromise peace
Behind his back. Would wonders never cease?
The PM had no choice but to concur –
Or to be steamrollered, if you prefer.

It was academic, in the event.
For Japan and Germany were hell-bent
On fighting to the last man, come what may.
Compromise never saw the light of day.

Renewal of the North Africa campaign

Rommel, now driven out of Libya,
Was set on defending Tunisia.
He failed, but the allies' progress was slow.
Despite making headway through Morocco
And Algeria, German resistance
Was strong. Rommel, at Hitler's insistence,
Held firm. For once North Africa was lost,
The Führer would be forced to count the cost:
The loss of Sicily a certainty,
With Italy a possibility,
Thus affording the allies a strong base
In southern Europe. Hitler would lose face
And the war to boot. Well, that was his fear.
1943: a critical year.

The defeat of Rommel

Allied forces advancing from the west
Had a tough old time. Rommel, at his best,

Was unstoppable. He was quite unfazed,
Leaving the allies confused and amazed.

Yet soon the game was up. Montgomery,
From the east, proved a stronger enemy.
With superior forces, he routed
Rommel at Médenine. Few now doubted
That this defeat, for Hitler, spelt the end
Of his African adventure. The trend
Was clear. Rommel, having been driven back,
On the 6th of March halted his attack.

Within three days he had left the campaign
And returned home. Jaundiced, sick and in pain,
He warned Hitler it was "plain suicide"
To stay in Africa. Well, you decide:
What do you reckon the Führer did next?
He ranted and raved; he was highly vexed.
Rommel had lost his nerve. What did he know?
The Führer was happy to see him go –
A defeatist and a loser, a disgrace.

No evacuation was to take place.
The Axis forces were made to fight on
Long after hope of victory had gone.
By May it was clear the end was in sight,
Holed up in the capital. Yes, that's right –
In Tunis, stuck on the northernmost tip:
No food, no relief, not even a ship.
Some even dubbed the place 'Tunisgrad' –
Gallows humour indeed. It was that bad.

The united allied troops pushed forward,
The fall of North Africa their reward.
It was all over by the 12th of May.
After five months of muddle and delay,

The Mediterranean, once again,
Was open to allied shipping. The pain,
Clearly, had been worth it. The first convoy
From Gibraltar (with cries of "ship ahoy!")
Sailed to Alexandria. Italy
Was on her knees, a stark reality,
Her people divided, demoralised
And spent. Sooner than Churchill realised
(Even he), they'd seek to give up the fight…
Some hope! For the Germans would set them right.
Italy was to be no walkover.

The North Africa campaign was over.
Few escaped to Sicily. The allies
Had blockaded the coastline, from the skies
And by sea, making evacuation
Well-nigh impossible. In frustration
(Yet with some relief?), the Axis armies
Surrendered in droves. Of all victories,
This was one of the sweetest, the US
Tasting, at last, the first fruits of success.

The number of Axis prisoners of war
Totalled 200,000, possibly more,
Including ten generals. That's quite a score.

On into Sicily

As had been agreed at Casablanca,
Sicily would be next, the sheet anchor,
As it were, of the allies' strategy –
Then, according to Churchill, Italy.

He called the Mediterranean Sea
(And Italy) "the soft underbelly
"Of the crocodile". He promised Stalin,
In the circumstances, an easy win
Were the allies to attack Germany
From the south. Well, as we shall shortly see,
This was wrong. A soft touch? Anything but.
Italy was to prove a "tough old gut".

On July the 10th, 1943,
Allied forces invaded Sicily.
Planning for 'Operation Husky',
So-called, had been painstaking and detailed.
Imagine, for a moment, had it failed:
Two great armies effectively stranded.

A massive allied task force was landed.
On the very first day, by nightfall,
Well over 80,000 men in all,
3,000 vehicles (possibly more)
And some 300 tanks had come ashore.
More troops followed over the next few days.
Half a million (the figures amaze)
Made up the total number by the end.
More than were necessary? Why pretend?

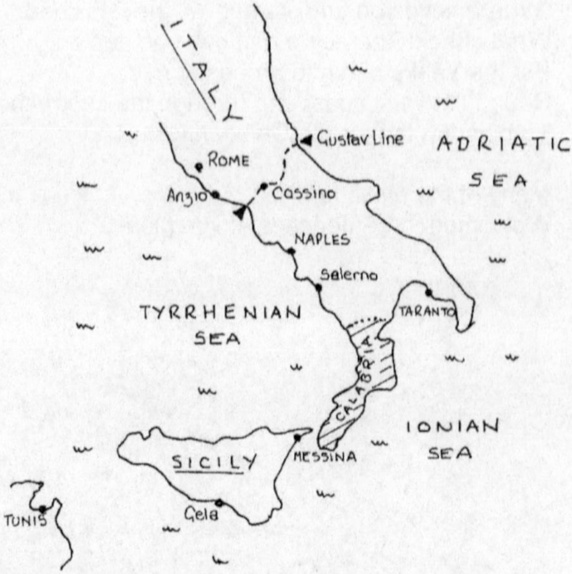

The Italians just melted away,
But the sturdy Germans, as was their way,
Put up strong resistance. Nevertheless,
They were taken by surprise. Their success
Was limited. They managed to hold back
An ill-fated American attack
At Gela, albeit briefly. They knew,
Sad to say, that their numbers were too few,
Yet the Nazis showed courage (nothing new),
Impeding Montgomery's slow progress
From the south-east. The British, I confess,
Were less than happy, behind the US
In reaching Messina, on the north tip.

A dubious display of comradeship
The Americans showed, when the British
Finally pitched up – the last to finish!

"Where have you tourists been?" the GIs cried.
What cheek! The nerve of it can't be denied.
For the Yanks had had an easier ride:
Round the west coast and through the central belt.
To be sure, the insult was keenly felt.

Many of the Mafia families
Welcomed the Americans, if you please.

Most of them had relatives in the States
And one of their particular pet hates
Was Mussolini. Man of the hour?
No longer. He was toppled from power
On the 25th of July. The King
Dismissed the dictator and (here's a thing)
Had the monster arrested. "*Benito*"
The headlines trumpeted "*e finito!*"

In a mere matter of weeks, Sicily
Was in allied hands. It seems a pity,
But the Germans, on this occasion,
Staged the perfect evacuation
From Messina across the narrow Straits –
Not something posterity celebrates.

Italy

General Eisenhower conceded
That a strong US force would be needed
For the invasion of Italy.
General Marshall fought this bitterly,
But was overruled. For such a campaign
Could be fought with the minimum of pain,
Eisenhower (and FDR) believed,
After Sicily. Churchill was relieved.
With the Italians in disarray,
The people would surely call it a day.

Hitler, it will come as little surprise,
Was livid and decided otherwise.
Stealing a march before his very eyes,
The allies must now be taught a lesson.
Under the mistaken impression
That the game was up, a shock lay in store
For the enemy. Hitler knew the score.

Hitler sends reinforcements

The Führer had been fortified, perhaps,
By his Italian ally's collapse.
Il Duce, increasingly unsteady,
Had let him down, but Hitler was ready.
He had sent reinforcements already
To northern Italy. Entering Rome,
The Germans found no government at home.

They rounded up more than 8,000 Jews
In a show of terror, the worst of news.
The King and Pietro Badoglio
(The new Prime Minister) fled, forced to go
In fear of their lives. Fascism was back.

A close call at Salerno

The Germans launched a fierce counterattack
Within two days of the invasion.
On this particular occasion,
The Americans had taken the lead.
General Clark (a maverick indeed:
It was he who'd beaten Montgomery
To Messina) disembarked from the sea
At Salerno, halfway up the west coast
(Roughly) to Rome. His troops could have been toast,
For the Germans were ready and waiting.
They fought like tigers, no hesitating,
As the General came within an ace
Of losing his men. At most he lost face,
But he diced with death, a proper disgrace.

Salerno was far from the perfect spot.
The mountains on both sides, like it or not,
Favoured the enemy. Clark lost the plot,
Proposing at one stage to re-embark.
Close to defeat, his options were stark.

Aerial reinforcements saved the day –
And allied naval gunfire. I should say
(Were I asked) that Dwight D. Eisenhower
Was lucky. Clark, the man of the hour?
Hardly. This was the nearest the Yanks got
To a complete wipe-out. To stop the rot,
The allies would need to consolidate.

Monty's progress

The British 8th Army, at any rate,
Under Monty was making good progress
Through Calabria, on to Taranto
And beyond. Fortifying Salerno
With the Americans, who was to know
That there would be eight long months still to go
Before they reached Rome? For progress was slow
And far more costly in casualties
Than could be borne. The Germans on their knees?

Far from it. Naples was taken, it's true,
Within three weeks. The Nazis (nothing new)
Had booby-trapped the ancient city.
Their miserable scorched earth policy
Led to shortages of water and food.
The people showed enormous fortitude
And defiance, though stricken with disease.

The campaign falters

The allies had expected the Nazis
To withdraw further north. Their near success,
However, at Salerno (what a mess!)
Had encouraged Hitler to draw the line
South of Monte Cassino. The great spine,
Down central Italy, suited him fine.
The enemy had to advance, at best,
On one side or the other, east or west.

No one had foreseen, it must be confessed,
Such sluggish progress. Victory was near…

Or was it? The combined allies, I fear,
Were miles from Rome by the end of the year –

Well over eighty. A whole world away.
Churchill was furious. He had his say
(As ever): "The stagnation," he fumed,
"Of the whole campaign" (as disaster loomed
On the Italian front, he assumed)
"Is becoming scandalous." Europe's fate,
He believed, hung in the balance. The date,
However, for allied landings in France
Had now been agreed. They would take their chance,
At long last, in May 1944.
It was that close: the crisis of the war.

The return of Mussolini

Hitler was stretched. The Führer's bizarre choice –
Deaf to many a more cautious voice –
To restore the morose Mussolini
To his old place in Fascist Italy,
And to defend that divided country
To the hilt, meant that Nazi Germany
Was starved of resources and under strain.

What, Goebbels asked, of the eastern campaign?
He even urged (how the Führer was vexed)
An accord with Stalin. Whatever next,
Raged Hitler! But there was trouble brewing
In the East. How were the Germans doing?

The continuing Russian campaign

Rather better than expected, sadly.
Stalingrad (for them) had ended badly.
Feldmarschall Paulus, to Hitler's horror,
Had capitulated. On his honour,
The Field Marshal saw which was the wind blew.
It was folly to go on. This he knew.
It was certainly not the Führer's view,

For the Germans were far from down and out.
Of this Hitler had not the slightest doubt.

Kharkov

The Nazis were not simply showing off,
When in February they took Kharkov
(For the second time), four hundred miles west
Of Stalingrad. They did their level best,
Stalin's Red Army, but they failed the test.

This was a significant wake-up call
For Uncle Joe. Stalingrad, after all,
Did not mark the beginning of the end.
It was perfectly foolish to pretend
That the Nazis were on the run. Kharkov
Was a serious setback. A mere trough,
However, fleeting and temporary,
Or a major reverse? Well, we shall see.

Stalin's caution

Stalin's advice from the military,
After Kharkov, was to stay defensive.
The enemy would launch an offensive,
This was a near certainty. They were right.

Hitler's fears

The Führer, for once, lay awake at night
With foreboding. His stomach, he confessed,
Turned over (it's true, no word of a jest)
At the very thought of the attack. Yes,
He fully admitted to nervousness,
This a change from his usual outburst
Of hysterical rage. Surely a first.

Kursk

The blow was most likely to fall at Kursk.
The Germans were ready to do their worst,
But the Russians were better equipped.
Confident they could have the Nazis whipped,
The Red Army generals, fit and keen,
Were more prepared than they had ever been.

Hard lessons had been learned. Four defence lines
Stretched back to a depth of fifty miles. Mines
Had been laid in strategic places. Tanks,*
Several thousand of them, joined the ranks.

---

*Russian factories, in 1943,
Built 24,000 tanks, astonishingly.
All in all, Soviet output (military)
Finally outstripped that of Nazi Germany.

The famed new model, the T-34,
Was tops. It effectively won the war.

On the morning of the 5th of July,
The Germans struck. It was pie in the sky,
But their earlier success at Kharkov
Had given them confidence. To cut off
Kursk (in its so-called 'bulge') was their intent,
From north and south. Now as far as it went
This might in theory have worked out well.
They made a direct assault from Orel
In the north and, in the south, Belgorod.
The fighting was fierce, honest to God,
The biggest tank battle in history.

Why the Germans lost is no mystery.
Russian hatred of the enemy
Knew no bounds. It was fury in the ranks
That made the difference. Mercy? No thanks!
By now most of the soldiers had seen
How diabolic the Nazis had been
To their prisoners, savage and obscene.

They had an inexhaustible supply,
Moreover, of men, all prepared to die
For the evil done to the Motherland.
Their anger was not hard to understand.
Civilians had suffered torture… rape…
From this terror there had been no escape.

A major defeat for the Nazis

The Germans, still with power to amaze,
Made an advance of ten miles in five days
From the Orel direction, as planned.
Then they came to a halt, wholly unmanned

By the furious Russian defence.
The fighting had been bloody and intense,
But with 50,000 casualties
And four hundred tanks damaged, if you please,
They had little choice. A twenty-mile dent
They made in the Russian entrenchment
To the south, but that's as far as it went.
The battle was lost. The Germans were spent.

Kursk was saved. On the 15th of July,
The Führer (his shame was hard to deny)
Called off the offensive. The proud army
Of National Socialist Germany
Had been beaten in the field. This was a first.
The Russians had shown a healthy thirst,
A lust for revenge. Something had to give
And now they took the initiative.
Any Nazi would be lucky to live
As they launched their own massive offensive,
Bitter, bloody, sustained and extensive.

Russian morale was fierce and high.
800,000 of their troops would die
Defending Kursk and in its aftermath.
A gruesome catastrophe. A bloodbath.
This represented four times as many
As the Germans. Lives were two-a-penny…
No. For of those who fell, every one
Was a beloved father, or a son,
Or a husband. The devil's work was done.

Russia on the march

The Soviet recovery began.
The Nazis were driven out, to a man.
Suddenly the armies were moving west
After two long years and all for the best.

In the face of the Russian attack
The German forces, as they were pushed back,
Laid waste all in their path. Orel was free
By August the 5th, 1943.
Belgorod followed. “Eternal glory,”
Declared Joseph Stalin, “to the heroes
“Who fell in the struggle against our foes
“For the freedom of Russia!” Who knows
Whether this breathtaking hypocrisy
Was noted? Russia was never free
Under Uncle Joe. It’s simply absurd.
Stalin nonetheless had the final word.

The relief of Leningrad

So be it. The Nazis’ place in the sun,
So brief, was over. Hitler’s day was done.
The Soviet war was as good as won,
Though it still took some time. Kiev was free
By November. Then, in January,
It was Leningrad’s turn. The tragedy
Of the shocking siege, a two-year-long grind,
Is that the dead of the allies, combined,
Were fewer in number than those who died
In Leningrad alone. Nationwide,
Throughout Russia (the record survives),
Over twenty million lost their lives.

The gas chambers at Auschwitz

In the summer of 1942,
Himmler visited Auschwitz. In his view,
Oświęcim (Polish) was the ideal place
For extermination: a showcase,
Built as it was on the main railway line,
Kraków to Vienna. Himmler, the swine,
Went to Auschwitz to study the design

Of the state-of-the-art crematoria
And the new gas chambers. His euphoria
Was patent. There were special chimneys
And furnaces. 'Advances' such as these
Were perfect. The architects aimed to please.
They succeeded. Work was well under way.
These foul edifices were here to stay.

All the camps were sited on railway routes.
When the trains stopped, the Nazi guards, the brutes,
Would sort the passengers into two groups:
Children (mark how low humanity stoops),
Women, the old, the infirm and the sick
To one side; to the other (a foul trick,
For they too would die when their strength and will
Were spent), those 'fit to work'. A bitter pill:
Separated on a railway platform,
Families wrenched apart. This was the norm.

The journey itself had been hell on wheels.
How can one possibly tell how it feels,
Herded into a cattle truck, no light,
No air, no sanitation, so tight
There is barely room to stand? Many died
On the journey. You will be horrified,
I know, that some folk had been given bread
To encourage them to 'sign up'. Instead
They suffered agony, starvation
And death. Their state of desperation
In the ghettos had weakened their spirits.
When they saw, written on the trucks, 'Auschwitz',
They had no idea what that name meant.
Most victims were relieved (if not content)
When told they were bound for 'resettlement'.

Those selected to be gassed straight away
Were soon to discover, to their dismay,

That they were being forced to get undressed.
Not unnaturally, they were distressed
And confused. They were told, to their surprise,
They were going to be 'de-loused'. More lies.
The chambers were shower rooms, they were told.

Freezing by now and shivering with cold,
The desperate victims were herded in.
As cool as you like, a guard took a tin
(Zyklon B) and, through a hole in the roof,
Shook in the insecticide – living proof
(Were it needed) of human wickedness
On a gigantic scale. Cries of distress
Rent the air. Some twenty minutes it took –
An eternity in anyone's book –
For the screams to die down. Now, don't suppose
The SS guards were the ones to dispose
Of the bodies. No, this hideous task –
I am sorry, I know you didn't ask –
Was assigned to other prisoners, Jews
In the main. Grim, but how could they refuse?

As a catalogue of iniquity,
Human wickedness and depravity
This terrible chapter of history
Has no parallel. It's no mystery,
Perhaps, why some people, more's the pity,
Prefer to draw a veil over it.
This is to nobody's benefit.

Gold from the teeth of victims was removed
Before their bodies were burned. Who approved
This vile practice? Why, Himmler, of course,
And his acolytes: no shred of remorse.
Spectacles, clothes (including underwear),
Shoes and suitcases, even human hair

(To be woven into socks or for wigs)
Were collected by the SS, the pigs,
And sent back to the Reich. Fillings and teeth?
Extracted after death? Beyond belief.

Dr. Mengele

Appalling medical experiments
Were undertaken, the very essence
Of evil. 'Work' on identical twins
By Dr. Josef Mengele, whose sins
Are infamous, leaves one shocked to the core.

Other poor victims, tens of thousands more,
Were exposed to hideous cruelty,
Suffering unspeakable agony
At his hands: 'tests' and operations;
Experimental amputations;
Exposure to impossible degrees
Of heat and cold; force-feeding, if you please,
Of sea-water… Awful atrocities.

The Warsaw ghetto

Resistance was futile. In '43,
However, the end of January,
The 70,000 surviving Jews
In the Warsaw ghetto struck back – bad news
For Himmler, who ordered that the ghetto
Be razed to the ground. It was a poor show
SS troops put up. Himmler was aghast,
As the bold insurgents fought to the last:
From the sewers and from the factories
They had occupied. Heroes such as these
Will never die. In despair the SS
Flooded the sewers. With greater success

They set fire to the buildings. The Jews
Threw themselves from the roofs rather than choose
Surrender. 'Parachutists' they were called
By the SS. I know you'll be appalled.

The brave defenders held out until May,
A mighty effort, I am bound to say.
In the fight, thousands had already died.
7,000 more (they were never tried)
Were executed immediately.
56,000, agony to see,
Were rounded up and shunted off, alas,
To Treblinka, to suffer death by gas.

Allied action?

Prisoners in the camps had smuggled out
Photographs, leaving the world in no doubt
Of the atrocities perpetrated
By the Nazis. But they hesitated

(The allies) to act. What could they have done?
They held talks! Anthony Eden was one,
Churchill's Foreign Secretary, who knew
What was happening, but what could he do?

The British government made a statement –
Little more, in effect, than a lament –
Expressing its "horror" and making plain
Its "detestation". He felt the pain
Of the Jewish people. He made a speech
In the House of Commons. Sorry to preach,
But the fact that the House stood (stirring stuff)
In support of Eden was not enough.

Those who would have bombed Auschwitz, however,
Were wide of the mark and far from clever.

There are Jewish critics who, to this day,
Disagree. But imagine the dismay
Had the camps been bombed and Jewish lives lost.
Would this have been an acceptable cost,
A fair and reasonable price to pay
For 'liberation'? A close call, I'd say.

It was clear to all, by '44,
That Germany was losing the war.
The killing rate, believe it or not,
Was accelerated. Some were shot;
Most were gassed. The wagons rolled in still
From Italy, Greece, Hungary… Kill,
Annihilate… Never stop until
Every Jew in Europe was dead.

Power went to Heinrich Himmler's head.
All hope of victory had long gone,
But the master race must soldier on.

Japan in trouble

The setback suffered by the Japanese
At Midway brought the country to its knees…
Or did it? Well, there was surely no room
For complacency. It spelt Japan's doom
In the long run. It was hard to pretend
This was not the beginning of the end.

Yet on the surface little had gone wrong.
The country still seemed remarkably strong.
The Japanese, as they'd planned all along,
With their conquest of the Dutch East Indies
Were rich in oil. They had conquered, with ease,
Malaya, so the world's rubber supply
Lay at their feet. It was hard to deny
Their triumph. Enormous reserves of tin
Were also seized. They were in this to win.
With their success in Burma, moreover –
No less, as we've seen, than a walkover –
China was completely isolated.
Next on the list? How they celebrated!

Yet even their massive reserves of oil
Were a prize that in time was sure to spoil,
And fast. These met their peacetime needs, it's true,
But war with the United States, they knew,
Would exhaust the supply, with no knowing
How it would end. They had to keep going.
There was no practical alternative,
Though something would finally have to give.

So it did and at a terrible cost:
Over three long years, thousands of lives lost
In a cruel, fierce, relentless campaign,
All to no purpose – the constant refrain.

US advances in the Pacific

The Pacific led to increasing strain
Between Britain and her US allies.
American Chiefs of Staff (no surprise)
Ignored (it seems, unilaterally)
President Roosevelt's declared policy
Of putting the defeat of Germany
Above that of Japan. In '42,
Fewer US resources (far too few)
Went to Europe than went to the Far East.
This was one reason, at the very least,
For the postponement, until '44,
Of the Normandy landings. Say no more.

There were two strategies for waging war
In the Pacific. Admiral Nimitz
Was in favour of a series of hits,
Intense and direct, on the Japanese
At the furthest point of their advance. These,
It was decided, should focus at first
On the Solomon Islands. A short burst,
Nimitz thought, would dislodge the enemy
From Guadalcanal and then Tulagi.

Guadalcanal

On the first of these, the construction
Of an airfield threatened disruption
To US sea communications
With Australia. These two nations
Were key allies. The struggle for Midway,
Indeed, had held the Japanese at bay,
Posing, as they did, a serious threat
To the continent. It was a safe bet
That enormous danger, the gravest yet,

Would follow from a Japanese air base
On Guadalcanal. It was no disgrace
That it took until 1943,
Six gruelling months, to drive the enemy
From the Solomons. Brutal and bloody,
The fight dragged on into February,
A battle royal on land and at sea.
Guadalcanal was called, pitifully,
The 'Island of Death' by the Japanese.

25,000 died. Figures like these
Testify to the sheer terror of war:
Men in their thousands, a hideous score.
Keeping a tally I truly abhor –
Which side lost fewer victims, which side more.
It hardens the heart and this I deplore.

Port Moresby

The second limb of US strategy
Was focused (at least initially)
West of the Solomon Isles. New Guinea
And Papua (the two, effectively,
One huge island) lay off the northern tip
Of Australia. Superb seamanship,
Noted earlier, meant that Port Moresby
Was saved (the Battle of the Coral Sea),
But it took until 1943
For the allied troops, in January,
To secure their foothold in New Guinea.

Jungle conditions

The enemy attempted to regain
Port Moresby, but they were foiled. The campaign
Was cruel, brutish and fought, in the main,

By Australian troops. Gradually,
In those first scary months of '43,
With great daring and dogged persistence
They overcame Japanese resistance
In Buna and Gona, two hundred miles
Up the northern coast. But there were few smiles.
Americans and Australians, both,
Suffered dreadfully. The dense undergrowth
Of the jungle was harsh and dangerous.

They succumbed to dysentery, typhus,
Dengue fever and malaria – the pits.
Their clothing, even their boots, fell to bits
In the humidity of the tropics.
Infections from insect bites and ticks
Caused skin to suppurate and putrefy.
Small wonder that so many had to die.

Food and resources were in short supply.
Airdrops often fell far wide of the mark.
The jungle, a fearful place in the dark,
Was full of noises. Ambushes were rife,
With the Japanese, you can bet your life,
Pitiless in their tactics. Left for dead,
They'd conceal themselves in corpses, it's said,
Then leap out and spring a surprise attack,
Shooting their hapless victims in the back.

General MacArthur

It was General Douglas MacArthur,
The other allied Supreme Commander
In the Pacific (oh yes, there were two,
He and Nimitz), who was certain he knew…
Everything! Where Nimitz was modest
And cautious, MacArthur (no contest)
Was a born self-publicist, pushy, proud
And thick-skinned. He never said it out loud,
But President Roosevelt he despised.

Few, indeed, would have been greatly surprised
Had he challenged FDR for office
In 1944. A mere novice,
MacArthur was a right-wing maverick,
To whom the President (who made him sick)
Was a covert Communist. Fantastic!

Republicans at home, the fools, backed him
As Supreme Commander (signally dim)
Over both the army and the navy.
Such an appointment would have been crazy,
Given his character. Far from lazy,
MacArthur was a zealot; shameless, too.
He belittled his rivals (nothing new),

Suggesting that the Ozzies in New Guinea,
Despite all evidence to the contrary,
Had evinced a cowardly reluctance
To get 'stuck in'. Talk about truculence!
MacArthur claimed, too, that the enemy
Was weaker in numbers. Sheer treachery,
To talk down the outstanding bravery
Of a sound ally. Barefaced knavery.

It took another eighteen months before
New Guinea was cleared (autumn, '44)
Of the Japanese. This was a grim war,
Hard-fought and bitter, a very long haul.
The Japanese had reinforced Rabaul,
North of New Guinea, a vital air base
On New Britain. In the desperate race
(Led by MacArthur) to the Philippines,
Rabaul was crucial. They had the means
(The US army and navy) to rid
Rabaul of the enemy. This they did,
But not until December, '43.
Many lives were lost on both sides, sadly.

What the madcap General craved, badly,
Were the Philippines, the next stepping stone
On the drive north. The campaign was his own:
Japan would never be overthrown
Until MacArthur returned in glory
To free the people! The same old story:
Personal pride, arrogance, vanity
And a monster ego. Insanity.

Death of Admiral Yamamoto

First things first. Admiral Yamamoto,
Since Pearl Harbour the nation's hero,

Was killed in April, 1943.
The Americans, fortuitously,
Had intercepted, *via* radio,
News of a journey that Yamamoto
Was taking from Bourgainville to Rabaul,
By air. Chester Nimitz put through a call
To Washington. Could he ambush the plane?
Licence was granted. America's gain
Was Japan's loss. Yamamoto's plane crashed
On Guadalcanal. The aircraft was smashed
To smithereens. A search party was sent,
A Japanese guerrilla contingent,
To find his mortal remains their brief.

They found the body, charred beyond belief –
Yamamoto, the Commander-in-Chief
Of Japan's Imperial Navy. Grief,
Horror… Words alone were inadequate
To sum up the tragedy. So be it.

His death was an irreparable loss.
One US Admiral was very cross.

He'd hoped "to lead the scoundrel" (as you do)
"In chains up Pennsylvania Avenue"
(So much for mercy) "with the rest of you
"Kicking him where it would do most good". Well,
At Pearl Harbour he had given them hell.

Admiral Isoroku Yamamoto
Received a state funeral in Tokyo.
This marked the end of the line. From now on,
Japan was on the ropes. All hope was gone
Of victory. Yamamoto had known
That the enemy could be overthrown
Only with a quick early knock-out blow.

So why did they carry on? Who's to know?
To honour Emperor Hirohito?
Probably. For every boy was taught,
From infancy, that a war must be fought
To the death. Surrender was a sin.
You died in glory. Never give in.

The Philippines

MacArthur considered himself kingpin.
This was a battle that he had to win.

By June, '44 (I'm skimming along,
I know), the General was well on song.
The conquest of New Guinea all but done,
A further victory still to be won
Was in the Philippines. You'll want to laugh,
But he among the allied Chiefs of Staff
Was the only one who advocated –
And what a furore he created
If crossed – the present liberation
Of the Philippines. Inspiration?

Hardly. Mere pride, as far as I'm aware.
MacArthur was even heard to declare
That the people "are waiting for me there".

Fellow commanders were close to despair,
Preferring to head straight for Formosa.
With the charm and tact of a bulldozer
MacArthur dug in his heels. Why object,
Pondered Roosevelt, to his pet project?
To refuse MacArthur, one understands,
Would have played directly into the hands
Of Republicans at home. For to date,
Thomas Dewey, their chosen candidate,
Was creeping up in the polls. Some argue
That the very best FDR could do
To ensure MacArthur did not speak out
Was give him his head. There is room for doubt
Whether the hard-fought Philippines campaign
Was necessary. Money down the drain,
Wasted resources, high casualties…
Clearing the islands of the Japanese,
However, was approved. The strategy
Was rubber-stamped, to MacArthur's great glee.

A 500,000 dollar present
From his chum, the Philippines President
Manuel Querzon, had nothing, of course,
To do with it. Some doubted this. What sauce!

The Philippines, you'll not be surprised to know,
Presented a huge challenge to Tokyo.
Easy to police, control and defend? No.
For here was a jungle archipelago
Of 7,000 islands. As campaigns go,
Japanese progress had been painfully slow.
To a good, patriotic Filipino,

The deadly two-year-long occupation
Was little less than an aberration.
Guerrilla groups on the small islands thrived,
However hard the Japanese contrived
To stamp them out. There was strong resistance,
As workers in Manila, for instance,
Passed on valuable intelligence
To their compatriots. US success
Owed much to their efforts. Nevertheless,
MacArthur, too, made limited progress.

The Battle of Leyte Gulf

Overconfident, I have to confess,
His troops landed on the island of Leyte,
South of the main island, Luzon. The date?
October the 20th, '44.
Was Douglas pushing at an open door?
I fear not. The Battle of Leyte Gulf raged
For four long days, two great navies engaged
In the biggest sea battle ever fought:
A total in warships (neither side short)
Of two hundred and eighty-two, that's more
(By seventeen) than in the First World War
Were involved in the Battle of Jutland.

The US put up an heroic stand.
The Japanese were the heavy losers:
Three great battleships, six of their cruisers
And four carriers were sunk. The US
Could celebrate an outstanding success:
Just two cruisers and one carrier lost.
They won the battle at minimal cost.

On land, the General's work was cut out.
The US navy, no shadow of doubt,

Had done him proud. MacArthur was now free
To give the Philippines their liberty!
This proved considerably more tricky
Than expected. Superiority
In the air still lay with the Japanese.

When they were finally brought to their knees,
In mid-December, their casualties
Were horrific: 60,000 or more
Killed in action was the final score.
10,000 more Japanese were to drown
When their transport vessels sank, going down
Off the coast of Leyte. The cost to the US
Was over 3,000, certainly no less.

The General, anything but modest,
Called the Japanese defeat "the greatest
"In the military annals" (no contest)
"Of the Japanese army". What a fool!
Best not to brag too early, as a rule.
He hadn't reached the largest island yet,
Luzon a tougher nut to crack, you bet.
Indeed, he'd planned a victory parade
Through Manila and was greatly dismayed
When told of 700,000 trapped
In the capital. His patience snapped:
Where was his audience? No, that's unfair.
When it came to sparing lives he did care.
Aerial bombing, he was well aware,
Would kill thousands. So, nothing from the air.

Hand-to-hand fighting was the only way
To dislodge the enemy. Day by day
The death toll mounted. I regret to say,
Their backs against the wall, the Japanese
Were guilty of foul atrocities.

Some 100,000 civilians,
That's over twelve *per cent* of Manilans,
Perished in the conflict. By March the 3rd,
It was over. MacArthur, you have my word,
Tried hard. However vain, however absurd,
He respected civilians, so I've heard.

The Philippines campaign, though, dragged on and on.
Even in the northern reaches of Luzon
General Yamashita fought to the last...
Or did he? His subordinates were aghast
When he surrendered, exhausted but alive,
On the 2nd of September, '45.
This, of course, was a day to remember:
That of the official surrender.

I'm surging ahead. We need to go back.
While the Philippines were under attack,
The small strategic island of Saipan
Was in US sights. The threat to Japan
Was real should the Yanks manage to storm
This island. Their troops were already warm,
Following their success in New Guinea,
And after Rabaul particularly.

Saipan

Saipan lay to the north; from Tokyo
Just nine hundred miles south. Those in the know –
The truth of this could hardly be overlooked –
Saw that their goose would be well and truly cooked
Should Saipan fall to the Americans.

The threat to Japanese civilians,
To all Japan's major towns and cities,
To her factories and facilities,

Was patent once control of their air bases
Was lost. Saipan was one of those key places
Pivotal to the outcome of the whole war.

On June the 15th, 1944,
American assault troops swept ashore.
Their courage never ceases to amaze.
Saturation bombing for five days,
Prior to landing, on the Japanese
Had served good notice that their enemies
Were on the attack. They fought to the last,
As ever, but this time the die was cast.

A paltry eighty-five square miles in size,
Saipan, as folk would quickly realise,
Became a graveyard. The foe, to a man,
Fell in the futile defence of Saipan:
25,000 Japanese. The dead
And wounded, according to what I've read,
Were 15,000 on the US side.
Civilians committed suicide
In large numbers. For Japanese women,
For the first time ever, and their children
Were caught up in the fighting. Now Japan
Was closer by the day and so began
The final stages of this tragedy.

It took three brutal weeks, more's the pity,
To take Saipan. You may be horrified,
But by the time the last Japanese died
US bombers were already prepared
To take off for the mainland. Few now cared,
It seems, for the fate of the Japanese.
Their proven catalogue of cruelties
Had hardened allied hearts and that's a fact.
Following Saipan, the US attacked

More strategic islands: Jima, Iwo –
A mere four hundred miles from Tokyo.
Then, in the last act of this grim drama,
Japan's nearest island, Okinawa,
Fell to the US in early July.

Kamikaze raids

Kamikaze pilots rained from the sky.
The young daredevils found this inviting,
The lure of death profoundly exciting.

They volunteered in droves, yearning to die.
"Send me! Send me!" was their desperate cry.
They did not ask for parachutes to pack,
Aware that they were never coming back.
They inflicted much serious damage
On US ships. That was their privilege.

US bombings

American bombing was relentless
Of Japan's towns and cities. I confess
That the measure of their alleged 'success'
Makes grim reading. Japan's wooden cities
Torched easily. Of all obscenities,
It was the burning down of Tokyo
That was the worst: a blazing inferno,
Sixteen square miles of the city flattened.

Later it seemed as if this never happened,
Despite the hideous casualties.
For this and other dreadful tragedies
Were eclipsed, if that's at all possible,
By something other – irresistible,
Mushroom-shaped and unimaginable.
That will end this chapter of our story,
A gravest event in human history.

The 'liberation' of Burma

Burma was now something of a sideshow,
But there are certain things you ought to know.
British morale, hitherto pretty low,
Slowly but surely began to revive.
Lord Louis Mountbatten kept hopes alive.
Heading the South-East Asia Command
(Newly created), he had one demand:
To end the stalemate and knock out Japan.
If anyone could, Louis was the man.

Furthermore, it was not just down to him.
Another key player, General Slim,
Commander of the new 14th Army,
Arrived, with the force of a tsunami,

To shake up the troops. Watchful, all-seeing
And committed to his men's well-being,
Slim was 'one of them'. The General cared.
He showed true courage. He never despaired.

For the British, Burma was a buffer
Protecting India. They would suffer,
The brave troops, in the Empire's defence –
Quite futile in the event (no offence),
Given that India's independence
Would be won in the very same decade.
Attlee guaranteed it. The pledge was made.

Be that as it may. 1944:
The Brits and Japanese were still at war.
To enter India by the back door,
Through Burma, by gaining a firm foothold
In Assam was the enemy plan – bold,
Focused and realistic. Mountbatten
Took the initiative: get at 'em!
This way, as far as Lord Louis could see,
Was the only viable strategy.

The British were fired up to a man.
They began their advance through Arakan
Early in '44 (the 9th of Jan).
The Japanese counterattacked in force.

Their men would never surrender, of course:
Their lives were the Emperor's. They despised
The British and were never more surprised
Than when they gave themselves up. To the death
The Japanese fought, to the very last breath.

So the British troops were rightly wary
Of the enemy. The jungle, scary,

Deadly, dangerous and dark, held no fear
For the Japanese. Breaking point was near
For the Brits: dysentery, diarrhoea,
Dengue fever and malaria (the worst)…
They abhorred the jungle. They swore, they cursed.
For every one battle casualty,
Malaria claimed one hundred and twenty.

The British advance

Yet the Arakan push, surprisingly,
Proved a success. It was a close-run thing.
The British came near to panicking
When the Japanese caught them napping
By capturing the Okedoke Pass,
Thereby encircling, as bold as brass,
One of their critical divisions.

Taking the bravest of decisions,
Isolated groups of men, surrounded,
Fought on. The enemy were astounded
As these pockets of resistance held out,
Against the odds. No shadow of a doubt,
This was a turning point. The order came:
No withdrawal. The Brits had upped their game.
Essential stores were dropped from the air.
These crack troops were not going anywhere!
They knew the consequence, one understands,
Of falling into enemy hands.

Japanese atrocities

Casualties were heavy. The Japanese
Committed most appalling atrocities.
At one British field hospital, if you please,
All were butchered: nurses, patients, orderlies,
Surgeons… The most hideous of tragedies.

Yet the myth of the Japanese superman
Was finally exploded at Arakan,
When some soldiers surrendered. Not all,
It's true. Their overall numbers were small
And most still opted to fight to the last.
Some, nonetheless, leaving colleagues aghast,
Had clearly had enough. It's hard to pretend
That this was not the beginning of the end.

On another front General Stilwell,
For the US, was also doing well.
'Vinegar Joe' was no friend of the Brits.
A difficult man, Stilwell won plaudits
For his brilliant work (nothing finer),
Opening up supply lines to China
By constructing a new road from Ledo
In the north – quite a feat, I'll have you know –
To join the Burma Road. For the Chinese
This offered a lifeline. The Japanese
Were driven back: total casualties
Numbered 4,000. There came in their wake
Gangs of labourers who, make no mistake,
Built this new road to the highest standard.
For Stilwell, conditions were as hard
As anywhere in Burma. We should pause
To honour Joe. He deserves our applause.

Wingate's Chindit expedition

Now a General, newly appointed,
Orde Wingate never disappointed.
His first Chindit expedition
Left him in a strong position.
Wingate failed, but those had been early days.
His courage and leadership won high praise.
Lessons were soon learnt. There were many ways

To overcome the Japanese. Again,
Wingate's relations came under strain
With his superiors. He didn't care.
Jealous were they? That was their own affair.
Orde was a man of passion and flair –
Above all, of imagination.

Japan's lines of communication
Were key, in Wingate's estimation.
Destroy these, the war in Burma was won
And Japan on her knees, all said and done.
With 10,000 men (ten times as many
As first time round and as good as any)
And 1,000 pack animals, well-fed
And well-supplied, you can take it as read
That Orde was bristling with confidence.
The Chindits' strategy, in essence,
Was guerrilla warfare. This made sense.

Death of Wingate

Yet, sad to say, there was trouble in store.
On the 24th of March, '44,
His plane crashed in the jungle. All aboard
Were lost. This the British could ill afford.
The fight went on. The Chindits, highly skilled,
Battled bravely. The Japanese were killed
In whole areas they thought were secure.
The jungle was their friend. Not any more.

Kohima

The Japanese launched their own offensive
Further north. Now something would have to give.
Their targets were Imphal and Kohima,
Both within the borders of India,
Lying north-west of the Chindwin River.

Kohima was the particular prize.
Taking it would cut the line of supplies
To Imphal, a key base for the allies.

The British (well, two thirds of their forces
Were Indian) were starved of resources.
Allied aircrew flew sorties, night and day,
Seeking to keep the enemy at bay,
But they kept on coming. Terror, dismay,
Frustration... However, come what may,
The valiant defenders won the day –
In the closest of calls, I have to say.

An intense hand-to-hand battle was fought,
Believe it or not, on a tennis court.
This was the front line. The Brits went flat out,
For the men were sure, no shadow of doubt,
That torture was their fate if taken alive.

In the desperate battle to survive,
They held out for seven weeks. From the air
Their supplies were replenished. Even there
They were lucky, with few aircraft to spare.
Finally Kohima was relieved (just),
As the Japanese, as they knew they must,
Fought to the last. The British garrison
Was outnumbered at first by four to one.

Fighting at Imphal was equally grim,
But the Japanese, in the words of Slim,
Would "never return". The Brits fought their way
Down through Burma. On the 2nd of May,
'45, their troops were back in Rangoon.
"We shall march, fight and fly through the monsoon,"
Mountbatten had promised. Take it from me,
His pledge was honoured. God bless Lord Louis.

The bombing of Germany

The 'strategic' bombing of Germany
Has given rise to great controversy.
Indeed, the revival of the question
Still gives historians indigestion.
Few can agree. What was the bombing for?
Was this the quickest way to end the war
Or was it a waste of resources, time
And brave pilots? Was Dresden a war crime?
Sorry, but you'll get no answers from me.

Bombing was a cruel necessity…
Or was it? Some swear it was a mistake.
If so, it was a sorry one to make.
Yet the Nazis had sought to 'coventrate'
British cities. Were the Brits to sit back
And take it, or go onto the attack?

What were the motives for such a campaign?
Revenge? Some thought this was plainly insane.

'Bomber' Harris

Sir Arthur Harris, again and again,
Claimed aerial bombing could win the war.
What, after all, was the RAF for?

This proved false. That is not, of course, to say
That bombs did not hasten in any way
The collapse of the Nazis. Be aware
That the truth is likely to lie somewhere
Between the two: bombing a tragedy,
Pure and simple, a dreadful travesty
Having no practical effect at all;
Or a crucial factor in the fall,
The ultimate collapse, of Germany.
Let no one claim either with certainty.

A country that could defend its air space
Was still a comparatively safe place.
So much the Battle of Britain had proved.

Nonetheless, the War Cabinet approved
RAF long-range bombing. They argued
(Like Harris later) that wars could be won
From the air. Massive damage would be done
To the heartlands of German industry,
Whilst shattering, simultaneously,
The morale of the people. However,
This bold strategy was far from clever.
The RAF were sadly ill-equipped
For daytime bombing. They were badly whipped
In their early attempts at daylight raids.
Their courage and daring were matched, in spades,

By the *Luftwaffe*. So, a halt was called
To daytime strikes. The public were appalled,
But with such high losses the campaign stalled.

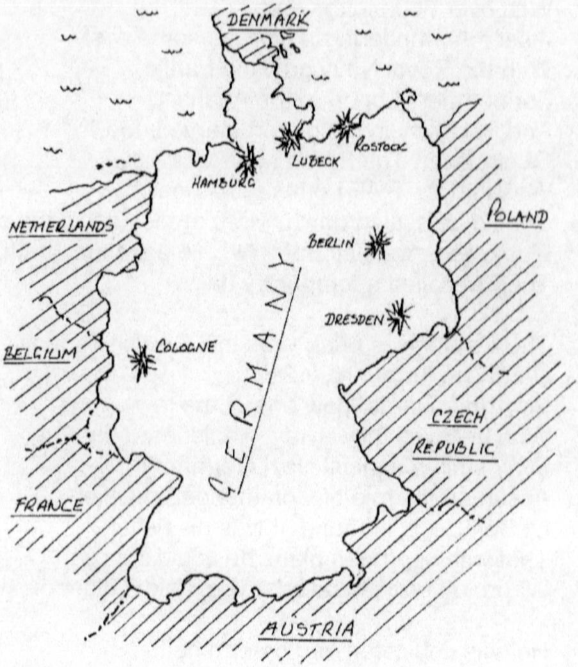

Night time forays, if anything, were worse.
Precision bombing? Quite the reverse.
A success rate of less than ten *per cent*
(Within five miles!) was as far as it went.
And the Nazi propaganda machine
Was laughing. Bombing hospitals? I mean!
Blasting such 'targets' was of course obscene,
But that was the hazard. These kinds of hits
Were no proper way to avenge the Blitz.

Yet vengeance was what people expected.
The RAF, revered and respected,
Did their best. By the end of '41,
However, the battle was far from won,
With over 700 aircraft lost.
It set folk wondering. This was some cost,
With the Royal Navy growing frantic
For bomber support in the Atlantic;
And the Army in the desert starved, too,
Of air cover. The Prime Minister's view
Was that the RAF bombing campaign
Should be scaled down. More money down the drain,
More men, more aircraft? No. To ease the strain,
The PM called a temporary halt.

The respite was brief. Was this Churchill's fault?
Hardly. In February, '42,
Sir Arthur Harris (now one of the few
Who believed fully – nay, wholeheartedly –
In air strikes against Nazi Germany)
Assumed the role of Commander-in-Chief
Of Bomber Command. It was his belief
That with upgraded plans he could succeed
Where others had failed – yes, he did indeed.

He was dedicated and determined.
The Germans, Harris explained, "sowed the wind"
With their bombing raids on British cities.
They were going now (a thousand pities)
"To reap the whirlwind". Phrases such as these
Gave Prime Minister Churchill the willies,
No word of a lie. Harris, if you please,
Was given his head. Night time raids resumed –
With Churchill's blessing, it's to be assumed –
On North Baltic ports. When the nights were fine,
Navigators could follow the coastline.

So reasoned Sir Arthur. Easy to find,
Even when pilots were flying half blind,
Lübeck was the first target. It burned well:
Half was destroyed, a veritable hell.
The following month it was Rostock's turn.
Horrified, the Germans watched their town burn.
This was the pattern for the next three years:
Indiscriminate bombing, it appears;
Few 'specific' targets – terrifying,
Reckless, heartless and unedifying.
Harris felt he had no alternative.
Was he right? Was he wrong? Well, as I live,
I have no idea. I wasn't there.
Yet given the poor results, I despair.

The 'Baedeker' raids

With Rostock and Lübeck beyond repair,
Hitler ordered 'Baedeker' raids, so-called.
The British people were duly appalled,

As the Germans sought to have the last laugh
By targeting such cities as York, Bath,
Exeter, Norwich and Canterbury.
These all featured in Baedeker,* you see,
And the raids were retaliatory,
Aimed at cultural landmarks, historic
And unique. You wonder what made him tick,
The Führer. The campaign, I'm glad to say,
Met with little success. To some dismay,
York's famous Guildhall took a direct hit,
And Bath's Assembly Rooms, but that was it.
Canterbury, Exeter and Norwich –
These cities sent a defiant message
To Göring's *Luftwaffe* and that's a fact.
Their great Cathedrals remained intact,
As did York Minster. All very good news.

The bombs, however, whatever one's views,
Took a deadly toll. The record survives.
The Baedeker bombings claimed many lives.
Some sixteen hundred civilians died,
With thousands more sadly injured beside.

---

*Baedeker was a famous travel guide,
Featuring sites of interest worldwide.
The volumes were published as a series,
Covering a large number of countries.
The guides embraced a whole host of cities,
With details of travel facilities,
Maps and background, with comprehensive lists,
Compiled by Europe's top specialists,
Of the best museums, art galleries,
Churches and other cultural glories.
So, when he opted to play the tourist,
The Führer was laughing. You get the gist?

50,000 houses, too, were destroyed.
The Führer, we're told, was highly annoyed
That the raids (in his view) proved such a flop,
His objectives frustrated. Did they stop?
Well, no. They staggered on from year to year,
With more 'collateral damage', I fear.

I detest that phrase. We should never try
To lapse into a careless 'by the by',
To soften the blow. For children will die,
Young men, women, the elderly, the sick.
They should never become a statistic.

The bombing of Cologne

On May the 30th, a calm, clear night,
Through a cloudless sky, as the moon shone bright,
One thousand bombers took off for Cologne.

Now, Albert Speer* claimed (he was not alone)
That they never expected such a raid.
The damage was horrific, I'm afraid.
Over five hundred died. Churches were razed,
Some (you'll be suitably shocked and amazed)
From medieval times or older still.
Half of Cologne's houses (a bitter pill)
And public buildings were lost. The homeless,
In their thousands, roamed the streets in distress.
Tramlines, sewers, electricity, gas,
All were disabled at a stroke, alas.

---

*The Führer's Minister of Armaments
And War Production, it was nonsense
Ever to believe that the dreadful Speer
Was innocent of war crimes. I despair
When I hear 'Hitler's architect' excused.
He exploited slave labour. He abused
The Jews. It is impossible to hold
That Speer knew nothing (this leaves me cold)
Of the 'final solution'. Absurd.
For Speer was convicted at Nuremburg
Of war crimes. He was to serve twenty years,
Yet upon his release he shed no tears.
Guilty of crimes against humanity,
He'd have none of it! As a man, you see,
Speer was a coward, an apologist
For the Nazi *régime*, far from honest,
A liar and a fraud. When on trial,
He was simply a man in denial,
Insisting that he knew nothing of it.
The Führer, indeed, would have had a fit.
Yet Speer must have put up a good defence
At Nuremberg. He pleaded his innocence
And narrowly avoided a death sentence.

The Cathedral was saved, God knows how
(Perhaps He does?). You can visit it now,
Standing proud in the new, restored city,
A fine example of antiquity,
Testament to the imbecility
Of war. Nonetheless, what truly mattered
Was this: public morale was not shattered.

German industry, too, was on a roll.
Despite the apparently awful toll
Exacted by the bombers at Cologne,
The British 'success' was overblown.
The Ruhr, Germany's industrial heart,
Remained resilient. Harris apart,
Many doubted the bombing strategy.
Sir Arthur, though, ploughed on quite happily.

Churchill and Roosevelt (in '43,
At Casablanca, in January)
Had little doubt. They were quick to agree,
In their preparations for D-Day,
That the allies should do more in the way
Of combining their efforts. Bombs away!
The US were ready to strike by day –
Their bombers were better equipped, okay? –
But with meagre success, I'm bound to say.
This caused, of course, not a little dismay.

Hamburg

Harris soldiered on the same old way.
Making use of improved technology,
From July to December, '43,
Sir Arthur (in revenge for Coventry?)
Focused his attention on Hamburg.
A tornado of flames, you have my word,

Followed his first attack. The summer heat
Rendered the devastation complete.
The city burned with ferocious ease.
It's said the temperature, if you please,
In centigrade, reached a thousand degrees.
30,000 died in the deadly blast,
Including many children (I'm aghast) –
Doubtless dismissed as 'inevitable'
By Harris. The bombing was terrible,
Horrifying, unimaginable…

The US Air Force had contributed
With daylight bombings. It's convoluted,
But even with their improved instruments,
And navigators, it was still nonsense
To reckon that bombers could win the war
Single-handed. However, on this score,
Albert Speer (in a post-war interview)
Claimed that the Hamburg raids, out of the blue,
Seriously damaged morale. His view
(And Speer would have known) was that Germany
Was nearly on her knees – yes, really.
Six more raids would have ended the war, fast.
But the allies stopped short. The shock soon passed.

Neither air force had the capacity –
This was sadly the stark reality –
To bear the losses currently sustained.

This is how it's usually explained.
Who am I to doubt it? Had they known,
Though, as Nazi Germany stood alone,
On the brink, how close she was to collapse,
The allies would have persisted… perhaps?
No, for sure. At the time, no one knew it.
The allies almost certainly blew it.

Berlin

Harris, however, with a war to win,
Continued on his own. Next stop: Berlin.
The bombing, from late August, '43,
To March, '44, destroyed the city...
Or did it? Well, that was Sir Arthur's plan.

It soon became clear, once bombing began,
That the great city was far too spread out
To suffer fire storms. Without a doubt
These had contributed to Hamburg's fate.

Now this caused Harris to miscalculate
When it came to Berlin. His hopes were high.
His words to his men, it's hard to deny,
Were clear: "You have the opportunity"
(I quote) "to light a fire in the belly
"Of the enemy and burn his black heart out."

Berlin, he hoped, would be the final bout.
Within six months the battle would be won.
The war would be over. All said and done,
The high explosive bombs, plus incendiaries –
Well in excess of 15,000 tons of these –
Still failed to bring the capital to its knees.

Many of its offices and factories
Kept working. Total German casualties
(Civilians) numbered 9,000 or more,
A monstrous figure I deeply deplore.
1,000 aircraft, a terrible score,
Were lost by Bomber Command. Finally,
Some two thousand, six hundred and ninety
(An incredible loss) aircrew were killed.
These courageous warriors were skilled,

Dedicated and selfless – true heroes.
What Harris had hoped to achieve, God knows,
But he failed. The people kept on going.
Where would it all end? There was no knowing.
Harris had expected an easy win.
Nevertheless, "*Berlin bleibt doch Berlin*".*

Bomber Command had been severely mauled.
So many aircraft lost! Their campaign stalled,
Though Harris would never admit defeat.

The US now started to find their feet.
Though briefly at risk of losing their shirt,
With unsuccessful raids over Schweinfurt
(In '43), they would fight to the finish
Over Berlin in support of the British.

The US 8th Air Force, lean, fit and keen,
Was now as strong as it had ever been.
Yet independent bombing was ended –
Sir Arthur was bitterly offended –
When Bomber Command was taken over
By Eisenhower. Ike, no pushover,
Ordered temporary suspension
Of the air campaign. This caused tension,
As you can well imagine. However,
The canny Sir Arthur, boxing clever,
Bounced back in February, '45.
One wonders how he managed to survive,
But the Air Chief Marshal, more's the pity,
Was steadfast, grim, determined and gritty.

---

*These were the words of a popular song:
"Berlin may be broken, but not for long".
How could Sir Arthur have got it so wrong?

He never believed that landings in France
Could win the war. If given half a chance,
He would wrap the whole thing up in a trice.
Aerial bombing alone would suffice.

The horror of Dresden

Dresden sadly paid the ultimate price.
Harris's superiors, I assume,
Allowed his bombing campaign to resume,
For Sir Arthur was the people's hero.
Even Churchill felt he could not say no.
Bomb Dresden from the air? Give it a go!

The Prime Minister, the old so-and-so,
After the event thought better of it.
The sheer, naked terror… He had a fit.
Yet Churchill, throughout the course of the war,
Had called for such bombings. He knew the score.
He'd approved the raid on Dresden, what's more,
As had the Cabinet just days before.
Such duplicity I deeply deplore.

'Florence on the Elbe', they called Dresden:
The finest of cities, all said and done,
Famed for its architecture, its treasure
And its art – precious beyond measure.
Dresden had not been bombed previously,
But now it was to suffer grievously.
On the 13th night of February,
2,700 bombs were dropped.
Firestorms followed. They could not be stopped.

The horror cannot be overstated –
Thousands of poor souls incinerated
In the horror the fires created.

High-explosive bombs, incendiaries…
It's no surprise that the casualties,
Over three terrible nights, exceeded
25,000. The raids succeeded…
Or did they? Factories were hit, it's true,
But did this justify (I'm asking you)
Such horrific, wholesale destruction?
Many were soon back in production,
As in Cologne earlier and Berlin.

I honestly don't know where to begin.
Most factories (even to say this hurts)
Were located on the very outskirts
Of the city. The raids were "justified",
In Harris's words (you'll be horrified)
Thus: "I do not regard, personally,
"The remaining cities of Germany"
(Did he mean all of them?) "as worth the bones
"Of one British Grenadier." The groans,
The tears, the pain, the agonising cries
Of thousands barely moved him. No surprise:
He'd the hide of the rhino, I suspect.

Churchill's reaction to Dresden

The Prime Minister was more circumspect.
The bombing of Dresden, Churchill declared –
I have to say, I wonder how he dared –
"For the sake of increasing the terror
"Under other pretexts" was an error.
In a frank admission (well, nearly),
He called Dresden "a serious query
"Against the conduct" (in hindsight you see)
"Of allied bombing". Retrospectively,
Churchill washed his hands of the whole affair.
How could he justify this? I despair.

He called it "an act of terror", no less.
The PM was later forced to confess,
When Harris objected to the remark,
It had been made in haste. The truth is stark:
Sir Arthur stuck to his guns. A war crime
The bombing of Dresden was called in time.

Churchill could not afford to be that frank.
In any case he had Harris to thank
For doing his dirty work. The poor man –
I say that advisedly; I'm no fan –
Was abused and made to carry the can.
In Churchill's victory broadcast in May
Bomber Command, to Harris's dismay,
Received no mention. I have to say
This was mean. But that was the PM's way.
The myth is perpetuated to this day:
Harris was to blame. No medal was struck
To mark the campaign, just Sir Arthur's luck.
Bomber Command was erased from the map,
Like Dresden – no accident; no mishap.
Offered no peerage, Harris made no fuss.
He suffered in silence. Is it for us
To judge? These old controversies drag on
After the leading players are long gone.

The Italian campaign

The frustrating stalemate in Italy
Had to be addressed. After Sicily
The allied advances, more's the pity,
Had petered out. With grim tenacity,
The Germans under Kesselring (gritty
And focused), by December, '43,
Had established the so-called Gustav Line
Sixty miles north of Naples, a clear sign

Of their iron determination
To prevent further infiltration
Into Italian territory
From the south. This now meant that Italy
At its narrowest point, from coast to coast,
Was strongly defended. What mattered most,
To Churchill, was simply to keep going.
Should the allies fail, there was no knowing
Where it might end. It now started snowing.
With all of the major rivers in flood,
Men and equipment got stuck in the mud.
Trench foot, frostbite, exposure… Not much fun,
An ugly reminder of World War One.

Breaching the Gustav Line

Italy's mountainous Apennine spine
Made it harder to breach the Gustav Line,
For troops could only advance on one side
Or the other. I'll leave you to decide:
How could they possibly spring a surprise?
The Germans would be waiting. The allies,
Therefore, devised another strategy.
They would neatly outflank the enemy
By making an amphibious landing,
Behind the Line. It's my understanding
That they would land by sea at Anzio
(North of the Line), while Monte Cassino,
A strategic point just south of the Line,
Would be stormed. These two assaults would combine
To achieve a definitive breakthrough.

In the event this proved only half true.
The allies had been badly mistaken:
Cassino was not easily taken.
For the German forces held the high ground,
With command of the field for miles around.

The allied attack, in January, **1944**
Failed. General Clark's US Fifth Army
Was repulsed. The General was barmy,
According to rumour. He was obsessed
With image. He would be seen at his best
At photo calls! One can only suppose
It was owing to his fine Roman nose
That his officers dubbed him, as a joke,
Marcus Aurelius Clarkus! This bloke,
Believe it or not, set his heart on Rome.

He reckoned that he would be half way home
Should he manage to land on Anzio.
There would then be twenty-two miles to go,
No more, before reaching the capital.

Anzio… and Churchill's despair

Cassino apart, Clark was on a roll.
The General was lucky on the whole.
When the US troops finally landed
At Anzio, far from being stranded,

As at Salerno, they were unopposed.
The Germans, it can only be supposed,
Had been caught napping. Clark was well on song,
Before, that is, things began to go wrong.

The General in charge of the attack,
Lucas, though pleasantly taken aback
By the easy landing (a total lack
Of Germans!), always liked to have a plan.
John P. Lucas was a cautious man.
Before any advance on Rome began,
The beachhead must be secured. He waited,
Therefore – some would say he hesitated –
For a week, giving time for Kesselring
To regroup. It's an astonishing thing,
But Clark defended Lucas. Anyway,
To both men's considerable dismay,
Kesselring recovered fast and moved south.

With both Clark and Lucas down in the mouth,
The chance of storming north through Italy
Had been lost. Churchill complained bitterly:
"I thought," he carped, "we had flung a wild cat
"Into the Alban Hills." Instead of that,
"We found a whale floundering on the beach!"

Stuck in London, who was Churchill to preach?
It's ironic, of course, but he was right.
It was close to one minute to midnight
For the Germans. For a sudden advance
On Rome, had Lucas dared to take a chance,
Would have proved an unexpected success.

The lancing of the 'Anzio abscess'
(Hitler's phrase) became top priority.
Kesselring, never one to say sorry,

Launched his counterattack. Hitler, it seems,
Was hell-bent on saving Rome (in his dreams).
Kesselring, pushing at an open door,
Was sent even more men than he asked for,
So desperate was the Führer. Quite mad –
And for Italy pitifully sad.

Anzio was now looking very bad.
With Kesselring's forces on the attack,
There seemed little hope of holding them back.
The US troops, though physically fit,
Had never seen anything quite like it.
Young and inexperienced, one unit
Simply caved in and gave itself up. Well,
This, you'd imagine, sounded the death knell
Of the campaign. Some were even paraded,
Prisoners, through the streets of Rome, degraded
And humiliated. Lucas was sacked.

The assault on Monte Cassino

Clarkus Aurelius, lacking in tact,
Now blamed him for the fiasco. A rout?
Not quite. But beyond all shadow of doubt
The buck stopped with Clark. There was one way out.
The Gustav Line must be breached. The 'hot spot'
Was Monte Cassino. To stop the rot –
And this showed how serious it had got –
The allies had to take the offensive.
They knew the damage would be extensive,
Not only to the town of Cassino.
The monastery, too, would have to go,
Way up the mountain. A long tale of woe.

So, on the 15th of February,
The allies – believing mistakenly

That the monastery was occupied
By the Germans and that they'd fortified
The building up to the hilt – bombarded
This ancient site, widely regarded
As a sacred icon. This made no sense.

The ruins gave a new line of defence
To the enemy. With better cover
They were able quickly to recover
And the Gustav Line was held. Anzio
Now hung by a thread. It was touch and go.

Kesselring had pledged, should his troops break through,
That they would have the honour (this is true)
Of escorting through the streets of Berlin
The allied captives. Massed waves were flung in
Of German infantry. The allied guns,
However, gave the enemy the runs.

Again, like something out of the Great War,
They fell back. Yet this was a no-score draw.
For the allies lacked the strength to prevail,
But on no account could afford to fail.
On Monte Cassino, without avail,
A massive blitz on the monastery
From the air – a terrible travesty
Of warfare – made little or no impact.
Three assaults; three failures. That's a fact.
In Cassino itself the battle raged
From house to house, thousands of troops engaged.
New Zealand forces lost 4,000 men.

The monastery destroyed by the allies

When the tables turned it was only when,
With great cunning, the allies leaked a plan
To land by sea north of Rome. Thus began
A German withdrawal from Cassino
To prepare for the landings. As leaks go,
This was clever. Outnumbered three to one,
The Germans were finally on the run
From Monte Cassino. A sustained burst
Of allied artillery did its worst.
The monastery fell. Forever cursed,
The allies broke through. The Poles were the first –
At the cost of massive casualties –
To reach the ruin. 'Triumphs' such as these
Always leave a nasty taste in the mouth.

The allies quickly moved up from the south.
The Germans were now in headlong retreat.
On the 25th of May (pretty neat),
The forces that had taken Cassino
Linked up with those cut off at Anzio.
Clark could now head for Rome. It was all go.

General Clark's focus on Rome

Yet Clarkus Aurelius, you should know,
To other officers' open dismay,
Allowed the Germans to get clean away
In his crazy determination
To reach Rome first. The consternation
This occasioned among the allies,
Brits and Yanks alike, comes as no surprise.
For he left the German lines of retreat
To the north wide open. Admit defeat?
No. For Kesselring was let off the hook,
A major error in anyone's book,
Free to establish, by hook or by crook,
A new, well-fortified defensive line
North of Rome. The Germans were in decline,
But still they lived to fight another day.

The madcap General Clark, come what may,
Was focused on Rome. On the 4th of June,
US forces, not a moment too soon
(In his view), entered the capital. Swell!
They met no resistance and just as well.

The General was denied his triumph.
Two days later (with a mighty 'hurrumph')
He learned of the allied invasion
Of Normandy. On this occasion
Clark missed out on his moment of glory.
All set to take his place in history,
He was never accorded due credit
For the 'fall of Rome' – well, as he read it.
For the US General (at first glance
The hero) was upstaged in northern France.
His huge ego took a terrible knock.
Alas, poor Clarkus! A horrible shock!

Voytek: Soldier Bear

A footnote. To return to Cassino
Just for a moment. As spectacles go,
A large bear carrying ammunition
Takes the biscuit. How on earth permission
To bring Voytek,* the bear, into Italy
Was granted was something of a mystery –
Until you met him! For Voytek's history
Was this. The 22nd Company,
Polish Army Service Corps (Artillery),

---

*Wojtek: the Polish spelling. Either way
It is pronounced the same. I have to say,
I prefer this to the one I'm using,
But fear it might be a tad confusing.

Soon after their release from Russia,
Found him in the mountains of Persia
As a helpless wee cub. As like as not,
His mother had been hunted down and shot.

The Poles adopted him as their mascot.
They offered him milk and built him a cot,
Which he quickly outgrew! A friendly lot,
They treated the bear as one of their kind,
With the happy result, I think you'll find,
That Voytek soon became one of the men –
Not just a mascot, but (ten out of ten)
A colleague and friend. Wherever they went,
The bear would go with them, ever content
On doing his bit for the regiment.

I kid you not. Despite his enormous size
And his habit of springing the odd surprise –
He loved to wrestle! – Voytek was gentle
And loyal. Some considered it mental
To take a bear all through the Middle East
And on to Italy. A worthy beast,
Voytek was determined to play his part
In the war effort. He made a strong start,
Raising the Poles' spirits and putting heart
Into the troops. But in 1944,
In Italy, at the crisis of the war,
Voytek decided he was ready for more.

In the assault on Monte Cassino –
Explosive and hazardous, as we know –
The Poles were charged with responsibility,
Under heavy fire from the enemy,
Of supplying the Polish artillery
With ammunition. This was dangerous,
But not for Voytek. "He wants to come with us,"

One of the departing contingent remarked
As their lorry drew up. “He looks proper narked
“To be left behind.” Voytek rested his paw
On his colleague’s shoulder, as he blocked the door!

Voytek goes to war

And this is how Voytek got to go to war.
He was frightened, of course, by the noise at first –
The relentless shelling and the sudden burst
Of explosives as the bombs fell all around.
The men shared his fear, but Voytek stood his ground.
He watched the troops unloading boxes of shells
And cartridges. Then someone noticed: “Hell’s bells,”
He cried, “he wants to help!” They gave him a crate.
Voytek took it. The bear didn’t hesitate.

He carried the shells to the men stacking them,
Oblivious to the guns attacking them.
He soon took part in the regular routine
Of unloading the lorries. Voytek was keen
And hard-working, ever plodding to and fro
With heavy boxes of shells. A war hero.

When he wanted to take a rest from duty,
He would roll on his back or climb up a tree.
Exposed to enemy fire, he’d risk it,
Only to be tempted down with a biscuit.

The famous Battle of Monte Cassino
Ended in victory (of sorts), as we know.
Voytek was honoured for his role. The logo,
Or badge, of the company featured the bear.
Before long his image was everywhere:
Against the background of a round steering wheel,
A bear holding a huge shell. How would he feel,

One wonders, had he ever been made aware
Of his fame? This great, affectionate bear
Could not have cared less. That's certainly my guess.
So long as he enjoyed comradeship, kindness
(And food!), Voytek the bear was well content.

Voytek's last years

Good company, safe in the regiment,
Was all that he asked. Voytek's later years,
I am sad to report, were laced with tears.
The Poles fetched up in Scotland, in Glasgow.
That was fine, but where were the men to go
After the war? For Poland was not free.
The Poles had exchanged German tyranny
For Russian oppression. Their dream
Had been to return home. Now, it would seem,
This was impossible. The troops dispersed –
Fortune was set to do her best, or worst,
As the Poles ventured forth to try their luck
In foreign lands. Voytek travelled by truck
(This breaks my heart) to Edinburgh Zoo.
His old friends wept; there were more than a few.
They had planned to parade him through Warsaw,
Their hero the bear, the crowd on a roar.

This was not an option any more,
For their beloved Warsaw was a wreck,
Reduced to ruins. No place for Voytek.
The dreams of the poor Poles had been shattered.

Voytek's safety was now all that mattered.
His colleagues did their best. For 'safe keeping'
Their chum went to the zoo. There was weeping,
To be sure, as their lorry drove away –
November the 15th the fateful day,
1947. What can I say?

Peter, his oldest friend, led him to the place,
A large cage, his new home. The bear licked his face.
Voytek knew he'd be back. He put his trust
In his best of friends, as he knew he must.

Poor Soldier Bear. His hopes turned to dust.
He was well looked after. Edinburgh Zoo
Is a fine place. His erstwhile colleagues knew,
Nonetheless, that demobilisation
Would never suit a bear of his station.
Did he suffer from heartache, frustration
And loneliness? It's difficult to say,
For the subsequent years he whiled away
In peace. He lived to nearly twenty-two.
He never complained, to give him his due.
Voytek's first five years, though, as an army bear
Were the best of his life. I'm fully aware
That the cynics will scoff. I don't greatly care.

A huge statue in Voytek's memory,
On the 70th anniversary
Of the Battle of Monte Cassino,
Was unveiled at Kraków. The world should know
Of his heroism and bravery.

Up in Edinburgh, too, for all to see
In Princes Street Gardens is a bronze statue
Of Voytek, walking (as soldier bears do)
With an army colleague. His bear logo,
The badge, can be seen (I urge you to go)
At the Imperial War Museum.
There are more monuments (you should see them):
One at Duns (Scotland); others in Warsaw
And Italy. This chapter of the war
Was bitter and bloody. At any rate,
Voytek gives us something to celebrate.

Piero della Francesca

We must leave Italy. Before we go,
However, we'll head for Sansepolcro.
Founded in the 11th century,
This town has a stunning inventory
Of painters, all of whom made history:
Birthplace of Raffaellino del Colle,
The great Matteo di Giovanni,
Santi di Tito, Angiolo Tricca
And, of course, Piero della Francesca.

An astonishing Renaissance fresco,
The *Resurrection*, by the maestro
Is still to be seen in Sansepolcro,
Set in a Tuscan valley, to this day.

Aldous Huxley, in a famous essay
In 1925, had this to say:
"It stands there before us" (here I concur)
"In entire and actual splendour,
"The greatest picture in the world." One man,
Another Brit, Tony Clarke, was a fan.

Clarke, an officer in the RHA
(Royal Horse Artillery), on his way
With his regiment's oldest battery,
The Chestnut Troop, north up through Italy,*

---

*This was after Rome had fallen. In retreat,
The Germans had now begun to find their feet.
Their resistance was stronger. Sansepolcro
Lay some two hundred miles north of Cassino
And one hundred and forty-five north of Rome.
Yet the allies were still very far from home.

Had orders from HQ to shell the town.
He recalled a work of art of renown,
The *Resurrection.* He'd read Huxley
And recalled his words particularly.

Now, it was standard army strategy,
When ridding a town of the enemy,
To launch an artillery assault first,
Usually a long, destructive burst
To soften up the target, as it were –
Or raze it to the ground, if you prefer.
Clarke was in no doubt, were this to occur,
That the *Resurrection* could be lost –
The "greatest picture in the world". The cost,
Needless to say, was unacceptable.
Should he bow to the inevitable
And follow orders? He had never seen
The fresco, but considered it obscene
To risk its destruction. Cassino,
He was sure, had been a hideous blow.
Was he simply now to 'go with the flow'
And compound that terrible outrage? No.

Were Germans in the town? Who was to know?
The officer took a colossal risk.
His commander ordered him to be brisk.
Clarke fortunately managed to stall him.
The image continued to appal him
Of the great fresco smashed to smithereens.
To my mind this is what true courage means.
Had the enemy not already fled,
Clarke would probably have been left for dead…
Along with his men. So… a work of art,
Against soldiers' lives? Where does one start?

How low do you have to be, how depraved,
To risk your men? The great fresco was saved,

Thank God. No British losses were incurred.
Tony Clarke was fortunate, take my word.

So was Italy, and the world to boot.
The Nazis would not have given a hoot
For the picture. Clarke would have had a fit
Had he not been able to rescue it.
For he had written in his diary:
The fate "of Monte Cassino shocked me".
Thanks to this young officer's bravery
And imagination, the fresco
Is there in the Museo Civico
In Sansepolcro for all to see –
Well worth a visit, take it from me.

D-Day

So, to June the 6th, 1944.
Britain and Germany had been at war
For nearly five years. Churchill, when France fell,
Exhorted her brave people to "sleep well.*
"Gather your strength for the dawn, for the dawn
"Will come". Generations yet unborn
Would thrill to these words. Now French hopes revived.
They had not slept well! The time had arrived.

---

*In his halting French, Churchill had broadcast
To the people of France. He was steadfast,
He was confident… A Francophile, of course,
"*Dormez bien,*" he urged. "*Rassemblez vos forces*
"*Pour l'aube, car l'aube viendra.*" Well said!
Morning would come, he took it as read.
"*Vive la France!*" Churchill's rallying cry
Was proof that freedom would never die.

For morning would "shine on the brave and true:
"*Vive la France!*" Of course, what nobody knew,
In those first weeks, was how long it would take
To liberate Europe. Make no mistake,
The Nazis would fight to the very last,
But their fate was sealed. The die was cast.
No longer "the end of the beginning",
The end was in sight. But the winning,
When it came, was a struggle to the death.

Preparations and strategy

D-Day. The allies barely paused for breath.
Preparations were meticulous.
It would indeed have been ridiculous
Had hard lessons not been learned at Dieppe,
In 1942: a fateful step,
Taken too early, at a fearful cost.
In excess of 3,000 men were lost
In an assault on the port's defences.
Mines, artillery, barbed wire fences…
Dieppe itself was clearly beyond reach.
Many poor souls were gunned down on the beach,
Thousands more wounded, a pity to see.
Hundreds walked straight into captivity.

Strategists took note. A great invasion,
Such as the one planned on this occasion,
Had to be plotted in the finest detail.
Operations otherwise were sure to fail.
An invading army coming ashore
At this, the crucial point in the war
Would face the most robust opposition.
It must first establish its position
On the beachhead. Taken altogether,
This was the greatest challenge. The weather,

Too, could hold the invasion force back.
Next they had to go onto the attack,
In order best to stop the enemy
From driving them straight back into the sea
Or (the more lethal possibility)
Shooting them down. This was the theory.
A safe landing was the priority.
Yet casualties were bound to be high
Whatever happened, and many would die.

Where was the invasion force to land?
The great port of Calais, on the one hand,
Was the obvious spot. Beyond dispute,
The Pas-de-Calais was the shortest route,
The fastest passage and the most direct.
Calais, however, as you would expect,
Was a Nazi stronghold. Simple enough,
You might imagine, to call Hitler's bluff,
To meet the Germans head-on in Calais
And face the consequences come what may.
D-Day would then have spelt 'Disaster-Day'.
There surely had to be a better way.

Normandy was less strongly fortified.
It was further (this could not be denied)
From England. Nonetheless, its shores were wide –
Generous expanses of sand indeed,
Fifty miles long. The landing craft had need
Of flat beaches to disgorge their supplies,
Men and equipment. It was surely wise,
Too, to opt for a site where victory
Would result, in all probability,
In gaining control of Cherbourg; also,
Hopefully, the other Channel ports. So,
Normandy it was. Rommel was relieved.
He agreed with the Führer, who believed

(Showing some sense for once) that Normandy
Was the likely landing ground. Even he,
However, was slow to make up his mind.

This error of judgement, I think you'll find,
Cost the Germans dear. East of the Seine?
West of the Seine? It's hard to explain,
But Hitler had everything to gain
From concentrating his troops in the west.
Yet the Führer failed to rise to the test.
The strain was showing. He was past his best.
He sat on his hands. Hither or thither?
Hitler for once was all of a-dither.

The allies, in a clever deception,
Did much to encourage the perception
That they would come by the Pas-de-Calais.
Strategic bombing, by night and by day
East of the Seine, towards the end of May,
Strengthened these expectations. Norway,
As part of a ruse dubbed 'Plan Fortitude',
Was another possible landing. Crude?
Well, Germany had kept, throughout the war,
Some 400,000 troops there. What for?
You may well ask! Playing on Hitler's fears,
The allies, knowing he would be all ears,
Sent signals in the utmost 'secrecy'
Of plans to invade across the North Sea!

By contrast, the bombing of Normandy
Was lighter than air attacks on Calais.
Hitler was duped. To the Germans' dismay,
When it came to the 6th of June, D-Day,
They were far from ready. Nevertheless,
They might have done better (only a guess)
Had it not been for the dreadful weather.

The weather

The allies, at the end of their tether,
Had planned to invade on the 5th of June.
The dire weather made them change their tune.
The troops had embarked; all had been prepared;
Eisenhower would have sailed… had he dared.
As the storm worsened, the crisis was grave.
Now they say that Fortune favours the brave,
But by the evening of June the 3rd,
The winds were terrible. You have my word,
D-Day was off! Even two days' delay
Threatened the enterprise – that is to say,
It would be straight back to base. Cue, dismay.

According to the tide and weather charts –
Reported with the heaviest of hearts –
It might then be weeks before the campaign
Could resume. Ike, under hideous strain,
Watched the lowering clouds, the wind and rain
With gloom and foreboding. He feared the worst.
At the final hour, D-Day was cursed…

Or was it? Chief meteorologist,
J. M. Stagg, spotted sunshine through the mist –
That is, metaphorically speaking.
The high winds showed some sign of weakening,
With the likelihood, by Tuesday morning,
The 6th, of a quieter day dawning.
Stagg nonetheless delivered this warning:
The calmer weather could last until Wednesday –
Any further it was difficult to say.

So, to his credit, Ike postponed D-Day
By just twenty-four hours. Stagg (oh, boy!)
Spoke of Eisenhower's look of pure joy,

His beaming face "a marvel to behold".
The General's decision was bold,
The bravest, one might say, of the whole war.
Forget talk of stalemate, a no-score draw:
Had Eisenhower backed his hunch and failed,
Allied strategy would have been derailed
In Europe for months – perhaps for ever.

Hitler for his part was far from clever.
I hinted that the inclement weather
Favoured Ike. Crazy? Not altogether.
For the fateful forecast that made him pause
Pandered to one of Hitler's fatal flaws,
Complacency. For the Führer (don't scoff)
Was sure the allies' plans would be called off.
Rommel visited Hitler at Berghof
To discuss tactics. That is to say,
He left his post. The previous day,
He'd celebrated his wife's birthday,
Setting off for Nazi Germany
With no pressing sense of urgency.

On the night of Monday, the 5th of June,
The Germans cancelled all patrols. Too soon?
I should say! The die was cast. At sunrise,
On Tuesday, they were in for a surprise.

The troops

Ike needed no further persuasion.
Code-named 'Overlord', the invasion
Went ahead as planned. Man of the hour,
The Supreme Commander, Eisenhower,
Led a force of astonishing power.
The number of Yanks in Britain by now
Exceeded one-point-five million. Wow!
There were troops from other allied countries
(Including pilots and aircrew). Of these,
A large contingent came from Canada,
With many others from South Africa,
Rhodesia, Czechoslovakia,
Belgium, Australia, New Zealand,
France (well, naturally), Holland, Poland,
Norway and Denmark. All would take a stand
In their resolve to defeat the Nazis.
Reports of their vile atrocities,
Death camps and similar obscenities
Seemed incredible: prisoners of war
Shot; civilians butchered by the score…
These (and much more) were what D-Day was for.

The equipment

Equipping Overlord was a huge task.
4,000 landing vessels, since you ask,
Were required, including assault craft.
Engineers and suppliers simply laughed –
At first. Did they manage? I'm curious…

They did! The pace was fast and furious.
To deliver in such large quantities,
In bulk, when ship-building facilities
Were at a premium, was little less
Than a minor miracle. This success
Was matched by other Overlord targets.
Now this is as impressive as it gets:
Tanks and vehicles (17,000);
New bombers and fighters (13,000);
Parachutes (well over 90,000);
Bombs and explosives (the figures astound)
In their millions – and all Europe-bound.

The allies could hardly have asked for more:
An armoury on England's southern shore.
The massive weight of it set Ike thinking:
Great Britain was only saved from sinking
By the barrage balloons floating overhead!

He had little sense of humour, it's been said,
So folk were surprised when he cracked a joke.
Ike on the whole was a serious bloke.

With his vast international force,
He had to play the diplomat, of course.
Eisenhower was certainly a gent.
Commander of the US contingent
In North Africa, he was diligent,
Imaginative and intelligent –
Well, 'sound', perhaps, was as far as it went.
Elected American President
In '52, Ike came to represent
All that was best in the United States.
(I apologise. I know that this grates
If you are a Democrat. What am I?
Well, I prefer to keep my powder dry).

Best known of Ike's commanders-to-be
Was our forthright friend, Montgomery.
Although a figure of controversy,
For now the cry went up: "Good old Monty!"

The Mulberry Harbours

Nothing was quite as extraordinary
As the two Mulberry Harbours, so-called.
Strategists, understandably appalled
Following the Dieppe disaster, stalled.

The dilemma was this. A smooth landing
Demands a harbour. My understanding –
And that of the experts, make no mistake –
Is that it is impossible to *take*
A port without obliterating it!
As a harbour, it is no longer fit.

To destroy the very facilities
That you require is, of all follies,
Perhaps the greatest. Problems such as these
Are insurmountable… Or so it seems…

Mulberry Harbours were the stuff of dreams.
Lateral thinking! Hazard the unknown!
You can't take a port by storm? Bring your own!
Two artificial structures, the size
Of Dover Harbour, were built. The surprise,
When they saw them, that these 'ports' engendered
In the Germans would be long remembered.
If anything won the war, it was these:
Two harbours built from scratch – the Mulberries!

Then there was PLUTO (nothing left to chance):
A Pipeline-Under-The-Ocean to France
(For 'Ocean' read 'Channel', but never mind).
Inspiration and genius combined,
PLUTO was a lifesaver, take it as read:
A flexible pipeline on the sea-bed,
Miles long, bringing petrol to the beachhead.

One million tons of fuel, it's said,
Were pumped daily to France under water –
Altogether quicker, safer, shorter
(And cheaper) than standard delivery
By tanker. It's no fluke of history
That D-Day proved to be such a success,
Despite the losses. A triumph, no less.

Bombing German supply lines

Sir Arthur Harris, I have to confess,
True to form, was a fly in the ointment.
For D-Day was a huge disappointment

To the Air Marshal. He could win the war
Simply by bombing, of that he was sure.
Otherwise what was the RAF for?

Sir Arthur's pig-headedness I deplore.
Air Chief Marshal Tedder, Ike's deputy,
Gave Harris the order, fortunately,
To support the landings with air attacks.

The Germans in France had to mind their backs.
Their supply lines were crippled, the railways
And bridges, in the all-important days
Leading up to the landings. The huge scale
Worried Churchill greatly. To no avail,
He sought from Roosevelt a guarantee
That French lives would be spared. A legacy
Of hatred Churchill feared, a tragedy.
FDR, alas, chose to ride roughshod
Over French feelings. This, honest to God,
Was an outrage. For the French Resistance,
With courage, grit and dogged persistence,
Were vociferous in their insistence
That they could do more, with minimal loss.

Roosevelt ignored them. De Gaulle was cross
(Very), but there was little he could do.
Later he raised a right hullabaloo
When it came to liberating Paris,
An opportunity too good to miss.

All that's for later. The point now is this.
In the so-called 'Transportation Plan',
Wherever a major French river ran,
Its bridges were destroyed – over the Seine…
Over the Loire… Travelling by train?
Forget it. The Nazis soon felt the strain.

French civilian casualties

15,000 French civilians died
In these attacks. De Gaulle was horrified.
Regrettably, the same number again
(Or more) during the course of the campaign
Lost their lives. The total number to die
In the whole war, in attacks from the sky
And from shelling on land, I'm sad to say,
Was 70,000 – some price to pay
For liberation. This was rather more
Than British non-combatants killed in the war
In air raids and from flying bombs. Churchill
Was mortified, truly a bitter pill.

Calais or Normandy?

The allies were ready, for good or ill,
To go. The German Commander-in-Chief,
Gerd von Rundstedt, was firm in his belief
That the enemy would land at Calais.

Rommel, greatly to von Rundstedt's dismay,
Disagreed. They differed on strategy,
Too. Rommel wished to face the enemy
On the beaches, to go on the attack.
His superior preferred to hold back,
Build up a reserve and consolidate.

The first rule of war: never hesitate.
Sure, in any case, the allies would wait,
Owing (as we've seen) to adverse weather,
Both commanders missed out altogether.
Not a question of 'where', but 'whether'
The allied invasion would take place,
Their state of readiness was a disgrace.

The German commander in Normandy
Was off on manoeuvres in Brittany,
While we're told (don't laugh) that his deputy
Was spending the night with his paramour.
No way to impress the Führer, for sure,
And certainly no way to win a war.

Ready to go...

Overlord's departure points stretched the length
Of England's southern coast. In massive strength
The troops assembled: from Falmouth, Dartmouth,
Weymouth and Southampton, through to Portsmouth
And Newhaven. There were jitters, of course,
But this was a fit, well-drilled fighting force.

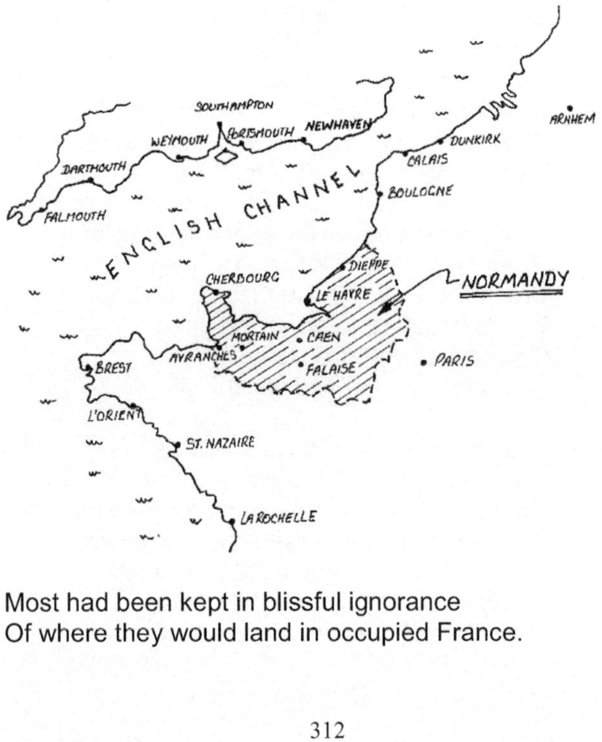

Most had been kept in blissful ignorance
Of where they would land in occupied France.

Officers and NCOs were aware,
But nobody else, of precisely where.
If the truth be told, they didn't much care.
After days of waiting, their one nightmare
Was further delay. It is my belief
That a huge collective sigh of relief
Went up as they came at last to embark.

Not for long. It was chilly. It was dark.
Each man had been served a hearty breakfast.
Soon their stomachs were churning. They were cursed
With seasickness. Let Hitler do his worst,
With their landing craft awash with vomit,
Did they dread coming ashore? Far from it!
Dry land, whether in Timbuktu or France,
Was better than this. They would take their chance.

The five beachheads

The beaches, from west to east, were 'Utah',
So-called, for the US, and 'Omaha';
Then 'Gold', 'Juno', and 'Sword' for the British
And Canadians. Fight to the finish!

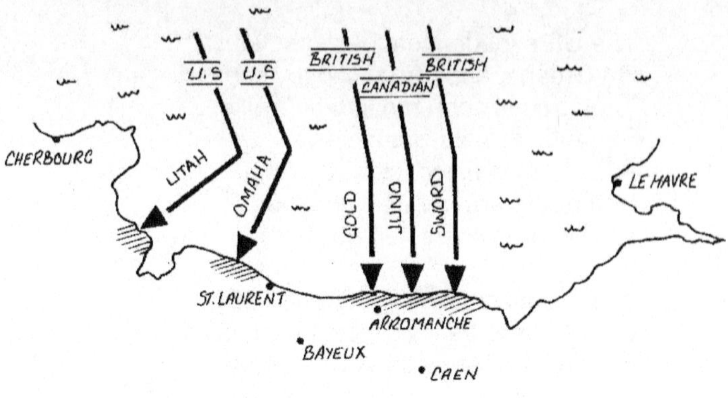

This was the resolve of the brave allies.
The landings came as a nasty surprise
To the Germans. Many came from the air.
More than 20,000, to the despair
Of the *Luftwaffe*, dropped behind the lines
By parachute. One of the clearest signs
Of the enemy's unpreparedness,
On D-Day, was their evident weakness
In defence. These parachutists were key
To the allies' aggressive strategy.
The majority of them would be lost.
Anticipated deaths (an awesome cost)
Were seven in ten. Intrepid? You bet.
For these predictions were sadly met.

A devastating naval bombardment,
Twinned with a massive air assault, was meant,
At the very least, to provide cover
For the allied troops. Soon to recover,
The furious Germans, though stupefied,
Aghast and amazed, quickly fortified
Their defences and began to fight back.

Omaha and Utah

The US experienced the worst flak.
On Omaha, apart from choppy seas,
Their troops soon ran into difficulties,
Suffering terrible casualties.
A German division, close at hand,
Had newly arrived. The expanse of sand,
Devoid of bunkers, left nowhere to hide.

It took until nightfall to stem the tide.
Losses were heavy. Bodies were piled high.
Hundreds of Americans were to die,

To achieve a beachhead a mere mile deep.
The agony of it. You want to weep.

The beach at Utah, on the other hand,
Boasting a similar expanse of sand,
Proved a more favourable place to land.
Prisoners were taken, I understand.
By sunset they had moved five miles inland.

Juno, Sword and Gold

The Canadians had a rough old time
On Juno. These crack forces, in their prime,
Found that the villages along the shore
Had been strongly fortified. Furthermore,
The Germans had contrived a clever maze
Of tunnels. It took a number of days
To establish themselves with confidence.
Yet these heroes still managed to advance,
As did the British on Sword. The high tide
Slowed the Brits down, while mines on the roadside,
With blazing vehicles blocking their path,
Had threatened a veritable bloodbath.

But the Germans (wrong-footed, remember)
Evinced a readiness to surrender.
So fighting on Sword proved rather shorter
Than expected. Given little quarter,
However, on Gold, one battalion,
Taken by surprise, had to battle on
For eight hours before making progress.
Another took twenty minutes (or less)
To move inland from the beach. You can see,
Then, that fortunes were mixed. The enemy
Were no walkover, that's a certainty,
Nor had they ever been likely to be.

By midnight on that first day, finally,
150,000 or more
Had somehow or other made it ashore.
The massive losses I deeply deplore:
Well over 8,000 casualties.
The Germans, apparently on their knees,
Had been forced back from the beaches (all five).
The Nazis, though, were still very much alive.

Churchill and the King

The PM, an unpredictable man,
Announced a bizarre and fanciful plan
To be among the first to land in France
On D-Day. His advisers looked askance
At this mad proposal, needless to say,
But Churchill insisted, as was his way.
His Chief Staff Officer, Hastings Ismay,
Was horrified and expressed his dismay.
This was sheer lunacy. But don't be fooled,
Churchill would never have been overruled
Had it not been for the King. For George, too,
Was itching to go. I mean, wouldn't you?
He made plans for the crossing, then withdrew,
Advised by his private secretary,
Lascelles, that no gift to the enemy
Would be greater than the loss of the King.

So George turned his mind to discouraging
Churchill. His argument was compelling.
The King, as the PM was well aware,
Was head of the Services. Was it fair –
Here George expressed himself most tactfully –
"That you should then go and do exactly
"What I should have liked to do myself?" So,
Thanks to the King, he opted not to go.

He toured the beaches six days later, though,
Taking lunch at Montgomery's HQ.

Ten days after the landings King George, too,
Visited Normandy. One of the few,
He also flew over to Italy,
Where the allied armies, more's the pity,
Were half-forgotten. As progress was made
In France, the southern campaign, I'm afraid,
Had been most unfairly left in the shade.

Allied progress

D-Day+1: the first priority
For keeping ahead of the enemy
Was the speedy build-up of troops, supplies
And vehicles. Before their very eyes,

Men watched the Mulberries towed into place.
Forces then poured in at a rapid pace.

Daily landings of troops, on average,
Numbered 35,000. Blockages
On roads inland, by D-Day+7,
Extended for fifteen miles. Great Heaven!
Traffic jams! Whoever would have thought it?
Whatever was needed, the ships brought it:
25,000 tons of stores per day;
5,000 vehicles… I have to say,
The Mulberries were the key to success,
One at Saint-Laurent for the US,
One at Arromanches for the British –
Allied lifelines from start to finish.

The Germans increased their strength in defence,
Though on Hitler's orders (which made no sense)
Seven available divisions
Were held back, one of those decisions
That gave some necessary breathing space
To the allies. For fear of losing face,
The Nazis fought hard to avoid disgrace
With the result that the allies' advance
Was frustratingly slow through northern France.

They made steady headway, nevertheless,
And were celebrating modest success
By June the 12th. All five beaches, no less,
Had been linked. The allies were well on song.
An area over sixty miles long
And twenty deep had now been occupied.
Their forces were well-armed and well-supplied.

Yet Eisenhower was far from dewy-eyed.
Ike, to his credit, was a realist:
The Führer still ruled with an iron fist.

Charles de Gaulle

For this was a most destructive campaign.
The people of Normandy suffered pain,
Ruin and loss. Bayeux, at any rate,
Gave the French one reason to celebrate.

For this ancient, medieval town –
Home of the great tapestry of renown –
Escaped relatively unscathed. De Gaulle,
The most famous 'Free Frenchman' of them all,
Arrived in Bayeux on the 14th of June,
The very first time (not a moment too soon)
That the General had set foot in France
Since June, 1940. He took his chance,
Championed the Free French and took his place.
In history. Pétain* was a disgrace.

---

*Pétain, tried and convicted of treason
After the war (with very good reason),
Was spared death. Later General de Gaulle
Summed up the Marshal's life, after his fall.
His course had been "successively banal,
"Then glorious" (generous words from Charles),
"Then deplorable, but never" (he said)
"Mediocre". Pétain died in his bed,
Aged ninety-five. "Glorious"? This was fair.
For Pétain, as you may not be aware,
Was a man of great military flair,
The undisputed hero of Verdun,
The bloodiest battle, all said and done
(Saving Loos and the Somme), of World War One.
Vichy was Pétain's ultimate downfall.
Puppet of the Nazis. That says it all.

More bad weather

Terrible Channel weather struck again
On June the 19th, stalling the campaign.
In the worst summer storms for forty years
The Mulberries were battered, raising fears
That all the recent gains would be reversed.

The foul conditions were roundly cursed,
As massive waves threatened to do their worst.
With grave damage to vital equipment,
Supplies were down by some eighty *per cent*.
Yet the harbours managed to take the strain…
Just. The traffic began rolling again
Sooner than expected. Three hearty cheers
For the brilliant British engineers!
Imagine, had they lost a Mulberry,
The scale of the vulnerability
Of the allies. A sense of urgency
Overtook Eisenhower. Out of sorts
During the storm, he knew that other ports
Were fundamental to the allied plan.
The Mulberries, so the argument ran,
Were the first ports of call (pardon the pun).
Cherbourg was priority number one.

Surrender of the Cherbourg garrison

Eisenhower made it his business
To make this an American success.
By June the 19th, they had made progress
Up the Cherbourg peninsula. The port
Held out strongly, but the Germans were caught.
The die was cast however hard they fought.
The garrison at Cherbourg surrendered
On the 26th, a date remembered
As marking the first major objective
To be captured since D-Day. Effective,
Focused and fearless, Dwight D. Eisenhower
Gave notice to the world of US power.

This was a cruel blow, without a doubt,
To the Führer's vain hope of holding out
In northern France: the crisis of the war.
25,000 prisoners or more
Were rounded up, including, to his shame,
The new commander of Cherbourg – by name,
Karl-Wilhelm von Schlieben. Most of the blame,
Though, fell on General Friedrich Dollmann,
The army commander. A broken man –
The Führer had long ceased to be a fan –
On the 29th of June, Dollmann died.
A heart attack? Or was it suicide?
He faced a court martial. You decide.

The port of Cherbourg was thoroughly wrecked
By the Germans – bombed, as you might expect,
And ruined. It was later in July
That the port became a source of supply,
And then only of limited value.
It was nonetheless a brilliant *coup.*
The Nazis suffered a severe whipping.
Cherbourg was open to allied shipping

By late August. Supplies came rolling in.
This was to prove a very useful win.

Montgomery's hesitant advance

Further to the east the British 'kingpin'
(Self-styled), General Montgomery,
Had his work cut out. He'd advanced slowly –
Too slowly was the American view.
The British would have had far less to do
Had they not dallied till the afternoon
Of D-Day on the beaches. All too soon
The Germans had built up their defences.

This was hardly the worst of offences
On Monty's part. It was part of his plan,
As the US drive on Cherbourg began –
At least so he said; should we trust the man? –
To keep Hitler's men away from the west.
This worked, as Monty did his level best
To engage the Germans at Caen. The test,
When it came, was long, relentless and hard.

Caen

Caen suffered terribly in this regard.
For German forces bound for the beachhead,
This was a key strategic base. Instead,
They found themselves under mounting attack
From the British, who seemed to have the knack,
When it suited them, of blasting a town
To smithereens. For Caen came crashing down.

With 8,000 tons of high explosive,
Dropped from 2,000 bombers, as I live,
It's not surprising something had to give.

Half of Caen was destroyed, at fearful cost:
Several thousand civilians lost –
Killed or wounded. If I'm not mistaken,
This was the worst assault undertaken
In support of ground forces in the war.
The world at large would have been in uproar
Had they known about it at the time.
Did the bombings amount to a war crime?
Who knows? They were claimed to be crucial.

Caen became known as 'the Crucible':
Little more than a bomb crater – rubble,
Smoke and ruin. Was Monty in trouble?
Far from it. For everybody knew,
Bar the ranks of the pessimistic few,
There was nothing now that Hitler could do
To win the war. Indeed, von Rundstedt's view
Was that hostilities should be ended.
This course he recklessly recommended
To the Führer! He was promptly dismissed.

Apparently, though, he must have been missed,
Reinstated as Commander-in-Chief
In the west within months. Beyond belief.
In March, '45, he was sacked again.
The reasons for this are hard to explain.
Von Rundstedt, it seems, was simply replaced
(By Kesselring), but was never disgraced.*

---

*He referred to Hitler, so I've heard tell,
As "that Bohemian corporal". Well,
That took some spirit, I do have to say,
Though the Führer knew he did anyway!
"Yes, but he's my best Field Marshal by far,"
He's quoted as saying. So, there you are.

Rommel's dismissal

Not only von Rundstedt, but Rommel too
(The famous 'Desert Fox') was of the view
That Hitler should bring the war to an end.
He told him so and it's hard to pretend
That the Führer was happy. However,
Hitler knew it would be none too clever
To dismiss Rommel, a Nazi hero.

In Normandy a fighter, flying low,
Spotted Rommel's car on the road below
And fired. The 17th of July
Was the date. Rommel wasn't killed (nice try),
But was badly injured, nevertheless.
He was forced to go home to convalesce.

The plot to assassinate Hitler

Three days later (events were moving fast),
A plot to kill Hitler appeared, at last,
To have been successful. Sadly, not so.
To conclude Erwin Rommel's tale of woe,
Hitler believed he was implicated.

The picture is rather complicated,
But Rommel was thought to have made contact
With the conspirators. What Hitler lacked
Was evidence. This had not in the past
Stopped him! But the public would be aghast
Should their favourite face execution,
Trial or no trial. The solution,
It did not take Hitler long to decide,
Was a choice between death by suicide
And a trial before the 'People's Court'.
Field Marshal Rommel, as he knew he ought,

Chose the former – rather more dignified,
For his money, to swallow cyanide,
Than be dragged before a kangaroo court
To be sentenced to death. As Hitler thought,
Rommel took the 'honourable' way out.
For the Führer himself, without a doubt,
This was a relief. Rommel, if you please,
Died, it was announced, of his injuries,
Sustained under fire in Normandy.
Hitler paid his debt to him, formally,
With a state funeral. Hypocrisy?
Well, I've heard of humbug, but honestly!

Claus von Stauffenberg

The young leader of the abortive plot
Was Claus von Stauffenberg. Like it or not,
Claus took part in the occupation
Of Poland. The colonisation
Of that poor unfortunate nation
Was "essential". The invasion
Of Russia he also supported.
At the highest level he consorted
With the Nazis. His reputation
For courage was an inspiration.
In Rommel's dangerous desert campaign
He lost his left eye (imagine the pain),
His right hand and two fingers of his left.
To his credit, Claus was far from bereft.
He'd never really known, he confessed,
What to do with ten fingers! At his best,
Von Stauffenberg could be a witty man.

Given his record, I am no great fan.
He was prey to the vile racist views
Of the Nazis. Yet the plight of the Jews

Began to offend his sense of justice.
Regrettably, though, it was not just this
That fed his hostile and bitter instincts
Against the Führer. His record still stinks.
Following D-Day, von Stauffenberg knew –
His thinking was shared by more than a few –
That the war was lost. The case for a *coup*
Was overwhelming. Hitler had to die,
Then the allies (this was pie in the sky)
Would negotiate an end to the war
In the west. Was he mad or what? There's more:
The Russian campaign would continue!

Von Stauffenberg (this is only my view)
Was a fantasist. Be that as it may,
He plotted to kill the Führer. The day?
July the 20th. He had access –
This was a prerequisite of success –
To Hitler in person, one of the few.
For the Führer's circle, his retinue,
Was tiny. He never went walkabout.
Assassination attempts were 'out'
As far as common Germans were concerned,
This a direct result of lessons learned
From earlier botched plots. A trusted aide,
Claus had shown courage. The case was made.
In his presence Hitler was unafraid.

The fateful day

To *Wolfsschanze*, the Führer's private 'Wolf's Lair',
Near Rastenburg (East Prussia). It was there
That Claus von Stauffenberg would do the deed.
With two bombs (the second in case of need)
He arrived at a top-level meeting.
This had been moved, due to overheating,

From its usual place (built of concrete)
To a wooden structure. This would defeat
Von Stauffenberg's objective, for the force
Of the blast was dissipated, of course,
As the walls of the room were blown out.

Hitler would have died, no shadow of doubt,
Had the crucial meeting taken place
In his concrete bunker. Claus's briefcase
Contained both bombs. All he now had to do
Was prepare them. He went off to the loo.

Priming two bombs is hard, I assure you,
With three fingers. He had done just the one
When he was summoned. The talks had begun.
He'd been missed. He put the case on the floor,
Close to Hitler's chair (he could do no more),
Then managed quietly to slip away…
He heard a massive blast. He'd won the day.

Hitler survives the blast

He later learned, to his utter dismay,
That the Führer lived. Claus had made his way
To Berlin, certain that Hitler was dead.
No one could survive such a blast, he said.
The crucial briefcase had been moved, though,
For no good reason (as far as we know),
Behind a table leg, further away
From its target. This, I regret to say,
Weakened the massive impact of the blast.

Claus arrived in Berlin. He was aghast
When he heard the news. There was little doubt
The game was up. Poor man, he was dragged out,
After a makeshift court martial, and shot –
One of the lucky ones. Another lot,
Co-conspirators (yes, there were a few)
Were 'tried' and condemned to death (nothing new)
By hanging... What exactly did they do,
The executioners? I tell you,
It was not pleasant. I shall draw a veil,
For once, over the grisly detail.

A film showing their final agony
Was enjoyed by Hitler. What staggers me
Is that this, the only viable plot
Against his life, collapsed. A craven lot,
The Nazis. They were cowards to a man.
The Führer was weaker, so rumour ran,
Following his narrow escape from death.
Yet were there further attempts? Spare your breath.
Though many opposed him, nobody dared.
Murderers... bullies... they were far too scared.

After the war Hitler's secretary,
Traudl Junge, recalled: "He looked funny...

"His hair stood up like a brush." He'd survived,
Nonetheless, and very quickly revived.
"His trousers were slit in small stripes. 'You see,'
"Hitler said" (this I find rather scary,
The words of a madman) " 'my fate has saved me
" ' For my mission.' " (he'd lost it completely)
" 'I am now to do what I must do'." Well,
The Führer would give his opponents hell,
Whether or not they were implicated.

Some 5,000, it's been estimated,
Were to suffer cruelly in the purge.
A prime excuse. When Hitler felt the urge,
Watch out! It all sprung from fear, of course,
But he showed not a single shred of remorse.

The Führer's decline

The plot left the Führer a damaged man.
From now on a steady decline began
In his physical health. It's hard to tell
If his mind began to decay as well,
For he'd always been implacably bad,
Not to be trusted and thoroughly mad.
Now at least there was comfort to be had
From the fact the Führer was far from fit.
In short, Adolf Hitler was losing it.

Rapid progress across France

Back to the campaign. The US success
After Cherbourg continued to impress.
They swept rapidly across from the west,
Before meeting stiff resistance at Brest,
The Brittany port. This was fortified
More strongly than expected. Many died

In the assault. It was only taken
After a month. The Germans were shaken,
But managed to hold on to La Rochelle –
Lorient, too, and Saint-Nazaire as well –
Until the end of the war. Nonetheless,
The Americans enjoyed more success
Inland. The rest of Brittany, no less,
Was theirs within weeks. Further to the east,
Nazi resistance effectively ceased
This side of Mortain. This was a surprise.
US forces could not believe their eyes:
No Germans at all! There was little doubt
The French Resistance had driven them out.

Was the US thrust not necessary?
A fair question. Very possibly,
Yet once the Nazis had been sent packing,
Who cared? For the French had US backing –
On the whole, at least. All that was lacking
Was a comprehensive German collapse.
This was far too much to hope for, perhaps,
For the progress made in those early days
Suffered a major setback at Falaise.

Temporary German recovery

Hitler was livid. The German malaise,
As he saw it, must be halted. Advance,
He ordered, west – to cut off (at Avranches)
US lines of communication.
An impossible operation!
German tanks: one hundred and forty-five.
Allied tanks: some two thousand. Saints alive!

The Germans edged back west, beyond Falaise,
Then stuck at Mortain. Some say, courage pays.

Well, not in this particular instance.
The move, made at the Führer's insistence,
Led his forces into an allied trap.
US General Patton, a sound chap,
Approached from the south, while Montgomery
Moved in from the north. Anyone could see
That the outcome of this pincer attack
Would be to form a sort of net, or sack.
The enemy would soon be on the rack:
No means of launching a counterattack
And no way of escape, no going back.

The Germans trapped

That was the theory at any rate.
Communications were less than great
Between the British and Canadians
(On the one part) and the Americans.
The Brits were blamed for being way too slow
And letting many escape. Who's to know?
Monty was being careful. Even so,
By the time the neck of the sack was 'tied',
Trapping the Germans, 10,000 had died.
50,000 prisoners were taken.

The German command was badly shaken.
Field Marshal Günther von Kluge, ashamed,
Guilt-ridden and demoralised, was blamed
For the catastrophe, the worst, some said,
Since Stalingrad. Within days he was dead.
The Führer feared he might negotiate
A surrender. Kluge did not hesitate.
Hitler, he was sure, would give him a rough ride.
Like Rommel before him, he chose suicide.

There was friction, though, within the allies.
Hordes of German troops, before their very eyes,

Managed to escape – 40,000, we're told,
An impressive number. Far from overbold
(An understatement), Bernard Montgomery
Was charged with allowing the enemy
To escape, with their equipment, scot-free
Before the neck of the sack had been closed.
The US, it can only be supposed,
Were disappointed, resentful and bitter.
Under General Patton (a big hitter),
Their troops had proved themselves quicker and fitter
Than the British. This was only the first
Of future fallouts, though perhaps the worst.

Falaise earned for itself the chilling name
The 'killing field'. Carnage… some claim to fame.

The liberation of Paris

Parisians sensed that liberation
Was at hand. The four years' occupation
And the curse of Nazi domination
Would soon be over. The situation
Was complex. Eisenhower's intention –
And that of FDR, I should mention –
When it came to Paris had been to bypass
The capital. The American top brass
Agreed. Paris would slow down allied progress.

The President, it seems, could not have cared less
For de Gaulle. Later he was forced to confess
That this was an error. Be that as it may,
Le Général, determined to have his day,
Inspired Parisians, as was his way,
To action. To Eisenhower's dismay
The Americans had no choice, after all,
But to join forces with General de Gaulle

To liberate Paris. The Germans pulled out,
Their flight from the capital never in doubt.

The 25th of August: the surrender
Of the 'governor', a day to remember.

The Führer had ordered the destruction
Of Paris. Ignoring this instruction,
General von Choltitz handed the city
To de Gaulle. In a spirit of unity,
The Communists backed the Free French. Even so,
It took some weeks before this long tale of woe
Was over. Thousands of collaborators
Were hunted down, Nazi fellow travellers,
Even some old Communists and that's a fact,
Supporters of the Nazi-Soviet Pact.

Some 10,000 were executed, we're told.
They were shown no mercy. The blood runs cold.

'Operation Anvil'

Nor was the allied campaign at a standstill
In southern France. 'Operation Anvil',
So-called (now renamed, for some reason, 'Dragoon'),
Landed hordes of troops, not a moment too soon,
Between Marseilles and Nice, on the Côte d'Azur.
The invasion was useless, to be sure,
In military terms for winning the war.
The Germans were on the run in any case.
They knew they were staring defeat in the face.

The landings in the south were of consequence,
Nonetheless. To Eisenhower it made sense
To draw the focus away from Italy.
One in the eye for the Brits, more's the pity.

These tidings also suited the Führer fine.
He now moved three divisions to the Rhine,
From Italy. Although Anvil was opposed
By the British, more favourably disposed
Were the French. The Republic might have been bled
To death had not the occupiers fled.
There was less time for the Nazis to rape,
Ravage and ruin. A lucky escape.

Romania changes sides and Bulgaria quits

The weeks of August, 1944,
Were charged with joy and hope. For there was more.
The very day Paris was liberated,
Romania in the east celebrated…
By changing sides. Hitler's oil supply
Disappeared at a stroke. Hard to deny,
A near-terminal blow. Only a few,
Toadies and acolytes, were of the view
That the war could possibly continue.

The Bulgarians had quit the field too,
Having left the Axis. The Finns (mark this)
Were negotiating an armistice
With Russia. Bad news everywhere
For the Germans. But did Hitler despair?
Amazing to say, apparently not.
He believed deep down he could stop the rot…
Or did he? Who knows what went on in the brain
Of this madman? Certifiably insane.

All over by Christmas?

The allies had achieved gain after gain.
Their swift progress was easy to explain:
A smart campaign and a German collapse.
The war would even be over, perhaps,
By Christmas. They were optimistic chaps,
The allies. Their troops could see at a glance,
Now the greater part of occupied France,
And Belgium, had been liberated,
That the war was won. Few hesitated,
Even the cautious Montgomery,
In predicting a speedy victory,
The home straight ahead of them already.

For the German defeat had been heavy
In France: forty-five divisions smashed,
Well in excess of 2,000 tanks trashed
And half a million German troops lost.
Now all that was left was to count the cost.

Few could deny the allies were on song,
Yet wiser heads had advised all along
That the best-laid plans could go badly wrong.
German resistance in places was strong.
They held out doggedly, but for how long?
Good question. Longer than expected!

Eisenhower in the ascendant

One seminal change which all respected
With the sole exception of Monty –
His nose put out of joint, quite possibly –
Was the assumption by Eisenhower,
Not before time, of sole personal power
Over the combined land forces, US
And British. Three fifths, remember (no less),
Of the two million allied forces
In France were American. Resources,
Supplies and vehicles, as well as men –
Most hailed from the United States. Who, then,
Could grumble if the war was US-led?
Monty should have kept his mouth shut. Instead,
The Field Marshal (recently appointed)
Expressed himself sorely disappointed
At his 'demotion', as he saw it.

Ike's caution

Take note, then, of how ill Monty bore it.
For Ike disagreed with him, most strongly,
On fundamental allied policy
Regarding the advance on Germany.
Monty nursed a near-manic certainty
That with one sharp thrust the war could be won.
The Nazis would be utterly undone
By a single attack behind the Ruhr,
Cutting off Germany's forces, for sure,
In Holland. He would cross the lower Rhine
In three places – as a theory, fine,
But nowhere near as simple in practice.

Eisenhower was unhappy with this.
An opportunity too good to miss
Or too clever by half? Far too reckless,

In his opinion. A broader front
He preferred. The Germans should bear the brunt
Of an assault the whole length of the Rhine.
Patience and caution would combine
To make a breakthrough more likely. What's more,
The Saar region, as well as the Ruhr,
Would be a plum target for the allies.

Monty put in his place

Monty reckoned Ike was taking the rise!
At one key meeting he got rather cross
And launched into a tirade. "I'm your boss,"
Eisenhower pointed out quietly,
Gently putting his hand on Monty's knee,
"You cannot speak to me like that." Monty,
At least, had the good grace to say sorry.
Whether he meant it or not, who's to say?

Somewhat, though, to Eisenhower's dismay,
Both plans in tandem would carry the day.
Pressurised from London, Ike said, "okay",
So Bernard Montgomery got his way.

Petrol shortages were causing delay.
This was a headache. The allied advance,
Impressively swift through occupied France,
Was slowing down. Outrunning their supplies:
The age-old problem. To no one's surprise,
Petrol trucks stretched back to the far reaches,
Miles away, of the Normandy beaches.

The Channel ports

Hitler still held the ports along the coast.
These were places the allies needed most:
Le Havre and Dieppe, Boulogne, Calais
And Dunkirk. Recklessly, as was his way,
The Führer ordered that these 'fortresses'
Should be defended. Modest successes
The allies achieved. Hitler was annoyed
That Dieppe, rather than being destroyed,
Fell to Canadian forces, deployed
Under Monty's command. Deliveries
Of petrol and oil, over the seas,
Began within days. On the other hand,
Le Havre, we're given to understand,
Under bombardment from land, sea and air
By the allies, took an age to repair.

Calais did not take long to surrender.
The town fell at the end of September,
As did Boulogne, under relentless fire.
As a working port, the outlook was dire.
By the time allied forces reached Dunkirk
The Germans had done their own dirty work,

And destroyed it. The place could not be saved,
So was abandoned. The Germans behaved
According to Hitler's orders. Depraved?
Well, to have left a Channel port intact
Would have smacked of folly and that's a fact.

On September the 7th, at long last,
Monty could plan his advance. As forecast
By Eisenhower and the doubters though,
Resistance was strong and progress was slow.
Brussels had been taken four days before,
And Antwerp the following day. The war,
Surely, would soon be coming to an end.

Disaster at Arnhem

This was too optimistic (why pretend?).
Monty advanced just ten miles in four days.
The Germans dug in. Tenacity pays.
The allies were no longer in pursuit,
But again under attack. Resolute
And refreshed, the enemy were ready.
Monty, normally composed and steady,
Wanted to be the first across the Rhine.
His tail was up, but where to draw the line?

On the 17th, the advance began.
To drop forces in Arnhem was the plan,
North of the Rhine, by air, having taken
Three bridges (if I am not mistaken,
Over the Maas, the Waal and the Nederrijn),
In order to bypass the 'Siegfried Line'
And sweep down to attack the Ruhr. Sadly,
From the very outset, things went badly.

The weather was poor. The parachute drop
In the Arnhem area was a flop,

Some troops landing up to eight miles away.
At Arnhem, to Montgomery's dismay,
It happened that a Nazi exercise
Was in full swing, an unpleasant surprise.
Poor radio communications
Played a part, as did strained relations
Between the British troops and the US.
Arnhem, in short, was a terrible mess.

To Monty's considerable distress,
On the 27th of September
Hundreds of Brits were forced to surrender
(A disaster) at the Arnhem bridgehead.
Hopes of victory by Christmas were dead.

6,000 allied prisoners of war
Were taken. 2,000, this I deplore,
Lost their lives in the fighting. Monty's plan
Was in ruins. A self-satisfied man,
Montgomery was always in the right.
Arnhem had been a simple oversight.

Code-breaking at Bletchley Park

The British people were kept in the dark
(Very hush-hush) regarding Bletchley Park.

'Ultra secret' were its works – code-breaking
And intelligence. There's no mistaking
Its vital role. For GC&CS,*
At Bletchley, was a brilliant success.
According to some, its activities
May well have shortened the hostilities
By two to three years. The casualties,
Imagine, had the war dragged on that long!
Some tens of millions or am I wrong?

Mathematicians were best suited
To code-breaking work. They were recruited
From Oxford ("men of the professor type")
And Cambridge. Also, when the time was ripe,
They were joined by proficient linguists
(In German and Japanese), physicists
And humble, but essential, typists.
Staff numbered a mere hundred and fifty
(A rough estimate) initially.
This figure was to increase rapidly,
Until, in the final days of the war,
There were 10,000 people, maybe more,
Working for the organisation.

In '41, there was occasion
For complaint. A group of the code-breakers –
Deeply concerned, far from trouble-makers,
The modest Alan Turing among them –
Wrote an urgent letter to the PM:
They were starved of resources. Such ructions
Were rare. Churchill issued swift instructions:
"Action this day!" he wrote. "Priority!
"Make sure they have all they want. Report to me
"That this has been done." Immediately,
The concerns of the 'boffins' were addressed.
Their bosses pulled out all the stops. I'm impressed.

---

*The Government Code and Cypher School.
I prefer the letters as a rule.
Its successor was GCHQ.
Who knows what that stands for? Very few.
Government Communications
Headquarters. Abbreviations
Are nonetheless better in my view,
So GC&CS will have to do.

The work was critical. Their first break came
When Dilly Knox's team (his claim to fame)
Unlocked the 'green' administrative key,
To Enigma, of the German army.
Having accessed this code successfully,
They cracked that of the *Luftwaffe*, the 'red',
So-called. Success didn't go to their head.
The German navy had tighter controls.
The whereabouts of their wolf-pack patrols
In the Atlantic were hard to locate.
British shipping suffered a dismal fate
After the Nazis toughened up their codes.
It took the Brits ten months to make inroads
Into their four-rotor Enigma. This,
To his credit, Turing made his business.

Breaking the German ciphers at Bletchley
(The Lorenz and Enigma), all agree,
Was vital to the war effort – at sea,
On land and in the air. In Normandy,
Details of Hitler's defence strategy
Were open to the allies, clear to see,
As soon as their codes had been decrypted.
It's almost as if it had been scripted.

The British even confused the Nazis
As to where the allies planned to land. These,
And similar 'surprises', were owing
To strong intelligence. There's no knowing
What the allies would have done without it.
They'd have lost the edge. No doubt about it.

The US valued the intelligence.
Eisenhower (this makes absolute sense)
Said it was "of priceless value to me".
Nobody understood better than he

The importance of sparing allied lives.
Thousands, he declared (the record survives),
Had been saved. The North Africa campaign,
At a critical time of greatest strain,
Could have ended in the loss of Cairo.
General Auchinleck (and he should know)
Thought Rommel might easily have got through
Had it not been for what the allies knew
Of his precise strategy and movements.

Bletchley was ever making improvements
In its systems. The famous 'Bombe' machines –
After brilliant work behind the scenes
By Turing and Gordon Welchman – were key
To identifying the settings, daily,
On the Enigma machines in Germany.

Their pioneering design, most certainly,
Led to the exciting development
Of Colossus, the first experiment
In digital electronic computing.
So, when your computer next needs 'rebooting',
Or is doing updates (however boring),
Spare a moment to think of Alan Turing.

Turing's fate

The great man died in 1954,
Aged just forty-one. I deeply deplore
The way he was treated. Turing was gay,
An abomination in his day.

In 1952 (quite recently),
Turing was charged with gross indecency.
His sentence (this I find hard to forgive),
Offered as a 'simple' alternative

To time in prison, was hormone treatment.
What this 'corrective' effectively meant
Was a sort of chemical castration.
Shame on British justice and the nation.

His punishment was wicked and depraved.
How many lives had Alan Turing saved?
The cruel injustice cuts like a knife.
Turing tragically took his own life,
Sixteen days before he turned forty-two.
He felt there was nothing else he could do.

Prime Minister Brown, in 2009,
Offered a public apology. Well, fine,
But a tad late. In 2013,
He won a posthumous pardon from the Queen.
Now Turing appears on the fifty-pound note.
Enough to keep Britain's conscience afloat?
I should say not. Too little, too late, sadly.
Alan Turing was let down very badly.

Plans for the future on the home front

The allies were clearly winning the war.
At home there was a thirst, by '44,
For reform. Just twenty-six years before,
The Great War had ended. Everyone knows
That far from being a 'land fit for heroes'
Britain became a byword for poverty,
Mass unemployment, want and misery.

All agreed, this time, it was not to be.
Hitler may have left the people reeling,
But now there was a popular feeling
That the peace must be won, not just the war.
If not, there was major trouble in store.

The Beveridge Report of '42
(A best seller) caused a mighty to-do
In Conservative circles. Insurance,
From cradle to grave? Beyond endurance!
Far too expensive; socialist to boot.

Its proposals were not designed to suit
The PM. Churchill was a slow learner
When it came to reform. The back burner,
That's where the Report, unfortunately,
Was destined. It would be up to Attlee,

In 1945, to breathe new life
Into Beveridge. Discontent was rife,
Nonetheless, even among some Tories,
When the Report was dropped. There were stories
Of potential rebels in the ranks.
These came to nothing. Rock the boat? No thanks.

The 1944 Education Act

Education, as far as one knows,
Was less likely to get up Churchill's nose
Or to tread on sensitive Tory toes.
Whether that's true, I'll leave you to decide.

R. A. Butler enjoyed an easy ride
With his breakthrough Education Bill.
Why didn't Labour go in for the kill?*
Because this was a reform to treasure,
That's why – a timely, progressive measure,
Designed to extend opportunities
To all classes and all communities.

Local Education Authorities
Were obliged (for the first time, if you please)
To provide, without charging any fees,
New levels of schooling. The primaries
(Five to eleven) and the secondaries
(To fifteen) replaced the elementaries
(Five to fourteen). 'Further education'
Was included, affording the nation

---

*The party was in coalition,
Of course – a delicate position
Had its members chosen to oppose it.
They didn't. In fact, quite the opposite.

A three-tier system. The secondaries –
This one of the less enlightened policies –
Were subdivided into grammar schools
And secondary moderns. The new rules
Allowed selection, unfortunately –
An exam to assess the ability
Of all candidates. Nobody caused a fuss,
Alas, over the dreaded eleven-plus.
Some eighty *per cent* were deprived of their dream,
Four fifths relegated to a lower 'stream'.

Nonetheless, the new Education Act,
Piloted through the House of Commons with tact,
Skill and great political intelligence,
Was a huge leap forward. It simply made sense.

A health service? What a load of old nonsense!
The BMA made not the slightest pretence
Of its horror. Health would sadly have to wait
Until July the 5th, 1948.
Remember, if you will, that glorious date.

Major Russian advances

The brave Russians were making progress
On every front. To settle for less
Than complete, all-out victory… No thanks!
With 30,000 guns, 5,000 tanks
And 160 divisions,
One of the Red Army's best decisions
Was to face the Germans at their strongest point,
Viz. the centre. Their troops did not disappoint.
With newly restored vigour, energy
And nerve, they surrounded the enemy
At Minsk. The Nazi resistance was poor.
It was clear they couldn't take any more.

Estonia, Latvia and Lithuania

100,000 prisoners of war
Were rounded up. To the north, Latvia
Was cleared of Germans, Lithuania
Was 'liberated' and Estonia
Recaptured. To the south, Romania
Had raised the white flag, while Bulgaria,
Her neighbour, had collapsed under the strain.
Most significant of all, the Ukraine
Had been freed and was Russia's again.

Germany was now clearly on the ropes,
A country of broken dreams and dashed hopes.
Over half a million Germans died,
In three short months, at the front. Horrified
As they were, back home in the Fatherland
Folk supported Hitler, we understand,
In his iron resolve to carry on.
For the people felt far from put upon.
The Führer still promised them victory
So they fought to the end, more's the pity,
And Germany's violent history
Was set to continue. A tragedy,
However, on an even greater scale
Was soon to unfold, a most sorry tale.

Poland

The Poles had ever been beyond the pale,
In Stalin's opinion; Hitler's, too.
Here's a good question: what do you do
When stuck between a rock and a hard place?

The fate of the Poles has been a disgrace
Throughout history, I'm ashamed to say.
From September the 1st, that fateful day

The Second World War

In '39 when Hitler did his worst,
To the end of the war the Poles were cursed –
And long after that if the truth be told.
Germans... or Russians...? The blood runs cold.

The facts. By August, 1944,
The Russians were knocking at the door
Of Poland's capital city, Warsaw.
The Red Army already occupied
The eastern half of Poland. For the tide
Was turning. The Germans were moving out.
The Poles were nervous, no shadow of doubt,
Of the Red Army. The Hitler-Stalin Pact
Had granted Russia (a sobering fact)
The part the 'invaders' occupied now.
They feared the consequence of this, and how.

The Polish government in exile
In London was strongly resolved, the while,
To establish its presence in Warsaw
In order to assert itself *before*
The Russians arrived. A new Poland
Would greet Stalin's forces, you understand,
As an army of liberation,
Rather than one of occupation.

So far, so good. The Russians, it seems,
Were quite accommodating. In your dreams!
As the German forces prepared to leave,
The Russians broadcast (can you believe?)
To urge the Polish Resistance to rise
Against the Nazis. Well, surprise, surprise!
The Red Army advance ran out of steam
As the Resistance surfaced. End of dream...

Or was it? The Poles were now on their own,
But the Nazis could still be overthrown,

Or so they believed. On August the 1st,
Warsaw was ready and the bubble burst.

The Polish Home Army

The Polish Resistance movement was strong.
For five painful years it had laboured long
For this moment. Communications,
Command structures, key preparations
For the manufacture of armaments,
Boy scouts as messengers… It all made sense.

The Polish Home Army, as it was called,
Was 400,000 strong. When it stalled,
As it sadly did, it was all owing
To Stalin. Why? There's no way of knowing,
For sure, but Uncle Joe could never trust
These Polish 'bandits'. Their dreams turned to dust
As Stalin sat on his hands. Now it's true,
His army (we know this is nothing new)
Had outrun its supplies. It had to rest.
But Stalin refused (this the acid test)
To support a vital allied airlift
To aid the beleaguered Poles. You get the drift?

The brave Polish Resistance got short shrift
From the Russians. Stalin had his eye
Fixed firmly on the future, that was why.

The Warsaw uprising

Some 200,000 Poles were to die
In the course of the Warsaw uprising.
The Führer (this is hardly surprising,
Once he had twigged what Stalin was doing –
Not doing, rather) ordered the SS
To crush the uprising. With ruthlessness,

Malice and considerable relish –
An image that Hitler was to cherish –
The Germans bombed Warsaw to smithereens.
This, be assured, is what tyranny means.

The Germans deployed their great siege gun 'Thor',
One of the deadliest of the whole war,
Each shell weighing over two tons. Hopeless
Was the struggle. The Poles had to confess
It was time to draw a halt. No one cared.
The world had forgotten them. They despaired.

The RAF could not fly in supplies
Until Uncle Joe came to realise
That his name was mud among the allies.
He was still not that bothered. For his spies
Told him that the Poles had enough to eat,
Killing horses and dogs (even cats) for meat.

The Resistance had to admit defeat.
The Germans accepted their surrender
'With honour'. Their generals, remember,
Were well aware that they had lost the war.
If they treated the heroes of Warsaw
As partisans, fit for execution,
Many were fearful of retribution
In any future settling of scores
After this, the most terrible of wars.
The spectre of their trial for war crimes
Was soon to loom large, a sign of the times.

Still, before that critical moment came,
Heinrich Himmler (the Nazi hall of fame
Would never boast a more cruel sadist)
Sensed an occasion not to be missed.
Children were murdered for sport, nurses raped,
Then killed, in their hospitals… Few escaped.

The Poles were suddenly very bad news,
Almost as dangerous as Europe's Jews.

Another 'treat' Himmler could not refuse:
Shortly before Warsaw was blown to bits,
65,000 Jews were sent to Auschwitz,
From the capital, to face certain death.

Did the allies intervene? Save your breath.
Some argue it was not that they wouldn't,
But rather, quite simply, that they couldn't.
I'm reminded of '39: a fudge.
Perhaps that's unkind. I'll leave you to judge.

Warsaw destroyed

After Warsaw was evacuated
The whole city was annihilated,
Razed to the ground. So, was Stalin to blame?
Hardly. For it was in the Führer's name,
And Himmler's, that Poland's capital fell –
Warsaw in ruins, an image of hell.

This ancient city laid to waste
Was nevertheless to Stalin's taste.
For the Polish Home Army's defeat
(The 'bandits') made his triumph complete.
An independent Poland? No more!
This heralded, sad to say, the Cold War.

Germany close to collapse

It was clear the Third Reich was on its knees.
Past victories were distant memories.
Yet morale remained surprisingly high
Among the people. It's hard to know why.

Hitler reduced the call-up age (don't laugh,
This is tragic) to sixteen and a half.

Military losses had been heavy.
Himmler announced a recruitment levy,
The *Volkssturm* (a sort of German Home Guard),
With ridiculously little regard
To age or fitness. Young boys and old men,
Over 700,000 of them,
Were recruited. Himmler was on a roll,
The idiot. *Eintopf* (or 'casserole')
These were called, to make his folly complete,
For his army consisted of 'old meat
And green vegetables'. They wore armbands –
There was no uniform one understands.
These poor souls were paraded through Berlin
By Goebbels. There was still a war to win.

The Ardennes: Hitler's final throw

With the Germans now on the defensive,
Hitler would launch no winter offensive,
Of that the allies were sure. They were wrong.

The Führer had been planning, all along,
A huge counterattack through the Ardennes,
Scene of his finest triumph. That was then...
This was now. His last gamble, nonetheless,
Threatened to be a startling success.

His plan was this. Less strongly fortified
By the allies, it could not be denied
That the Ardennes was the ideal place
For a breakthrough. The US (a disgrace)
Had four weak divisions stationed there.

Their strongest units were deployed elsewhere,
Mainly to the south. Soldiers complained
Of boredom, which can only be explained
By the fact that nobody expected
An attack. The region was neglected,
Owing to laziness, complacency
And arrogance. It is easy to see
How this came to pass, but it was folly.

The neglect, of course, suited Hitler fine.
His enemy had still to reach the Rhine.
If his great breakthrough of 1940
Could be repeated (I'll tell you for free,
A victory won in an afternoon),
His troops, inspired by their good fortune,
Would sweep rapidly north, retake Antwerp,
Cut off the British (another Dunkirk)
And win the war! It really could work!

His generals, to a man, were appalled.
Their forces, they knew, would be badly mauled.
Hitler, though, had spoken. Give it a go.
Those were his orders. They could not say no.

The allies taken by surprise

The Germans struck their unexpected blow
On December the 16th. You should know –
It rather sticks in my throat to say so –
That Monty had put in, the day before,
For Christmas leave. Was there trouble in store?
Far from it. Few had their minds on the war.
Monty played some golf (I forget the score).
Ike, in a rare show of emotion,
Was celebrating his promotion
To 5-star General. Later (don't laugh)
He graced the wedding of two of his staff
With his company. At allied HQ,
In Versailles, they'd nothing better to do
Than discuss the tragic air accident
In which Glenn Miller was killed – so recent,
So raw (and equally out of the blue).

When news of the German attack came through,
General Bradley was of the clear view
That this was a mere 'spoiler' (nothing new),
Calculated to increase tension
And distract American attention
From more pressing concerns. I should mention,
In passing, that it was Bradley's privilege
To join Ike in a rubber or two of bridge,
After dinner, before retiring to bed.

The following day, it has to be said,
Bradley was better informed. Ike saw red.

The German advance

The balance of forces favoured Germany,
A menace to the allies, most certainly.
Their strength in divisions numbered thirty –
Ten armoured units and twenty infantry.
These compared with a mere four for the US.
Surprise was the key to their early success.
They were one hundred and thirty miles, or less,
From Antwerp. Poor Bradley was forced to confess
That the allies were in one heck of a mess.

The German advance was swift, relentless
And bewildering. The mass surrender –
An event too painful to remember –
Of 7,000 US troops occurred
In the first few days. Ike, you have my word,
Was furious, but he kept a cool head.
Sidelining Bradley, he ordered instead
Our old chum Monty to take command
Of the forces to the north. Well, I'll be darned!
Against all the odds the Brits were in demand.

To the south, Patton turned his troops about –
By ninety degrees. Ike had little doubt
That the Germans could be fatally trapped
In a pincer move. Their strength would be sapped,
Their morale to boot, by lack of supplies –
They ran out of fuel: surprise, surprise! –
And their weak and inferior manpower.

Patton saves the day

This was General Dwight D. Eisenhower
At his brilliant best. Man of the hour,
However, was Patton. At Ike's behest,
Like his boss he also rose to the test.

He turned his army round on a sixpence.
The General had a kind of sixth sense –
Patton's instincts were as good as any –
That if he could delay the enemy
Until the heavy cloud cover lifted,
The balance would be totally shifted
In the allies' favour. The bad weather
Had forestalled any attack whatever
By US or British planes from the air.
The weather, one pilot said in despair,
Was for days "sitting right on the treetops".

The Ardennes was the mother of all flops
For Hitler nonetheless. On Christmas Eve
The cloud lifted: blue sky, can you believe,
To the allies' delight, on Christmas Day.
Conditions were perfect. Bombs away!

The enemy had made it all the way
(Almost) to the Meuse. To Hitler's dismay,
His troops were sitting ducks. In disarray,
They could only await the great onslaught.
A battle lost, but valiantly fought?
Who can say? For they never stood a chance.
This was Hitler's final gamble for France.*
His top generals could see at a glance
That the war was lost. To the bitter end
The Führer fought on. It's hard to pretend

---

*Most of the Ardennes is in Belgium,
Not France – a classic error made by some.
Yet with France, too, at risk, all I can say
Is it doesn't much matter either way.
In '44, when the Germans attacked,
It was just the Belgian part in fact.

That his pig-headed imbecility
Did not compromise his ability
To defend the Rhine. If he had rested,
Paused and regrouped... Instead, he invested
All his resources, equipment and men
In this ill-fated push through the Ardennes.
Arguably the war came to an end
Six months early. An unscheduled godsend.

Bernard Montgomery strutted about,
Resolved to leave no one in any doubt
That he, Monty, and he alone had won
The battle. Far from a figure of fun,
His desire to take all the credit
Ruffled some feathers. As Churchill read it,
'The Bulge'* was "the greatest" (this he swore)
"American battle of the war".

Another terrible winter

The conditions that winter were tough.
As if fighting alone was not enough,
The men had to endure freezing rain
And heavy snowfall. Imagine the strain.

---

*So-called after the 'bulging' salient
That represented the furthest extent
Of the German advance. The vital town
Of Bastogne won itself lasting renown
As an isolated US 'pocket'
Within the salient. Like a rocket,
Patton raced to the scene. No ifs, no buts,
This small town refused to surrender. "Nuts!"
Was General McAuliffe's reaction,
To Ike's amusement and satisfaction.

15,000 so-called 'cold injuries'
Were reported, instances, if you please,
Of trench foot, pneumonia and frostbite.

With slush and mud by day, and frost by night,
Life was insufferable. Those left alive
By the end of January, '45, **1945**
(The battle over) were lucky to survive.

Over 90,000 US soldiers fell,
Killed, wounded or missing – a veritable hell.

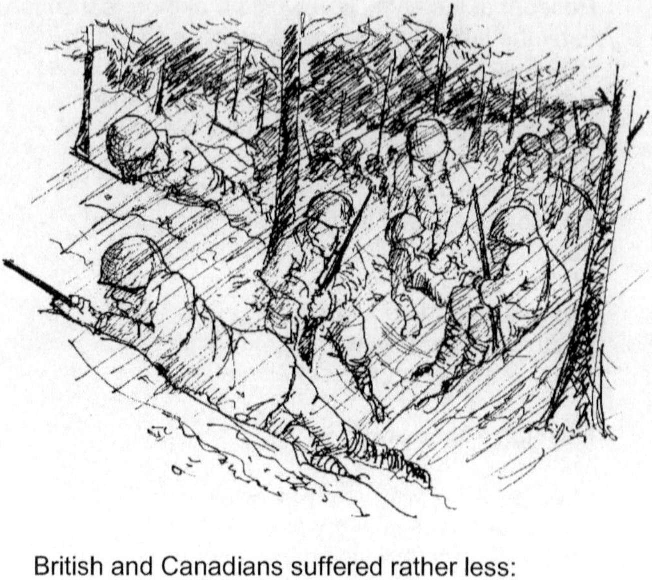

British and Canadians suffered rather less:
Fourteen hundred casualties. These, I confess,
Were enough. Germany's losses, reportedly,
Exceeded 85,000. The enemy,
Defeated and thoroughly demoralised,
Were close to collapse and I am not surprised.

Stalin's new offensive

The Battle of the Bulge had proved expensive
For the western allies. Stalin's offensive,
Planned for the 20th of January,
Was brought forward. Eisenhower's deputy,
Sir Arthur Tedder, had been sent to Moscow
To argue the allied case for Uncle Joe
To strike early. "The battle in the west
"Is very heavy" (Churchill at his best) –
"I regard the matter as urgent." Stalin
Was happy to agree. As sharp as a pin,
He leapt at the chance. It would make perfect sense
If, by the time of the Yalta conference,
Scheduled for the first week of February,
He controlled most of Poland. Most certainly
This was his main motive for striking early.
Churchill welcomed Stalin's "generosity",
As he saw it. He saluted a "fine deed".
He allowed himself to be duped. Fine, indeed!

Stalin's cynicism, frankly, makes me sick –
Duplicitous and opportunistic –
But that, sad to say, is what made him tick.
Since when were dictators altruistic?

Russian superiority

The Red Army was vastly superior
To the Germans in every area:
Six to one in tanks, seventeen to one
In planes. The campaign was as good as won.
They had five or six times as many men.
Guns? More, by a factor of one to ten!

On the 12th, the great offensive began.
The Red Army was ready, to a man,

To wreak revenge for the hideous crimes
Committed by the Nazis. Wicked times.
Marshal Zhukov's forces made rapid progress,
Averaging sixteen miles a day (no less).
After only a week they entered Warsaw.
Stalin, in his dreams, could not have wished for more.
Marshal Konev stormed into Silesia,
Further to the south, his progress easier,
If anything, than Zhukov's. After the Ruhr,
This was the centre of industry. The war,
By now, was lost, of that the people were sure…

Or were they? Clearly not. The Germans fought on
Long after all chance of victory had gone.

Zhukov and the Russians were all smiles.
Within weeks they were a mere forty miles
From Berlin, before Stalin called a halt.
Now this was certainly nobody's fault.
Progress, if anything, had been too fast,
With Zhukov's advantage too good to last.
The old issue of outrunning supplies
Was the big risk. This policy was wise.
Eisenhower was nowhere near Berlin.
There was no danger of Ike going in
Before the Red Army. On Stalin went,
However, further south. He was hell-bent
On ridding Europe, as fast as he could,
Of Nazis. After the war (touching wood)
He would keep the spoils, for his country's good.

Hungary and Austria overwhelmed

By the second week of February,
Stalin's troops had overwhelmed Hungary,
Having finally taken Budapest.
Although the Germans did their level best

To stand firm in Austria, Vienna fell
In April, this a particular bombshell
For Hitler. The Führer also knew full well
That the war was lost, but could never say so.
The horror, alas, had a long way to go.

Yalta

I'm running ahead. In February,
The allied leaders, the so-called 'Big Three'
(Franklin D. Roosevelt, Josef Stalin,
Winston Churchill), still with a war to win,
Met (sadly for the last time) at Yalta.

FDR and Churchill were in Malta,*
Briefly, on their way to the conference,
But Roosevelt feared that Stalin's absence
Might falsely lead Uncle Joe to suppose –
This would really have got up his nose –
That the pair were ganging up against him.

---

*Churchill attempted to make light of it.
Stalin, to be sure, would have had a fit
Had he known. "No more let us falter!"
Churchill wrote to FDR. "From Malta
"To Yalta! Let nobody alter!" Well,
The PM for once failed to cast his spell.
The US President turned a blind eye
To Churchill's blandishments. Still, a nice try.
It remains something of a mystery –
If not to most people, at least to me –
Why, when Churchill came to write his *History*
(Called *The Second World War*), he did not try verse.
It clearly appealed and he could have done worse.

Indulging the PM's every whim
Was not to the President's taste. Churchill,
Indeed, was destined to struggle uphill
At Yalta. FDR was past his best.

The meeting was to prove his final test.
Soon he would die. The PM was depressed.
He referred to "this new, disgusting year" –
Russian dominance was his big fear,
In central Europe and even beyond.

The new mood, however, 'across the Pond',
To which FDR was quick to respond,
Was to withdraw American forces
As soon as possible – men, resources
And finance. In Churchill's considered view
This was dangerous, but what could he do?

His choices were limited. Joe Stalin,
On the other hand, was the new kingpin:
Powerful, assured and articulate.

FDR in decline

Roosevelt was manifestly unfit:
Prematurely old, increasingly frail
And clearly sick. Churchill fought tooth and nail
For Poland. To nobody's great surprise,
The Russians refused to compromise.

Their forces were now in complete control
Of the country. Stalin was on a roll.
His own puppet government was installed
In Warsaw: the 'Lublin Poles' they were called,
Under Stalin's thumb. Churchill was appalled
When Poland's 'free' government-in-exile
Was rejected (such was Uncle Joe's style)
As partners in any new government.
This, as I understand it, is what's meant
By 'possession is nine tenths of the law'.

The Poles abandoned

Stalin was pushing at an open door
In the case of Roosevelt. The old man
Came out as something of a Stalin fan.
He was slow to fight for the Poles. His aim –
Here, to his credit, he won lasting fame –
Was to bring Stalin and Churchill on side
Over his treasured UN. You decide:
Would the President have risked suicide,
Politically, had he irked Stalin
Over Poland? He declined to cave in
(Strong here, at least) over his pet project,
The United Nations. As you'd expect,
Stalin played a blinder. Uncle Joe knew,
As only the 'best' of dictators do,
Precisely what he could get away with.
He agreed to FDR's plans forthwith.

Poland was destined to go down the pan.
I was a devoted Roosevelt fan
Until this moment. This was a sell-out.
The Poles were condemned, no shadow of doubt,
To membership of the Soviet Bloc
In post-war Europe. This came as a shock
To all freedom-loving Poles. For the war
Began in Poland. What had it all been for?

It makes me sick. I can't take any more.
Stalin gave his solemn word (yes, he swore)
That the provisional government
Of Poland (by which he patently meant
The Lublin Poles) might "possibly" include
Non-Communist Poles. Sorry to be rude,
But this assurance was utter claptrap.
A free Poland disappeared from the map
As Roosevelt fell into Stalin's trap.

This sorry saga was one long mishap.
Churchill was a thoroughly decent chap
When it came to the Poles. What could he do?
Little or nothing. This was Stalin's *coup*.

Russian fears

Twice during the twentieth century
The Russian people's security
Has been threatened from the west. Their history
Has been of terror. It's no mystery,
Therefore, why the Russian government,
In the person of Stalin, was hell-bent
On establishing a strong buffer zone
By way of protection. This, alone,
Explains Stalin's position – my view,
I know, but to give Russia her due,

We should ever remember the horror
Suffered by her people. Paranoia?
Hardly. Never forget the men they lost,
The women and the children. What a cost.
They had their own interests to consider
In the peace. Little wonder they were bitter.

Crossing the Rhine

Further west events were gathering pace.
Dresden, as we've seen (an utter disgrace),
Was cruelly bombed. Waves of migration,
From the east, doubled the population
Of this great, historic city at a stroke.
A "severe case of over-bombing", no joke,
Resulted in some 25,000 dead.
It had all rather gone to Harris's head.

The people of Dresden suffered dreadfully,
But transport and industry? Less terribly –
An awful irony. Within a few days,
Factories were back on their feet, the railways
Were running and the city functioning.
Well, so much for allied strategic bombing.

Further west still, to prepare for the crossing
Of the Rhine, the massed air forces ranged at will.
Before the ground troops could go in for the kill,
Transport hubs were struck in preparation.
Roads and rail tracks suffered devastation
From rockets, bombs and aerial fire. The task
Was to clear the decks of Nazis, since you ask,
Before the allied armies crossed the river.

Churchill (and Monty) were all of a quiver.
Their purpose was to sweep up the Baltic coast
To achieve the goal that they coveted most,

The German capital, as soon as they could.
Ike insisted (had he been misunderstood?):
Proceed as agreed, as a good ally should,
And advance on a broad front. Forget Berlin.
The Russians, he assumed, would be first in
And this the Americans took on the chin.

Quite a risk, thought Churchill. Be that as it may,
As Montgomery was battling his way
Towards the Rhine, the Yanks found a route across,
Via a bridge at Remagen. At a loss,
Monty was speechless – in fact, extremely cross!
But what could a fellow do? Ike was the boss.

On March the 7th, with fourteen casualties,
The Americans crossed the Rhine. Their enemies
Fled before them. Poor Montgomery, if you please,
Didn't make it across until the 23rd.
Livid (imagine anything quite so absurd),
He swallowed his pride as General Patton's tanks
Swept a path before him. Sparing in his thanks
Was Monty. There was discontent in the ranks!

The German collapse

The Rhine was soon clear of Germans – that's both banks,
East and west. Only a few short weeks elapsed
Before Nazi morale completely collapsed.
By mid-April all their forces in the Ruhr
Had surrendered. They couldn't take any more:
Some 300,000 prisoners of war.

From the Dutch border in the north (where to start?)
To the Black Forest, Germany's very heart,
Her towns and villages suffered the same fate
As had those of France and Russia of late,

And Poland, Yugoslavia, Greece… These burned,
As Berlin would, before the enemy learned
That resistance was futile. Some were content
To raise the white flag. Yet wherever they went
The troops met hordes of refugees flooding west,
Their choice between communism, I suggest,
In the east and a free Europe. No contest.

The death of Franklin Delano Roosevelt

On the 12th of April, Roosevelt died.
Goebbels was ecstatic. "That's it!" he cried,
"That's it!" He believed it would turn the tide.
The Führer's joy, too, was unqualified.
A compromise peace, he thought, with the west
Was now assured. Stalin was past his best.
The Nazis and their new western allies
Would pool resources and spring a surprise
On Russia. The war would carry on
In the east. Now that FDR had gone,
The new President, Harry S. Truman,
Would fall in line. He was only human
After all! According to Hitler's spies,
Truman stood ready to antagonise
Stalin, as a staunch anti-Communist.
Franklin D. Roosevelt would not be missed.

All poppycock, of course. While it was true
That Truman was rather less keen to woo
The Russians than Roosevelt had been,
There was no American 'change of scene'.

The Russians close in on Berlin

All was set fair for the Führer's downfall.
Hitler, now with his back against the wall,

Understood there was little he could do
But withdraw to his underground HQ
Beneath the Imperial Chancellery
In Berlin. In his world of fantasy,
Hitler continued to direct the war
From his bunker. Knocking at Berlin's door
Was the Red Army. They were closing in.
By the 16th of April, Joe Stalin
Ordered the main offensive to begin.
By May the 1st, Berlin was a ruin.

Nazi resistance, believe it or not,
Was strong. Meanwhile the Führer feared a plot
By Hermann Göring and Heinrich Himmler,
Offering terms (or something similar,
The details are hazy) to the allies.
Göring, he reckoned, was taking the rise,
Stepping, he said, into the Führer's shoes.
This was not for Hitler the best of news!
"To give *me* an ultimatum," he raged,
"That really is the end." He had aged,
He was sick, he'd probably had a stroke,
But his staff still quaked when the Führer spoke.

Hitler prepares for the end

In case he should settle on suicide,
Hitler had ordered Himmler to provide
The wherewithal: capsules of cyanide.
Doubting now his former trustworthy aide,
The Führer paused. He was sorely afraid
That Himmler may have played a dirty trick –
Hard to believe, but far from fantastic –
And provided poison (hard to forgive)
That only knocked him out. He might still live,
To be taken to Moscow in a cage,
Perhaps… Yes, he was in a right old rage.

Animal lovers should now turn the page.
He took leave of his beloved Blondi,
His dog, second only (yes, honestly)
In his affections to Eva Braun.

Hitler fed her a capsule. Lying down,
The poor dog instantaneously died,
Painlessly, we hope. This was cyanide.

Death of Mussolini

Elsewhere events were coming to a head.
In Italy Mussolini was dead,
His body hanged upside down, in Milan,
From a lamppost. The final phase began,
As American forces crossed the Po
On the 23rd. A long way to go?

Thanks to brave partisans, happily no.
They and the allies stormed through Italy,
Liberating city after city:
Turin and Milan, Genoa, Venice…

The beleaguered Nazis (surprising, this)
Fought on until, on the 2nd of May,
They surrendered. On the following day,
Monty took Hamburg, which perhaps explains
Why Denmark (to the relief of the Danes)
Stayed free, thank Heaven, from the dreaded sphere
Of Russian influence. Shed a tear,
If you will, for the likes of Latvia,
Estonia and Lithuania,
Members of the Soviet Bloc, I fear
(Until modern times), for many a year.

US and Russian armies meet

April the 25th was historic.
US progress had been meteoric.

The Yanks and Soviets met at Torgau,
On the Elbe. Both east and west, for now,
Were comrades in arms. This did not last long,
But the allies for once could do no wrong
As they swept all before them. United
In triumph – war-weary, but excited –
The men exchanged cigarettes, chocolate…
And slaps on the back. They had done their bit.

Hitler commits suicide

Back in the capital time was running out
For the Führer. In his underground redoubt
He married his young mistress, Eva Braun.
He dictated his last will (taken down
By Traudl Junge, his secretary),
Still swearing revenge on his enemy,
The Jews, and the capitalist system.
He charged his successors, in their 'wisdom',
To adhere to the Nazi laws of race.
His final testament was a disgrace –
No surprises there. Hitler named in his place
Admiral Karl Dönitz as his successor.

He then gave instructions to his dresser,
His trusted valet, after he was dead
To burn his body. They should fight, he said,
"For the coming man". An odd thing to say,
But Hitler was having a rotten day.
Did anyone care? Be that as it may,
He and 'Mrs. Hitler' both slipped away.
It was then Traudl Junge heard a shot –
From the Führer's pistol as like as not.

Goebbels' little boy, who was also there,
Turned to Traudl (both sitting on the stair) –

Fräulein Junge, of course, was well aware
Of the event – and was quick to declare,
In his innocence: “That was a bullseye!”
With his five sisters he was soon to die
At the hands of their mother. Poisoned. Why?
Who knows? The horror is hard to deny.
Explain such evil? I shan’t even try.

The 30th of April was the day
Hitler shot himself. Good riddance, I say.
Eva Braun, discovered slumped by his side,
Had joined him in committing suicide.
Adolf Hitler’s twenty-four-hour bride
Had swallowed a capsule of cyanide.
Their two dead bodies were then dragged outside,
Doused in petrol and set alight. Their fate
Was sealed, sadly over twelve years too late.
Goebbels, Martin Bormann following suit,
Clicked his heels and gave the Nazi salute.

The Russians’ bitter fight for Berlin

The battle for Berlin was hard-fought, long
And bitter. Nazi resistance was strong
To the last. They struggled on, street by street,
Russian victory only complete
After two gruelling weeks, which is why,
Alas, final casualties were high.
All told, 100,000 were to die
From the Red Army alone. Cue, dismay.

It was only on the 2nd of May
That the Berlin garrison surrendered,
A day that will ever be remembered
In Europe. Dönitz did his level best
To secure a surrender in the west,

While continuing the war in the east.
He sought an accord, at the very least,
With the western allies at the expense
Of the Communists. Well, that was nonsense,
And Dönitz knew it in his heart of hearts.

Unconditional surrender

Although this was hardly the best of starts,
Piecemeal surrenders followed thick and fast.
On May the 4th, Montgomery, at last,
Took the surrender, at Lüneburg Heath,
Of forces in the north, this in the teeth
Of unexpected opposition.
Three days on, the German position
Was spelt out at Eisenhower's HQ,
In Rheims. General Alfred Jodl knew,
For Germany, what he now had to do.

His surrender was unconditional.
Terms were agreed, as was traditional,
With no strings attached. The following day,
At Zhukov's HQ, on the 8th of May,
In Berlin, the same document was signed,
The Nazis now conclusively resigned
To defeat. Victory in Europe Day
(VE Day) was the 8th. As was his way,
Churchill celebrated without delay.

VE Day

The PM was exhausted. On a roll,
To be sure, the war had taken its toll.
On VE Day he took lunch with the King,
With much mutual congratulating,
As indeed was only appropriate.
At 3 that afternoon Churchill saw fit

To broadcast to a grateful nation.
A great service of celebration
Was held at the Church of St. Margaret,
Westminster. Then the whole War Cabinet
And all the Chiefs of Staff, to their credit,
Trooped off to the Palace. The King and Queen,
In a special tribute rarely seen,
Led Churchill out onto the balcony
To greet the people (an amazing sea
Of faces, of smiles…) to a roar of cheers,
The like of which had not been heard for years.
Eight appearances he was asked to make,
Enough for an old man for goodness' sake.

The two young Princesses, make no mistake,
Took part in the fun. Pretty and single,
The King allowed his daughters to mingle
(Chaperoned, of course) with the crowds that night,
Londoners at large. Sharing their delight,
Sisters Elizabeth and Margaret Rose
Had the time of their lives (one can only suppose).

The Holocaust

While western Europe was celebrating,
Allied soldiers were 'liberating'
The death camps in the east. The suffering,
The agony, that confronted them there
Caused anguish, nausea and bleak despair.

The liberators sadly came too late
For millions. For most had met their fate,
Already, at the hands of the SS.
They had no hope. Starvation, sickness
And disease, among the few left alive,
Meant that most were far too weak to survive.

Auschwitz

It was in January, '45,
(The 27th) that the Soviets
Stumbled on Auschwitz. They'd been laying bets
How long it would take them to reach Berlin,
Three hundred miles distant. Where to begin?

This was the last death camp operating.
The Nazis began obliterating
Evidence of their foul deeds in the face
Of the enemy advance – just in case,
You understand, after the war ended,
They were charged with their crimes. They pretended,
Or tried to, that the camps did not exist.

To this day such delusions persist
In some minds – which is why it's down to us,
Future generations, without fuss
Or fear, to keep alive the memory
Of the terror in perpetuity.

As the Red Army closed in on Auschwitz,
The fleeing Germans (this the very pits)
Herded most of the inmates, mainly Jews,
On a death march to Germany. This 'ruse',
As they saw it, was hopeless. For the news
Of the Nazi death camps had been spreading.

The allies found what they'd long been dreading:
Those too weak to march had been left behind.
Was this, one wonders, more (or less) 'unkind'
Than making them leave? I think you will find,
Alas, that it made little difference.

They cowered, scared to offer resistance,
In hideous conditions: decrepit,
Ragged, skeletal… Primo Levi said it
(An Auschwitz survivor): "everywhere
"On the frozen soil", in utter despair,

The "patients... dragged themselves" (Levi's terms,
His own) "like an invasion of worms".

How could humanity have sunk to this?
Did the people know? Ignorance is bliss,
The saying goes. From the very word go
The average German went with the flow.
Had ordinary folk dared to say 'no'
To Hitler, the Nazis' rise to power
Could have been scuppered within the hour.

This is the lesson: zero tolerance
To racism. Never give it a chance.

The Hungarian Jews

As late as March, '44, Germany
Assumed direct control of Hungary
And, with apparently no time to lose,
Sent three quarters of a million Jews
To their deaths. Himmler was duly impressed.
Just two months earlier he had addressed
An audience of high officials,
Including admirals and generals,
And reminded them of the "sacrifice"
His troops had been making. Let that suffice.

All this is truly terrifying stuff.
I've reached my limit. Enough is enough.

The numbers defy belief. Uncle Joe –
The basest of tyrants as tyrants go –
When confronted by stark reality
Observed that "one death is a tragedy,
"A million a statistic". Not so.
For fourteen million deaths (this I know)

Represent that number of tragedies:
Mothers and children, fathers, families,
Sisters and brothers. Figures such as these
Can numb our minds if we allow them to.

The host of other victims

It is up to all of us, me and you,
Never to let this happen. The gypsies;
Those with physical disabilities
(And mental); Russian prisoners of war;
Ethnic Serbs, Croats, Muslims by the score;
Polish civilians (non-Jews) and more;
Homosexuals; Jehovah's witnesses;
And six million Jews. Never forget this:
Each was an individual. Statistics?
No. The allies would hit the Nazis for six…
Eventually. The stage was now set
For victory. They were closing the net.
The Nazis had been defeated… and yet,
The peace would be fragile. Never forget,
Racism is an ever-present threat.

Victory over Japan

As you know, Victory in Europe Day
Was celebrated on the 8th of May.
It took a further sixteen weeks, at least,
Before the Japanese, in the Far East,
Were defeated. Their final surrender,
Declared on the 2nd of September,
Was called 'Victory over Japan Day'
By President Truman. I have to say,
His remarks caused not a little dismay
After the first ever* atomic bomb fell
On Hiroshima, a veritable hell.

The atomic bomb

"This is the biggest thing in history,"
Announced the US President. To me,
This proud statement is the epitome
Of breathtaking insensitivity.
This the 'biggest thing'? Bragging, patently.

100,000 perished instantly.
The final bomb, dropped on Nagasaki
A mere three days later, claimed more lives. Still,
Nuclear fall-out from the blasts would kill
Many thousands of others. Japan's will
Was broken. Emperor Hirohito,
To the horror of General Tōjō
(Former Prime Minister), after deadlock
Among ministers, as firm as a rock
(For once), sided with the peace faction –
This the first independent action
That the Emperor had ever taken.
The Japanese were badly mistaken,

---

*Not strictly true. You will be interested
To know that a prototype bomb was tested
In July. There were only three in all.
The second one, which triggered Japan's fall,
Was dropped on Hiroshima, then the third
On Nagasaki. It's far from absurd,
But had the Japanese not surrendered,
The two bombings would have been remembered
As costly failures. Harry Truman
Would have been pilloried: less than human,
Reckless, unfeeling and cavalier.
Instead the public applauded, I hear.

It later emerged, in what they believed.
They would doubtless have been highly relieved
Had they known that the mighty US
Had run out of atomic bombs, no less,
Staking all they had on Nagasaki
And Hiroshima. The land of the free
Took a gamble, a calculated risk.

Harry S. Truman, determined and brisk,
Shaped the future. Sadly, as we turn the page,
We must come to terms with the nuclear age.

Bibliography

Paul Addison, *The Road to 1945* (Pimlico, 1994)

Paul Addison, *Winston Churchill* (Oxford University Press, 2007)

Jonathan Bastable, *Prime Ministers – Amazing and Extraordinary Facts* (David and Charles, 2011)

Antony Beevor, *The Second World War* (Weidenfeld & Nicolson, 2012)

Angus Calder, *The People's War. Britain 1939-1945* (Pimlico, 1969)

Winston Churchill, *Painting as a Pastime* (Odham's Press Ltd., 1949)

Terry Coleman, *The Old Vic* (Faber & Faber Ltd., 2014)

Bryan Forbes, *That Despicable Race – A History of the British Acting Tradition* (Elm Tree Books, 1980)

Kenneth Harris, *Attlee* (Weidenfeld & Nicolson, 1982)

Richard Holmes, *The World at War* (Ebery Press, 2007)

David Howell, *Attlee* (Haus Publishing Limited, 2006)

Roy Jenkins, *Churchill* (Macmillan, 2001)

Primo Levi, *If This is a Man* (translated by Stuart Woolf) (Abacus, 1987)

Graham Macklin, *Chamberlain* (Haus Publishing Limited, 2006)

David Marquand, *Britain since 1918 – The Strange Case of British Democracy* (Weidenfeld & Nicolson, 2008)

Keith Middlemas, *The Life and Times of George VI* (Weidenfeld & Nicolson, with Book Club Associates, 1973)

Geoffrey Morgan and W. A. Lasocki, *Soldier Bear* (Collins, 1970)

Kenneth O. Morgan, *The Twentieth Century (1914-2000)* (in *The Oxford History of Britain,* ed. Kenneth O. Morgan – Oxford University Press, 2001)

Charles Loch Mowat, *Britain between the Wars, 1918-1940* (Methuen & Co. Ltd., 1955)

A. J. P. Taylor, *English History, 1914-1945* (Oxford University Press, 1965)

A. J. P. Taylor, *The Second World War. An Illustrated History* (Penguin Books, 1976)

G. M. Trevelyan, *A Shortened History of England* (Penguin, 1959)

Gerhard L. Weinberg, *World War II – A Very Short History* (Oxford University Press, 2014)

The World at War (Thames Television: 1973-1974). Series Producer: Jeremy Isaacs. Writers: Neal Ascherson, Peter Batty, Charles Bloomberg, Courtney Browne, Angus Calder, Charles Douglas Home, Jeremy Isaacs, Stuart Hood, Jerome Kuehl, J. P. W. Mallalieu, Laurence Thompson, David Wheeler, John Williams. Directors and Producers: Alan Afriat, Peter Batty, Ted Childs, Michael Darlow, David Elstein, Raye Farr, Jeremy Isaacs, Jerome Kuehl, Susan McConachy, John Pett, Hugh Raggett, Ben Shephard, Martin Smith, Peter Tiffin, Phillip Whitehead. Music: Carl Davis. Narrator: Laurence Olivier. Chief Historical Advisor: Dr. Noble Frankland DFC.

RHYMING HISTORY
The Story of England in Verse

EARLIER VOLUMES IN THE SERIES

Volume One: 55BC – 1485
THE ROMANS TO THE WARS OF THE ROSES

An entertaining, ironic and accessible journey through our history from the first arrival of Julius Caesar in 55BC to the defeat of Richard the Third at Bosworth Field in 1485.

An ebook of Volume One and a CD of excerpts are also available.

Volume Two: 1485 – 1603
THE TUDORS

From Henry the Seventh to Queen Elizabeth, this volume spans one of the most exciting, turbulent and colourful periods of English history.

Volume Three: 1603 – 1649
THE EARLY STUARTS AND CIVIL WAR

Where James the First was intelligent and astute, his son was obstinate and rash. Charles the First plunged his kingdom into bloody civil war.

Volume Four: 1649 – 1660
CROMWELL AND THE COMMONWEALTH

This volume charts the early success and final decline of the new Commonwealth, closing with the triumphant return of Charles the Second to reclaim his lost kingdom.

Volume Five: 1660 – 1685
CHARLES THE SECOND AND THE RESTORATION

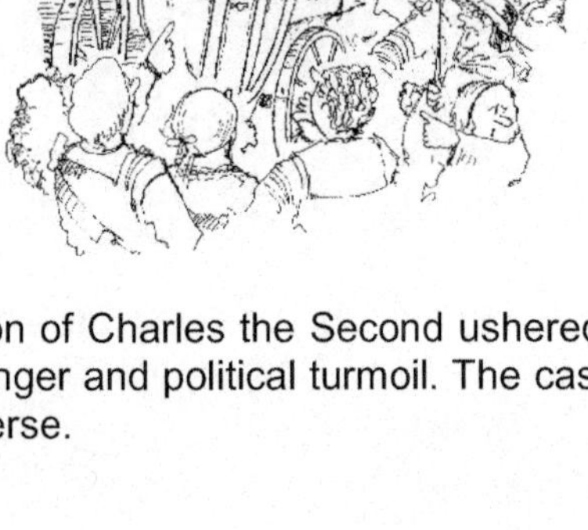

The Restoration of Charles the Second ushered in a new age of scandal, danger and political turmoil. The cast of characters is rich and diverse.

Volume Six: 1685 – 1688
JAMES THE SECOND, THE FORGOTTEN KING

James the Second was headstrong, vain and inept. He inherited a kingdom at peace, but rebellion was in the air. The Glorious Revolution was about to begin.

Volume Seven: 1688 – 1714
GLORIOUS REVOLUTION,
THE LAST OF THE STUARTS

In the Glorious Revolution, King William and Queen Mary were invited to reign jointly. When Queen Anne died childless, the Stuart dynasty drew to a close.

Volume Eight: 1714 – 1760
THE EARLY HANOVERIANS

The accession of George the First ushered in an era of change. The turbulent reign of George the Second ended with the celebrated Year of Victories.

Volume Nine: 1760 – 1789
GEORGE THE THIRD AND THE LOSS OF AMERICA

The reign of 'Farmer George' was the third longest in British history, but the first signs of the King's madness were beginning to show.

Volume Ten: 1789 – 1837
THE LAST OF THE HANOVERIANS

These were momentous times: the rise of Napoleon, the Great Reform Act and the abolition of the slave trade. With the death of William the Fourth, the Hanoverian era was at an end.

Volume Eleven: 1837 – 1858
THE EARLY VICTORIANS

The Victorian Age was one of vision, enterprise and conflict. The Great Exhibition heralded a time of progress and invention, but the Crimean War and the Indian Mutiny were soon to cast long shadows.

Volume Twelve: 1858 – 1901
THE LATER VICTORIANS

The death of Prince Albert left Victoria bereft. This was a great age of achievement, dominated by political rivals Gladstone and Disraeli. The Queen's final days were overshadowed by the Boer War.

Volume Thirteen: 1901 – 1922
THE EDWARDIANS AND THE GREAT WAR

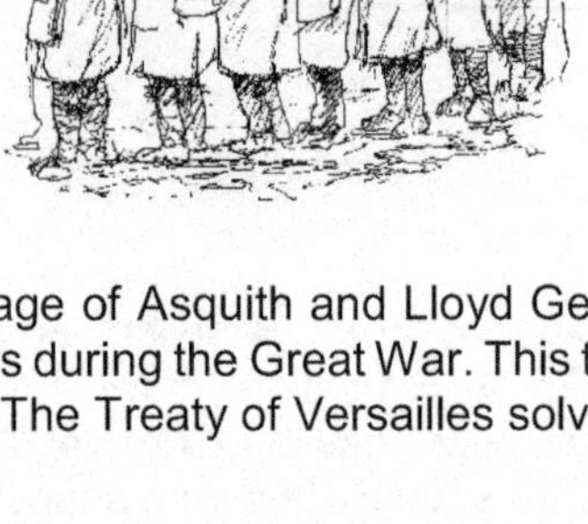

This was the age of Asquith and Lloyd George, Britain's two Prime Ministers during the Great War. This terrible conflict tore Europe apart. The Treaty of Versailles solved nothing.

Volume Fourteen: 1922 – 1939
DEPRESSION AND THE SHADOW OF WAR

As the German economy collapsed, the terror of the Nazis was total. In Britain the National Government avoided bankruptcy, but nobody could resist the rise of Hitler.

TO BE PUBLISHED IN 2023

Volume Sixteen: 1945 – 1964
ATTLEE TO WILSON

Attlee's post-war government teetered on the edge of economic collapse, but its achievements were historic. Macmillan boasted that we had never had it so good, but by the mid-sixties Britain's weakness was all too apparent.

Please visit our website for excerpts from all these volumes and for news of performances of the verse.

www.rhyminghistory.co.uk

Printed in Great Britain
by Amazon

31944438R00225